INSIGHT GUIDES

The world's largest collection of visual travel guides

CZECH&SLOVAK
REPUBLICS

Edited by Alfred Horn

Updated by Melanie and Chris Rice

Managing Editor: Tony Haliday

Editorial Director: Brian Bell

APA PUBLICATIONS

Part of the Langenscheidt Publishing Group

L

ABOUT THIS BOOK

When Communism crumbled in 1989, so too did many of the states on which it had been founded – including the former Czechoslovakia. The forces of separatism that split the country in two were as predictable as they were inevitable. Through most of their history, the Czechs and the Slovaks had not lived together; Czechoslovakia became their common country only after the collapse of the Habsburg empire in 1918. But being "Czechoslovak" never had much appeal for either group and, since January 1993, the Czechs and Slovaks have been citizens of their own independent states: the Czech Republic and Slovakia.

The photojournalistic approach of Apa Publications lends itself perfectly to destinations in a state of flux. Its editors were planning this book as the tumultuous events of the early 1990s took place and this latest edition of *Insight Guide: Czech and Slovak Republics* incorporates a full update on what has been happening in these rapidly changing destinations.

As project editor of this book, **Alfred Horn** assembled an expert team of writers and photographers. Horn, based in Cologne, first visited Czechoslovakia in 1965 with his school class and has since been back countless times. He has a particularly intimate knowledge of Bohemia, so in addition to his editorial duties he was well placed to write the chapters on the "Golden City" of Prague and the famous spa towns of Western Bohemia.

To provide an authoritative account of the region's past and present, he chose predominantly native authors and photographers to work on the book, and hired a leading Prague jour-

Volf

Pavlík

nalist, **Jan Jelínek**, as adviser to the project. Jelínek, managing editor of the Prague newspaper *mladá fronta dnesn*, liaised between Horn and the local authors and helped to ensure that this book benefited from friendly cross-border cooperation.

Jelínek engaged specialists for the feature essays as well as the cities and regions. **Petr Volf** researched the complex but fascinating history of the region. While the Czech Republic and Slovakia have their own individual histories, many developments were common to both countries. The chapters tell you where their destinies merged, and where and why they split.

Boris Docekal lives and works in Moravian Jihlava and is well acquainted with life in the small towns and villages. He wrote the revealing article on rural life. **Josef Tucek**, a top environmental journalist in the former Czechoslovakia, highlighted in his chapter the especially tense relationship between ecology and economy in two countries in the midst of such dramatic change.

Jan Plachetka supplied the articles on theatre, literature and music, all of which have an illustrious and venerable tradition, particularly in the Czech Republic.

Bronislav Pavlík covers Central Bohemia; his expertise on the area enabled him to give a vivid account of some of the magnificent destinations within easy reach of Prague. **Jan Cech**, who lives in Plzen, highlights in his article on Western Bohemia some of the common historical ties between his homeland and Germany.

Hana Vojtová, from Ústi nad Labem in Northern Bohemia, describes her fascinating homeland, not omitting to point out some of its serious environmental problems. **Irena Jirku** outlines

Horn

Jelinek

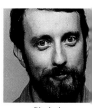

Plachetka

Jirku

Rose

a tour of Eastern Bohemia, where she lives and works in Hradec Králové, a town steeped in history.

Joroslav Haid, a wine connoisseur from Brno, describes his personal experiences from the wine cellars of the delightful little towns of Southern Moravia.

Petr Zizka, from the industrial town of Ostrava in Northern Moravia, brings alive the multicultural traditions in this region bordering Silesia in Poland. **Ondrej Neff**, one of Bohemia's best-known science-fiction writers, is also a specialist in Czech and Slovakian internal affairs. For this book, he provided material for the article "Czechs and Slovaks", describing the sometimes uneasy relationship between the two peoples.

Rudolf Procházka is press secretary of the prime minister of Slovakia. A trained journalist, he lives in the capital Bratislava, but knows his homeland not only from the perspective of a political commentator but also as a person who really appreciates the outstanding natural beauty of the region.

A number of German authors were also assigned to assist with the project. **Kerstin Rose**, a travel writer from Frankfurt, relates her experiences on an evening stroll around Prague and in addition provides a host of useful information for the concluding Travel Tips section.

As a student in Prague, the theologian **Werner Jakobsmeier** from Munich witnessed the dramatic events of 1968–69 at first hand. He contributed his expertise to the articles dealing with life today in the Czech and Slovak republics, with religion, theatre and architecture, and wrote the fea-

tures on Jaroslav Hasek and Smetana. He also edited the Travel Tips section and undertook the intricate task of inserting into the text a baffling variety of Czech accents.

Wieland Giebel, a former Insight Guides editor now based in Berlin, examines the situations of the various minorities living in both the Czech Republic and Slovakia. **Annette Tohak**, from Bonn, guides readers through the romantic nooks of the beautiful Southern Bohemia.

Chris Pommery in Prague provided valuable information concerning the momentous developments that led to the emergence of the two independent states, and **Peter Cargin** of Fipresci contributed helpful hints concerning the future of the Karlovy Vary Film Festival.

In the established tradition of the Insight Guides series, this book mesmerises with its superb photography. Together with their Munich colleague **Werner Neumeister**, the internationally recognised Prague photojournalists **Mirek Frank**, **Oldrich Karásek** and **Jan Ságl** offered the publisher a dazzling selection of shots for the final selection.

The book was translated into English by **Jane Michael-Rushmer**, and production was masterminded in Insight Guides' London office by **Tony Halliday** and **Dorothy Stannard**. Proofreading and indexing was completed by **Mary Morton**.

The update material for this new edition was gathered by travel writers **Melanie** and **Chris Rice**. As Eastern European specialists they have travelled extensively throughout the region. Chris Rice has a PhD in Russian History and knowledge of several East European languages.

Jakobsmeier

CONTENTS

CONTENTS

Maps

WELCOME

While breaking up is always hard to do, the formalities marking the final parting of the Czech and Slovak republics were completed with relative ease in January 1993 when the two states went their own separate ways. They had been married once before, over 1,000 years ago, in a kingdom called Greater Moravia. Although that didn't last very long either, it does at least show that despite their cultural and linguistic differences, the Czechs and Slovaks have common links that go back a long way. Their destinies have also been closely bound with the rest of Europe, by a complex network of historical and cultural ties.

For centuries Bohemia played a central role in the Holy Roman Empire; under Charles IV, Prague became one of the greatest capitals of Europe. The Czech religious reformer Jan Hus can be mentioned in the same breath as Wyclif, Calvin and Luther; the compositions of Smetana and Dvorák form part of the world repertoire of classical music. In "Golden Prague" the European tradition has not been relegated to dusty history books, but has remained full of life and atmosphere to this day. The town is no lack-lustre museum of medieval urban architecture, but an international arena throbbing with vitality which still manages to retain its charm and flair under the assault of millions of tourists.

Prague has long occupied a prominent position on the tourist trail; as far as the rest of the Czech Republic is concerned, however, the boom is still to come. Karlovy Vary – the elegant Karlsbad of days gone by – and Marienbad, where emperors and tsars, as well as luminaries such as Goethe and Chopin took the waters, are refurbishing their manicured promenades and nostalgic spa hotels. Beyond the historic towns and cities lie the forbidding castles and romantic river valleys of Bohemia and Moravia. All are just waiting to be explored.

Slovakia has yet to be discovered. As far as history and culture are concerned, until 1918 the country's destiny was always more closely wound up with events in Hungary than with the course of mainstream developments further west. After the Turks invaded the Hungarian heartlands, Bratislava even became Hungary's *de facto* capital. During the long reign of the Austro-Hungarian emperors, when the Czech lands of Bohemia and Moravia were politically and economically so powerful, Slovakia was relegated to the position of impoverished neighbour. Despite subsequent industrialisation under the communists, the country remains essentially rural in character, and is proud of its enduring traditions and folklore. It also possesses some splendid scenery, including the High Tatras, which are among the most spectacular mountains in Europe.

Preceding pages: panel paintings in the Chapel of the Holy Cross in Karlstejn Castle; wintertime in the Krkonoše (Giant Mountains); first snows in the High Tatra; the ruins of Strecno Castle stand sentinel above the Váh (Slovakia); facades on the Old Town Square in Prague. Left, generations of tradition in Slovakia.

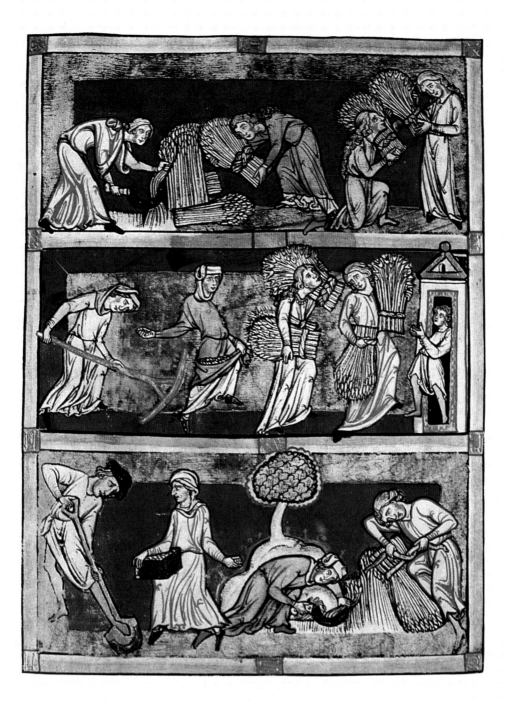

The frontiers of the Czech lands and Slovakia did not assume their present boundaries until this century, and yet the region can claim a long history as one of the focal points of Central European civilisation and as a bridge – or sometimes a watershed – between the cultures of eastern and western Europe. Furthermore, the Czech lands of Bohemia and Moravia lay at the crossroads of the traditional trade routes from the Atlantic coast to the Black Sea and from the Mediterranean to the Baltic. This valuable strategic position gave the entire continent a vested interest in the region's history.

Archaeological excavations have produced fine examples of pottery, testifying to the fact that Moravia and Slovakia were the homes of settled communities as much as 25,000 years ago. During the fifth millennium BC the members of the Danube civilisation practised extensive agriculture. The potter's wheel was discovered in about 3,000 BC; by 2,000 to 1,500 BC the members of the Únětice culture living near Prague had discovered how to smelt bronze and hence how to produce tools and weapons. This technology also allowed them to make religious cult figures and intricate jewellery.

The first Slavs – the earliest ancestors of the present-day Czechs and Slovaks – settled in the region from the 6th century AD onwards. Their migration route across Europe from the east brought them through the Carpathian Pass, the Moravian Gate and the Tisa valley, until they reached the area which was subsequently to become their new home. Here they encountered the Celts, who had been in the area for many years, as well as groups of Germanii who had also gained a foothold in the region.

The gradual assimilation of the original inhabitants marked the beginning of the political history of the Western Slavs. To protect themselves against the warlike incursions of the nomadic Avars they first formed a tribal association. They chose as their leader the Frankish merchant Samo, who had built up a powerful private army to protect his trading caravans. But no sooner had they beaten off the Avars, than they were attacked on their western flank by the king of the Franks, in 637. In the subsequent Battle of the Vogastisburg, the Slavic army won the day, and the Western Slavs proceeded to establish an extensive kingdom, though this quickly disintegrated after the death of Samo.

Christianity spreads: More clearly defined and better organised was the state of Great Moravia, which grew up after 833 in the regions of modern Moravia and Western Slovakia and expanded to include all of Bohemia, the southern part of modern Poland and the western part of modern Hungary. Thanks to his good relations with Byzantium, Prince Ratislav was able to arrange for Christian missionaries to be sent by the rulers of the Byzantine Empire. The arrival in 863 of two learned brothers, Cyril and Methodius, the apostles of the Slavs, was a key event in the subsequent political, religious and cultural development of the re-

Preceding pages: an old engraving of Karlsbad. **Left,** tribes from the regions of present-day Moravia and Bohemia formed a feudal state around AD 1000: a depiction of the harvest at that time. **Right,** a figure from the Libuše legend of the founding of Prague at Vyšehrad.

gion. They not only converted large numbers of the population to the new state religion, but also developed the Slavonic Glagolitic script. Once the Pope had given his official blessing to their accomplishments, permission was granted for sermons to be given in Slavic after the lesson had been read in Latin. This concession was crucial to the rapid spread of Christianity.

But Prince Svatopluk, the most notable ruler of this early state, was soon forced to recognise the superior strength of his neighbours, the Franks, and to grant additional rights to the western Church. A Swabian bishop was installed in his capital, Nitra, and the followers of the Slavic apostles were

nation, together with an alliance with Saxony lost him the support of the Bohemian ruling classes. Their resistance became more determined when Henry I started to enslave the Slavs east of the frontier with Saxony.

The prince's own brother, Boleslav, led the conspiracy against him. He was personally responsible for Wenceslas' murder in 935. Boleslav then succeeded in creating one of the most powerful states in Central Europe. He ruled over Bohemia, Moravia and parts of Slovakia as well as Silesia and Southern Poland. But he had to defend his kingdom against repeated attack by the Holy Roman Emperor, Otto I. After the death of Boleslav I (c. 967) and with the support of the

expelled. At the turn of the 10th century the state came under increasing threat from the Magyars, and finally collapsed following a crushing defeat at their hands near Bratislava in the year 907.

German dominance in Bohemia: The princes of Bohemia had already asserted their independence. Under their rule, the Czech Premyslid dynasty gradually emerged as the supreme power in the whole of Bohemia. Although the first of the Přemyslid leaders, Prince Wenceslas (Václav), was able to assert himself as sole ruler over Bohemia, he was forced to swear allegiance to the German emperor Henry I in 929. This subordi-

Pope, Boleslav II succeeded in stabilising the kingdom. He was also responsible for the founding of the Bishopric of Prague in 973.

Boleslav's successor, Břetislav (1035–55), tried to defend the borders and even to extend his realm. His principal achievement was the permanent union of Moravia and Bohemia. But for the German emperor, Henry, the united kingdom represented an unacceptable threat; in 1041 he forced Břetislav to recognise Bohemia's dependence on the German rulers who endeavoured to maintain the Czechs' position as vassals in a state of subordination to the empire. In this they were frequently assisted by local noblemen. Even the Přemyslids approached them for support in quarrels concerning the princely throne. This provided the German rulers with a welcome excuse to play an active role in Czech affairs. However, the Přemyslids were able to maintain their autonomy even in the most difficult situations. They were also experts at turning the repeated problems of the Germans to their own advantage and offered their services as reliable allies.

The 13th century saw a fundamental change in the status quo. In 1198 Otakar was crowned the first king of the Czechs; in 1204 Pope Innocent III also recognised the title. A further milestone was reached in 1212, when Emperor Frederick II ratified the Sicilian Golden Bull. This confirmed all the privileges which the Přemyslids had achieved to date and emphasised the unity of the land inhabited by the Czechs, which meant that the nation was finally granted official recognition at international level, and became a power to be reckoned with.

Pushing out the frontiers: The second half of the 13th century was dominated by the political and military successes of King Přemysl Otakar II (1253–78). His power, which rested securely on the vast wealth derived from the silver mines of Bohemia, rose steadily until he reached a position of hegemony in Central Europe. After his victory at the battle of Kressenbrunn in 1260 he succeeded in advancing into Hungary, occupying Bratislava and pushing the frontiers of Bohemia as far as the Adriatic.

The compliant attitudes of both the pope and the emperor show the extent of Otakar II's authority; not without reason do the chroniclers of the period call him the Golden King. He died in 1278 in the midst of the Battle of Dürnkrut, fighting against Rudolf of Habsburg, who considered the Czech king to be his greatest rival.

His death unleashed a crisis concerning the succession, but the situation became more stable when the claims of King Wenceslas (Václav) II to the Polish throne were recognised. His young son Wenceslas III tried to continue the expansionist policies of his forbears, but he was assassinated during his Polish campaign in the year 1306.

The Přemyslid dynasty ended with his death, since he was the last male heir of the line. The following years were characterised by bitter fighting for the throne of Bohemia, which had become the most lucrative sinecure in Europe. Forming an alliance with the Czech aristocracy, Duke John of Luxembourg was in a position to swing the balance of power in his favour.

His marriage to the heiress of Bohemia, Elizabeth, the younger daughter of Wenceslas II, added a note of legitimacy to his claims; when he stood with his armies before the walls of Prague on 3 December 1310, the citizens offered no resistance. He was crowned king of Bohemia the following year.

John's character was full of contradictions; he was a swashbuckling soldier who devoted more energy to waging war than to ruling his kingdom. This resulted in a perpetual drain on the national finances, but also led to a weakening of his own position within Bohemia, where the aristocracy was becoming progressively more discontented. The loss of confidence in the crown and the internal crisis within the Czech provinces soon reached major proportions. The hopes of the aristocracy and bourgeoisie alike were concentrated in the person of the crown prince Charles, John's son. They were not to be disappointed.

Left, replica of St Wenceslas' crown in the National Museum in Prague. **Above**, St Cyril and Methodius as depicted by the Slovak artist Fulla.

Charles IV was born in Prague in 1316 and spent much of his early childhood playing on the banks of the Vltava. As a small boy he was sent to Paris to the court of his uncle, the king of France. His tutor during these years was the future Pope Clement VI. Although he was christened Wenceslas, Charles abandoned his baptismal name and adopted that of his role model, Charlemagne. He studied at the university of Paris and travelled extensively in Europe, learning at first hand the languages and cultures of the different na-

tions. His first wife, Blanche of Valois, was an equally worldly and influential partner.

Charles's early years were marked by a tempestuous relationship with his father. At one point he even took refuge in Italy, entering the service of the Doge of Venice as the leader of an army of mercenaries. Following a reconciliation, his father proclaimed him governor of Bohemia and Moravia. Although he was only 17 at the time, Charles already had considerable experience of life. From now on he dedicated himself to the task of bringing new prosperity to the country.

Charles's first real success was the elevation of the bishopric of Prague to the rank of archbishopric in 1344. The support of the pope was instrumental in this, and in securing his nomination as king of Germany in place of the excommunicated Louis IV, in 1346. His father, now suffering from blindness, died in the saddle at Crécy only six weeks later, and Charles became king of Bohemia in 1347.

The Golden Bull: It was now understood that the German imperial crown was based on the crown of Bohemia, and in 1355 Charles travelled to Rome, where he was duly crowned emperor. Although throughout his reign he was mainly concerned with his native Bohemian lands, as these provided his greatest source of strength, Charles did not neglect his imperial duties. In 1356 he proclaimed the Golden Bull, a kind of imperial constitution. It confirmed the right of the seven electors to choose the German king; in return, the emperor acknowledged their absolute jurisdiction within their own territories, and decreed that the rule of primogeniture was henceforth to govern the laws of inheritance and succession. These statutes eliminated a potential source of strife for the emperor and ensured the loyalty of his most powerful vassals.

Whilst the rest of Europe seemed in danger of sinking into chaos, with England and France engaged in the mutually destructive Hundred Years' War and Italy shattered by petty intrigues and civil wars between its minor princes and city states, Charles cleared the way for making his native country the hub of his newly acquired empire. The conquest and purchase of further territories and his four marriages (each of which brought him increased power and additional land) as well as the skilful negotiation of the marriage of his son, Sigismund, to the daughter of the King of Poland and Hungary, strengthened his sphere of influence and gradually shifted the centre of political power within his empire in an easterly direction.

Charles actively encouraged the growth of the cult of St Wenceslas, the national patron saint. The "Lands of the Crown of St Wenceslas", which apart from Bohemia and Moravia also included Silesia, Lusatia and for a short while even Brandenburg, acquired increasing relevance in the empire.

A booming economy: Bohemia was located on the crossroads of the trading routes between Venice and the Baltic countries as well as those between Flanders and Kiev and the Byzantine Empire. Under Charles the standard of the existing roads was greatly improved. The Vltava and the Labe (Elbe) provided access to the North Sea and the additional markets of the Free Imperial Cities and the towns of the Hanseatic League.

New settlers were persuaded to make their

city where he had been born into a thriving European metropolis. He summoned the best architects of the time to his capital on the banks of the Vltava for the construction of the Cathedral of St Vitus. In 1348 he founded in Prague the first university in central Europe, the Carolinum and enlarged the city's area by the establishment of the New Town.

The king was generous in his support of the church. No fewer than 35 new monasteries were established throughout Bohemia and Moravia, and many old churches were

homes in the country, thereby encouraging the renewed use of agricultural land which had been allowed to lie fallow, and increasing the manufacturing potential. Charles spoke German as well as Czech, and despite large numbers of German immigrants, he managed to prevent the outbreak of ethnic and nationalist conflict.

Prague becomes capital: Charles raised Prague to the position of capital of the Holy Roman Empire, gradually transforming the

Left, Emperor Charles IV made Prague into the capital of the Holy Roman Empire. **Above**, the Emperor with the imperial insignia.

rebuilt. This feverish activity was not without its disadvantages, however; the underdeveloped taxation system placed a disproportionate burden on the poorer classes, heightening the social tensions between the masses on the one hand and the aristocracy and the church on the other. This growing problem was to lead ultimately to the Hussite rebellion during the 15th century. But in spite of these difficulties Charles IV was one of the outstanding figures of Czech and European history. During his reign Bohemia and Moravia flourished as never before, so that the era was described even by contemporaries as the Golden Age.

55

Kez ye biskupem se nazwali a od powew giniti żupaty Ambroż
v pane nezissi nworz pastezi zmnank sulu v wlk. Naurzi wbm
ze knize w wrodze żprelaty wpilati gisk wsinkne S. Bernath

Charles was succeeded as German emperor and king of Bohemia by his eldest son, Wenceslas IV (1378–1419). The latter unfortunately lacked his father's talent and energy. He allowed Germany to slide into anarchy and was ultimately deposed as emperor by the electors in 1400.

At home in Bohemia, his main problem was the church, which during the reign of his father had still been a reliable pillar of support for the ruling house. The English reformer, John Wyclif, had already openly challenged the authority of the church as a secular power. By virtue of the marriage of Wenceslas's sister Anne to King Richard II of England and the ensuing close contact between the two countries, Wyclif's revolutionary theories spread rapidly throughout Bohemia.

The blatant self-enrichment and extravagance of the senior clergy, the bigoted attitude of the priests and the prevailing situation in the abbeys and convents, where monastic rules were openly defied, now called for decisive action on the part of the monarch. But Wenceslas IV was not a decisive man and entrenched himself in a diehard conservative position.

In Prague, the centre for critical theologians was not the university but the Bethlehem Chapel in the Old Town, erected in 1391 to accommodate up to 3,000 of the faithful. The sermons were often held in Czech – an almost unprecedented act of boldness for the time, but one which greatly increased their appeal to the ordinary people. A new generation of Czech and German-speaking preachers arose, amongst whom Jan Hus was to become the most famous.

Fuel to the Fire: Hus's death at the stake in 1415 (*see Jan Hus box, page 33*) gave rise to a storm of indignation and protest throughout the whole of Bohemia. In Prague, a defensive league of aristocratic supporters of the Hussites from Bohemia, Moravia and Silesia was quickly formed. Together they asserted their belief in the freedom of the

word of God and protested against the violent death of Jan Hus.

Their petition, addressed to the council, was eventually signed by 450 noblemen. The Hussite movement also found widespread support amongst the working classes, both within the towns and in rural areas. What had initially started out as an internal reform movement within the church rapidly developed into a broadly-based protest movement pitted against the power of the monarchy, the Catholic Church and the supremacy

of the Germans throughout Bohemia.

The first Defenestration of Prague: The violent overture to what was to turn into 20 years of conflict took place even before the death of Wenceslas. At the end of July 1419, the citizens of Prague, led by Jan Želivský, threw several councillors from the window of the New Town Hall when they refused to release a number of Hussite prisoners. Unrest spread: the Hussites occupied the Town Hall and elected their own councillors. Wenceslas confirmed the appointments, but when he died soon afterwards the Bohemian throne was claimed by his half brother Sigismund, the German king responsible for Hus's death.

Left, the Pope as depicted by the Hussites (around 1500). **Above**, Jan Žižka (died 1424), the commander of the Hussite army.

For Sigismund the Hussites' actions were sufficient justification to start a crusade against the heretics. During the following year, at the head of an army, he laid siege to the city. By employing guerilla tactics, however, the Hussite "soldiers of God", under the command of their heroic leader Jan Žižka, were able to put the attackers to flight. Žižka, whose military experience included fighting for the British at Agincourt in 1415, had been chosen leader of the popular party in 1419. Having conquered Emperor Sigismund's army and captured Prague after the Battle of Vítkov Hill in 1421, he proceeded to erect a fortress at Tábor, which became the centre of the Hussites' utopian religious state. The

Hussites overran and plundered not only Bohemia, Moravia and Slovakia, but also Austria, Bavaria, Saxony and Brandenburg. The imperial army, hurriedly called up, was defeated by Žižka and his forces in a succession of decisive battles.

The Council of Basle finally took up negotiations with the Hussite leaders, at which point a schism developed within the movement. The moderate Utraquists, supported by the nobles, agreed to a compromise in the Four Articles of Prague in 1433, which contained acceptance of their principal requirement: the administration of the communion to the laity in both kinds (i.e. both bread and wine). The radical Taborites, on the other hand, fought on under their general Andrew Procop until, in 1434, they were defeated in a battle at Lipany by the combined forces of the Catholics and the Utraquists.

And so, after almost 20 years of Hussite wars, the moderate Czech Utraquists were the clear victors. For the next 200 years the power of the Catholic Church was to remain at a low ebb, despite the fact that the majority of the population was Catholic – or at least professed to be. The Germans, who had hitherto enjoyed political and economic superiority, lost both power and possessions; furthermore, they were forced to settle in the frontier regions of the country. Their dominant position was taken over by the Czech nobility and upper middle classes; the poorer people still had no say in the government of the country. The devastation of war drove farmers and peasants even deeper into debt and subservience.

And yet, the religious and social revolution represented by the Hussite movement remains the first reform movement to have a broadly based political impact on Europe as a whole. Its influence on the development of Bohemia's neighbours was to be long-lasting. This was one of the key episodes in Czech history, in particular because it was the first time that there was widespread support for the foundation of a separate Czech state – even though it was unsuccessful.

The new order arising from the end of war was personified by George of Poděbrady and Kunštát, who as leader of the aristocratic Utraquists, was to rule from 1439 as imperial administrator, and from 1458–71 as king. But George could not bring lasting peace to Bohemia or revive prosperity. After his death the Bohemian Estates elected Prince Vladislav of the Polish Jagiellon dynasty as king. In 1491, in the Testament of Bratislava, the succession to the throne of Bohemia and Moravia was granted to the House of Habsburg. When the king's son Ludwig died without issue fighting against the Turks in 1526, the country passed into Habsburg hands. Together with Austria it was to remain under their rule until 1918.

Above, the Bethlehem Chapel in Prague was where Jan Hus preached his damning sermons in the Czech language. Right, a portrait of the great reformer.

JAN HUS

Master Jan Hus, the preacher and philosopher whose teachings formed the foundation of the revolutionary Hussite Movement, is one of the legendary characters of Czech history. More than any other national hero, he was an inspiration to the common people. His name crops up in folk songs, he is the hero of several plays and in recent years he has even been the subject of films. The anniversary of his death, on 6 July 1415, is still celebrated as a national festival of remembrance.

Jan Hus was born in 1371 in the village of Husinec in Southern Bohemia. He studied at the local school and went on to Charles University, from which he graduated in 1396 with a Master of Liberal Arts degree. Two years later he was appointed as an ordinarius professor. In 1400 he was ordained priest and became the first Czech rector of the Charles University in 1409.

During his youth he began to devote his attention to the written works of the English theologian and reformer John Wyclif, who attacked the secularisation of the church and demanded a return to the doctrine and practices of the early Christian communities. Wyclif considered that the only real sign of membership of the church was an exemplary lifestyle; he acknowledged the Bible as the one true foundation of faith. Hus developed Wyclif's thesis further, emphasising the social aspects.

The unadorned Bethlehem Chapel in Prague, to which Hus was summoned as preacher in 1402, proved an ideal forum for disseminating his message to the widest possible audience. In order to get his points across, Hus, who was a brilliant rhetorical speaker, developed his own, often unconventional methods. He delivered most of his sermons and commentaries in Czech, even going so far as to write a number of texts on the walls of the chapel. He translated hymns and religious songs, thereby enabling a wide spectrum of churchgoers to take an active part in the service. One by-product of this approach was that Hus modernised spoken Czech, elevating it to the level of the written language. Hus found widespread support amongst many German-speaking theologians of the time; they even endorsed his demands for equal rights for the Czechs in Bohemia, seeing it as a justifiable pastoral and social affair.

But what had begun as brotherly criticism of the Catholic Church soon developed into a vitriolic attack upon the institution as he saw it. Hus's passionate demands for a return to the traditional poverty of the clergy and a general improvement in the moral standards of public life aroused the enmity of the upper echelons of the priesthood as well as causing animosity on the part of those members of the aristocracy who saw their privileged lifestyle about to disappear.

The conflict reached a head in 1411, when Hus castigated the sale of indulgences as amoral charlatanism. There were public demonstrations for and against his theories; the church excommunicated Hus and forbade him to exercise his priestly office, although he continued to preach at the Bethlehem Chapel and to teach at the university. But when he lost the support of King

Wenceslas IV, who shared in the proceeds of the sale of indulgences, Hus left Prague and began to preach in rural areas; here he found time to examine his doctrines in greater depth and to publish them under the title *De ecclesia*, in 1413.

During the spring of 1414 Sigismund, the King of the Germans, challenged Hus to declare his position before the Council of Constance. He was promised a safe passage and so, against the advice of many of his friends, Hus set out to attend. His hearing before the council developed into a fierce theological dispute; in the end, the conservatives won the day and Hus was found guilty of heresy. When he refused to recant his beliefs he was burned at the stake. ■

After the Hussite wars Bohemia's frontiers remained inviolate, but within the country itself unrest continued to ferment. An uneasy peace ensued when George of Poděbrady, the leader of the Utraquist aristocracy, came to the throne in 1458. He earned a place in the annals of European history with his proposals for a general treaty of non-aggression involving all the countries of Europe including Turkey. The plan was never realised because of the rivalries between the various rulers, but it was the first attempt of its kind and served as a model for future alliances.

George of Poděbrady was the last Czech king. Between 1471 and 1526 he was succeeded by the Jagiellon dynasty from Poland. Under their rule the power of the upper aristocracy resumed its former strength. With the coronation of Vladislav II Jagiello as king of Hungary in 1490, Slovakia, which had been part of the Hungarian kingdom ever since the destruction of Greater Moravia in the 11th century, was once more included in the union with Bohemia and Moravia.

In 1526, following the death of the young Jagiellon King Ludwig while fighting the Turks in the Battle of Mohacs in Southern Hungary, the throne of Bohemia and Hungary passed to Ferdinand von Habsburg, thus marking the start of a period of almost four centuries of Habsburg rule over Bohemia, Moravia and Slovakia. The Habsburgs concentrated political power in the hands of the king, supported by the Catholic Church and a handful of powerful magnates.

Ferdinand, who was also crowned Holy Roman Emperor in 1556 following the abdication of his elder brother Charles V, attempted to strike a balance throughout his vast empire between Catholics and Protestants. At the same time, however, he actively supported the Counter-Reformation in the lands of the Bohemian crown by summoning the Jesuits to Prague. The Jesuit Collegium Clementinum, founded by the king, gave the

Preceding pages: The Battle of Austerlitz, in which Napoleon defeated the Habsburgs on 2 December 1805, is reenacted every year. <u>Left</u>, George of Poděbrady, the last Bohemian king (1458–71). <u>Above</u>, Rudolf II of Habsburg.

Bohemian capital a Catholic university, and its reputation was soon to outstrip that of the Carolinum.

From Vienna to Hradčany: Even this could not prevent the Catholics sinking progressively into a minority within the lands of the Bohemian crown; by the end of the 16th century at least 80 percent of the population claimed to be Protestant. Ferdinand's son, Maximilian II, found himself beset by almost insurmountable problems in the face of increasingly violent religious quarrels within

his kingdom. His successor, Rudolf II (1576–1611), was more interested in the arts than in affairs of state – his collection of the visual arts included masterpieces and curiosities from all over the world. Although born in Vienna, he moved his official residence to Hradčany Castle in 1583, thereby initiating unexpected economic prosperity in Prague.

In 1593 the Turks attacked again following a long period of truce and the Habsburgs had difficulty keeping them at bay. Matthias, Rudolf's younger brother, eventually took over command of the army and managed to conclude a new peace with the Turks in 1606. The emperor, now mentally deranged, died in 1612, one year after he had been forced to abdicate the Bohemian throne in favour of his power-hungry brother.

The Bohemian Estates could only make temporary capital out of the family quarrel; in 1609 Rudolf had granted them complete freedom of religion and various other privileges in a *Letter of Majesty* – advantages which they had to defend against Matthias. The conflict intensified as both sides attempted to secure their positions by means of alliances: the Catholic princes formed the League, the Protestants the Union.

The second Defenestration of Prague: The religious time bomb finally exploded on 23 May 1618. In accordance with an old Bohe-

chose Friedrich of the Palatinate as their new king. The insult hit deep, for with the election of the leader of the Union it seemed as if the empire would not only lose Bohemia itself, one of the central countries of Europe, but also that the balance of power on the continent would be tipped in favour of the Protestants. The Emperor and the Catholic League reacted immediately by sending in a powerful army under General Tilly.

The Thirty Years' War: The Battle of the White Mountain, before the gates of Prague, took place on 8 November 1620. It was decided within the space of a few hours. Friedrich, the "Winter King" – so called because his reign had lasted for less than one

mian custom, the rebellious representatives of the Bohemian Estates threw two of the emperor's men and their secretary from the window of the chancellery in Hradčany Castle. This second Defenestration of Prague unleashed the Bohemian War, which was soon to develop into the Thirty Years' War involving all of Europe.

Occupying the throne of Bohemia at the time was Ferdinand II, who became king of Hungary in 1618 and Holy Roman Emperor a year later. This fact no longer interested the self-confident Protestant Bohemian Estates; they declared Bohemia an electoral monarchy, deposed Ferdinand and in August 1619

year – was forced to flee, losing all his electoral privileges within the empire. The enemy troops had little difficulty overcoming the hastily erected barricades; for weeks they plundered and destroyed everything they could lay their hands on. Hundreds of people were indiscriminately condemned to death or driven into exile, from ringleaders to people who had not even been involved.

Ferdinand tore up Rudolf's *Letter of Majesty* with his own hands, expelling all non-Catholic priests from the city and forcing the aristocracy and citizens alike to return to the fold of the Catholic Church. During the following years the Catholic Church soared to new heights of power, achieving an authority it had failed to enjoy since the Hussite Revolution. Protestant intellectuals, such as the famous philosopher and teacher Jan Amos Comenius (1592–1670), the bishop of the Bohemian Brethren, were forced to leave their native land.

Even after this fearful blood-letting there was no peace within the country. Merciless persecution and local uprisings continued to shatter Bohemia and Moravia and, following the intervention of Sweden, the war entered a second violent phase. This was the hour of Albrecht von Wallenstein, also known as Waldstein, a Bohemian nobleman who had converted from Protestantism to Catholi-

assassinated in 1634 in Cheb. Even without him, the imperial army won a decisive victory over the Swedish forces near Nördlingen; with the Treaty of Westphalia of 30 May 1635, the stifling peace of the Habsburgs descended on this part of Europe.

Under the Habsburg yoke: The failure of the rebellion had catastrophic consequences. The Habsburgs could now expand their absolute power without fearing any resistance; they moved the centre of political power once and for all to Vienna. Although nominally retaining their independence, the lands of the Bohemian crown became a provincial backwater, a situation which had disastrous effects on what had once been a buoyant independ-

cism in 1606 and had earned his military spurs as an officer under General Tilly. Having been awarded supreme power over all imperial armies, Wallenstein reached the zenith of his power when his opponent, Gustav Adolf, was killed in the battle of Lützen, near Leipzig, in 1632. But wary of his ambitions for power, his enemies soon closed rank and persuaded the emperor to denounce him; Wallenstein was ultimately

Left, the Defenestration of 1618. **Above left**, the Vladislav Hall in Hradčany at the time of Rudolf II (detail of an engraving by Aegidius Sadeler, 1607); Albrecht von Wallenstein.

ent culture. This was most obvious in the field of literature; Czech came to be regarded as the language of urban working people and rural peasants while German came to dominate lawyers' offices and literary salons alike. From 1763, university lectures were mostly held in German; it was not until 1791 that a chair of Czech language and literature was established at Prague University.

The economy, also largely controlled by the Germans, suffered badly from the devastation of towns that had prospered on their flourishing trade and skilled craftsmen. The tightening of serfdom in the country slowed down productivity and prevented a rapid revival. Peasants whose farmsteads had survived the war were now faced with the burden of paying feudal dues and socage (service) to the nobility so exorbitant that their very existence was threatened. The personal freedom of the individual was severely restricted: not only every marriage, but also the practice of a trade or the attendance at a place of further education had to be given the official seal of approval.

An era of tolerance: The status quo remained unchanged until the reign of the Empress Maria Theresa, who was crowned Queen of Bohemia in 1743 in Prague. Her son, Joseph II, who from 1765 ruled Bohemia jointly with his mother, was responsible for a new to become the most profitable economic region within the Habsburg empire. The manufacture of textiles provided the basis for an accelerated exploitation of industrial resources. Before the turn of the century an English spinning machine was inaugurated in Northern Bohemia. A few years later, steam-driven machinery was widely used in Brno and Prague. The attractive products of the glass-blowing and porcelain manufacturing industries conquered the European market; heavy industry followed in 1821 with the first iron blast furnace.

The national revival and revolution: The rapid economic expansion failed, however, to remove social and national tensions. Above

tolerance which permitted the existence of faiths other than Catholicism and allowed Jews to leave the ghettos.

Of more far-reaching importance for the subsequent development of the country was the edict proclaiming the abolition of serfdom in 1781, a move which paved the way for a liberalisation of the economy and society as a whole. The release of workers to satisfy the rapidly growing requirements of firms and businesses was as much a prerequisite for the industrial revolution as the improvement and expansion of educational opportunities.

Bohemia and Moravia rapidly expanded all, the language dispute continued to seethe, for Czechs and Slovaks alike demanded official recognition for their languages, and parity with German. The dispute provided a continual source of strife: for example, when the Czech aristocracy was gathered in Prague for the coronation of King Leopold II, they refused to speak anything but Czech in protest at the language policy of the Habsburgs. The resulting discord shattered the hopes for harmony of the new monarch, who had travelled to Prague specially for the occasion.

In spite of a number of concessions the Czechs and Slovaks were unable to reach agreement; indeed, they believed that the discrimination against their language was a symptom of the lack of respect for their nationality and an attempt to wipe out once and for all their cultural identity. Nationalism became the dominant theme of the revolutionary years 1848–49. But although all the movements were directed against absolutism and centralism, there was a conflict of national interests and goals.

It was the main goal of the German Nationalist Movement that it should create a united Germany. Even those Germans who lived in Czechoslovakia aspired to this goal. They automatically assumed that Czech territories should be part of a united Germany. This idea met with violent opposition on the part

First Slavic Congress in June 1848 in Prague. He demanded the transformation of the Austrian monarchy into a national federation, in which the united Slavs were to have decisive influence. But the Slavic rulers were uncoordinated. When unrest broke out in Prague and barricades were erected in Vienna, the imperial troops were soon able to regain the upper hand.

During the spring of 1848, Slovakian society supported the results of the Hungarian revolution. Their representatives voted for Slovakia to assume an autonomous position within the framework of a federal Hungarian state. Although encouraged by the Habsburgs's centralised administration, these

of the Czechs themselves, who in their turn sought allies amongst the other oppressed Slavic peoples and who – like the Czech delegation from Bohemia – turned down the invitation to attend the German National Assembly in St Paul's Church in Frankfurt on the grounds that they were not Germans. This attitude found expression in the doctrine of so-called Austroslavism.

The historian František Palacký had himself elected speaker of the movement at the

Left, life in the Jewish quarter around 1900. **Above**, a Czech farmer and his wife at the turn of the century.

Slovakian nationalist demands met with opposition on the part of the Hungarian revolutionary government, which instead used all its influence to assert a Hungarian Nationalist policy. After the creation of the dual monarchy of Austro-Hungary in 1867, the Hungarian government resumed control over Slovakia, and its policy of Magyarisation stimulated many Slovaks to emigrate, particularly to the United States. Slovakia remained a province of Upper Hungary right up to 1918.

A president from Moravia: After 1848 Czech political representatives supported the federalisation of the monarchy. When Austria rejected such demands out of hand, more radical suggestions gradually gained support. Towards the end of the 19th century a generation of self-confident professional politicians emerged and the various sections of Czech society, increasingly aware of their group and class interests, formed independent political organisations.

By the turn of the century, German national groups began to demand the unification with the German empire of areas settled predominantly by Germans; the radical Young Czechs, on the other hand, demanded a Czech state within a federation with Hungary and Austria as well as unity with the Slovaks. The new trend was known as Politi-

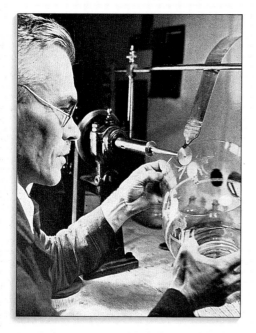

cal Realism; its most famous representative was Tomáš Garrigue Masaryk, who was to become the first Czech president.

Masaryk (1850–1937) was born in Hodonin in Southern Moravia, the son of a Slovak father and a German mother. He attended the German grammar school in Brno (Brünn), later studying philosophy and philology in Vienna and Leipzig. He was an academic educated in the best German cultural tradition. At the age of 32 he was summoned to the newly founded Czech University of Prague, created by the division of the venerable Charles University.

In 1891 he was elected leader by the Young

Czechs, and in 1907 he became leader of the People's Party in the Austrian Imperial Parliament. He established a reputation as a moderate politician devoted to a humanistic ideal of statehood. When war broke out, he emigrated in turn to Rome, Geneva and Paris, convinced that he had to fight for an independent Czechoslovakia from abroad. Together with Eduard Beneš, he founded a Czechoslovak National Council, from which a provisional government was created in 1918. In 1917 he had organised the Czech Legion, which earned a fine reputation among the Allies for their assistance during the anti-Soviet intervention.

Whilst the Allies initially saw Masaryk as no more than a useful instrument in their anti-Habsburg propaganda machine, Masaryk gradually succeeded in convincing the leaders of the Entente powers – the United Kingdom, France and the United States – of the viability of a united Czech and Slovak state, which he saw as the best antidote to Habsburg arrogance and German lust for power. It was Masaryk's greatest achievement that he succeeded in bringing to the conference table the scattered Czechs and Slovaks, an achievement which culminated in the Pittsburgh Convention of May 1918 containing the joint statement of the Czech and Slovak leaders in support of the foundation of a common federal state.

At the eleventh hour, Emperor Charles I of Austria attempted to save what was beyond repair: on 16 October he announced the transformation of his empire into an alliance of sovereign nations. Only a few years previously the Slavic nations would have greeted such a move with boisterous enthusiasm – but now it was too late. On 28 October the Czechoslovak Republic was proclaimed in Prague; on 14 November, three days after the emperor's abdication, the National Assembly elected Masaryk as the president of the new nation. Over 14 million people – 5.5 million Czechs and 3.1 million Germans, 3.5 million Slovaks and 750,000 Hungarians, 460,000 Carpathian Ukrainians and 70,000 Poles in areas without clearly defined boundaries, not to mention 200,000 Jews and other minority groups – unexpectedly found themselves part of a new country.

Above, Bohemia grew famous for its fine cut-glass. Right, a tram in Prague (1913).

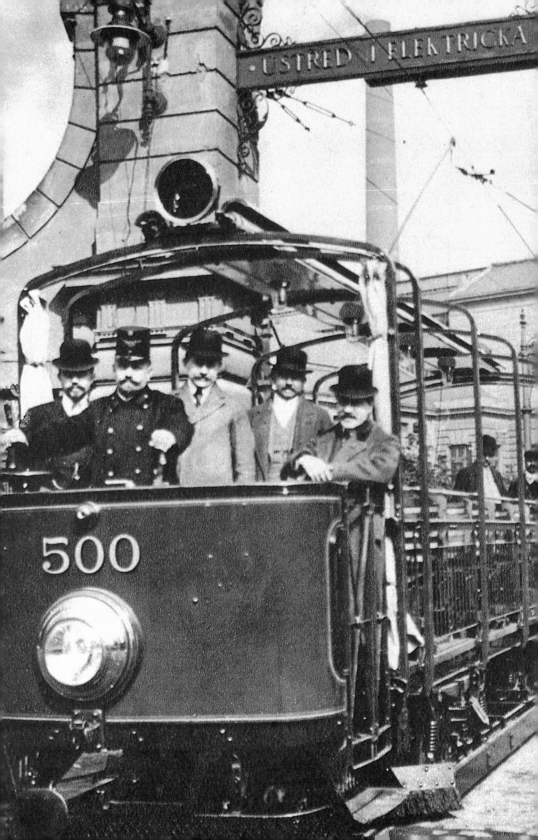

FROM REPUBLIC TO PROTECTORATE

The section of society which set the tone in the new independent state of Czechoslovakia was the Czech bourgeoisie. During those first years, it devoted its energies to transforming Prague into the capital of a modern European industrial country.

But it soon became evident that the country had inherited a number of basic structural problems stemming from the centuries of non-autonomous development: whilst the well-developed consumer goods industry found its market reduced in the first instance from the vast area occupied by the former Habsburg Empire to the much smaller internal market of Czechoslovkia, the country's heavy industry suffered from the lack of previous development and proved inadequate to supply the demands of the internal market. Even during the boom years of the 1920s the planners were unable to make any fundamental changes to this imbalance; after the advent of the Great Depression, there was neither the time nor the money for far-reaching reform. Agricultural development suffered a similar fate. The potential of the comparatively intensive farming industry was squandered by the inadequate attempts at land reform; the victims of the spreading crisis were above all the small and medium-sized farmers, especially those living in the ethnically mixed border regions.

The period of the Great Depression exacerbated the ethnic conflicts, which had remained a perpetual problem within the new republic. On the one hand, Czechoslovakia was a state with a democratic constitution, offering religious and ethnic minorities a high degree of protection and therefore providing asylum to growing numbers of political refugees from the increasingly authoritarian countries whose borders it shared: Germany, Poland and Hungary. On the other hand, the ruling Czech elite was not prepared to keep the rash promises it had made to other minority groups within the country.

Preceding pages: mine workers start their shift in Jáchymov. **Left,** Tomáš Masaryk, the founder and first president of the republic. **Above,** the double-eagle of the Austro-Hungarian monarchy was thrown out of the castle's window in 1918.

The Slovaks and the Carpatho-Ukrainians, who had been bold enough to join in the common adventure of Czechoslovakia in 1918, felt they had been cheated of their promised autonomy. And instead of cultural autonomy the German-speaking population found itself faced with wide-ranging discrimination in public life, culminating in the closure of the German university in Prague in 1934. There were already signs that a storm was brewing within the country when the new republic came face to face with

dramatically deteriorating conditions on the international scene.

Collapse and German rule: From the beginning the state's founders and first two presidents, Tomáš G. Masaryk from 1918 to 1935, and Eduard Beneš from 1935 to 1938, had seen the hegemony of France's position within the continent of Europe and the cooperation with the victorious Entente powers as a guarantee of Czechoslovakia's survival. But the Treaties of Versailles, St Germain and Trianon (1918, 1919, 1920), which determined Czechoslovakia's international frontiers, soon proved to be a very shaky barrier in the face of new territorial demands on the part of neighbouring countries. The Little Entente, the alliance formed in 1922 by the Czech foreign minister Eduard Beneš with Yugoslavia and Romania, both equally threatened by Hungary's quest for land, provided some temporary stability on the southeast flank. Nonetheless, everyone was aware that the biggest danger threatening Czechoslovakia lay to the west and north, where not only the Germans but also the Poles were demanding more land. Furthermore, both countries were able to exert considerable pressure on account of the minority groups actually living on Czech territory.

As early as November 1918, the German-speaking areas of Bohemia and Moravia creased his demands in the Karlsbad Programme of 24 April 1938. The basic tenets were self-administration, equal rights and reparation; during the local authority elections in May of that year the party won 92 percent of all German votes. When, under pressure from the western powers, the Prague government intervened, Henlein demanded the Anschluss with the German Reich.

The Munich Agreement: During the late summer, Britain's special envoy, Viscount Runciman, tried to act as arbitrator in Prague. He recommended the relinquishment of the German-speaking areas. During the discussions with Neville Chamberlain which followed, Hitler agreed to making 1 October

declared themselves part of "German-Austria", upon which Czech troops had used force to break up the local and provincial government apparatus. In 1933 Konrad Henlein founded the Sudeten German Home Front as an umbrella organisation for all German nationalist organisations in Czechoslovakia. In the 1935 elections, as the leader of the Sudeten German Party, he won 68 percent of all German votes, thereby becoming the head of the strongest group within the parliament in Prague. Henlein now demanded autonomy for the regions inhabited by German settlers in Bohemia and Moravia. After discussions with Hitler, he clarified and in-1938 the date for the transfer. Under the chairmanship of Mussolini, the Munich Agreement was signed by France, the United Kingdom and the German Reich on 29 September 1938.

Chamberlain and Daladier were convinced that they had thus ensured peace within Europe; the Soviet Union criticised the treaty but was neither able nor willing to risk war. Czechoslovakia was not consulted, and was forced to look on passively when, on 1 October, German troops in official support of human rights marched into the so-called Sudeten German Gau, to the jubilant cheers of the German populace. Poland and Hungary also took advantage of the favourable conditions to annex border areas. The Little Entente collapsed. On 5 October Beneš resigned and fled into exile in England.

The Protectorate of Bohemia and Moravia: Not content with this triumph, Hitler was anxious to "deal with the rest of Czechoslovakia", as a secret order of 21 October 1938 reveals. He encouraged the continued territorial demands of Poland and Hungary, and incited the Slovaks to proclaim their own independence. In Berlin on 15 March, by means of undisguised military threats, he forced the national president of Czechoslovakia, Emil Hacha, to sign an agreement confirming the creation of the National Protectorate of Bohemia and Moravia. Just a few hours later on, German troops marched into Prague.

Formally speaking the Protectorate remained a state under the protection of the German Reich; it had, however, no independent policies in the realms of foreign affairs, economics and defence. It retained its own head of state and a puppet government for home affairs, justice and culture. This secured the cooperation of some of the 7.3 million inhabitants.

The true power lay in the hands of the German protector, whose seat of administration was in Prague. The governing body not only organised the arrest and deportation of Jews but also devoted considerable efforts to silencing the Czech intelligentsia. The closure of schools and universities, institutes of culture and newspapers, the ban placed upon the choice of some professions and the enforced deportations took a heavy toll amongst teachers, academics, artists and journalists. The world-famous Barrandov Studios were forced to devote themselves to making propaganda films, such as the shallow comedies about the passionate Matjuschka and her handsome young lieutenant, designed to keep the troops at the front entertained and happy.

The Nazis employed the same thorough approach in their efforts to turn the Protectorate into an impregnable centre of armaments production and industry. Weapons would continue to be manufactured here

Left, Tomáš G. Masaryk promulgated the independent Czechoslovak Republic in Philadelphia, on 18 October 1918. **Above**, the staircase in the National Museum in Prague.

right up to the end of the war, owing to the limited range of the Allied bombers.

Massacre at Lidice: The workforce was lulled into submission by high wages and comparatively favourable working conditions. Since repression within Czechoslovakia was almost complete, resistance efforts had to be steered from abroad. The attempt on the life of the deputy Reichsprotector Reinhard "the hangman" Heydrich on 27 May 1942 was the work of a group of émigrés. Upon instructions from the government in exile in London, they parachuted into Prague and threw a bomb at Heydrich's car. They were finally shot in their hiding place in the Church of SS Cyril and Methodius. Not content with a

wave of executions and arrests in Prague, in retribution the Gestapo shot all adult male inhabitants of the mining village of Lidice on 10 June 1942 and sent the women and children to concentration camps.

On 5 May 1945 the citizens of Prague rose in united rebellion against the German occupying forces. Three days before the end of the war they directed their pent-up anger against the Sudeten Germans too; most of the latter were forced to leave their homes; of a total of some 3 million, only 200,000 stayed. When the victorious Red Army came, it was rapturously greeted by the populace, who believed the moment of freedom had come.

The Protectorate of Slovakia: The majority of Slovaks, deeply disappointed at the policy of the Prague government in the nationalities question, had watched more or less passively the threatened dismemberment of Czechoslovakia. The strongest voice was the fiercely nationalist Slovakian People's Party under the leadership of the Catholic priest Jozef Tiso. Slovakian politicians who spoke out in favour of cooperation with the Czechs quickly lost the support of the people.

On 6 October 1938, as a consequence of the Munich Agreement, Slovakia proclaimed itself an autonomous unit within the federal Czecho-Slovak state. Tiso was appointed prime minister. Early in the following year,

Hungary, which had entered into an alliance with Germany.

The most tragic chapter in the story of the German-Slovakian protective alliance was the active cooperation of the Slovakian government in the persecution and extermination of the Jews. Some 110,000 Slovakian Jews were mercilessly handed over to the Germans and sent to concentration camps. Only when the Vatican's protests became unequivocal did Tiso abandon the practice. In 1944 the approaching Red Army incited the populace to active resistance against the Fascist regime; in August, even Čatloš, the Minister of War, defected to the resistance with some sections of the army. But assisted

however, he demanded complete sovereignty for Slovakia. Hitler announced his support for this move on 13 March 1939 in Berlin; the following day Tiso declared the state to be fully independent.

Hitler made the Slovaks pay dearly for this favour; on 23 March 1939 the state was forced to place itself under the protection of the German Reich, relinquishing all claims to independent foreign, economic and defence policies. Further humiliations followed in the form of the construction of German defences in Western Slovakia, complete cultural autonomy for the German minority population and territorial concessions to

by German troops, the regime was able to remain in power for some months longer. On 4 April 1945 the Red Army entered Bratislava; in the Košice Programme of 5 April the resistance leaders under communist leadership proclaimed the fraternal unity of the Czech and Slovak peoples and demanded the nationalisation of key industries and financial institutions. Tiso was executed on 18 April 1947 in Bratislava.

Above, to the indignation of the populace, German troops marched into Prague on 15 March 1939. **Right**, a tour of the concentration camp in Terezín (Theresienstadt).

50

THE GHETTO OF TEREZÍN

The little town of Terezín (Theresienstadt) nestles idyllically in the valley of the Labe (Elbe) at the foot of fertile volcanic hills. The pretty surroundings are deceptive, however; today, for most citizens of the Czech Republic, Terezín is a symbol of man's inhumanity to man.

The *malá pevnost*, the little fortress overlooking the town, was built by Emperor Joseph II at the end of the 18th century as part of the line of defences protecting Austria against Prussian aggression. Because of the alleged military urgency of the project, the entire complex was completed within only 10 years. Paradoxically, however, it never proved necessary for the castle to serve its true purpose. During World War I it was used as a prison; when the Nazis invaded Bohemia, they used it for the same purpose – but this time for the imprisonment of Jews.

During World War II the German occupying forces created in Theresienstadt a notorious walled ghetto for Jews. Shipment of Jewish captives into Theresienstadt began in November 1941. Accordingly, the entire non-Jewish population of the town, numbering some 3,700, was hurriedly resettled elsewhere in order to make room for the new arrivals.

The Nazis claimed that the camp they were building here was a Jewish settlement with its own administration. When the International Red Cross insisted on visiting a concentration camp, the delegation was sent to Theresienstadt where it was treated to a week of cultural entertainment. It was, of course, a propaganda lie designed to deceive the rest of the world; for a long time, however, many Jews also believed in it and failed to flee to safety.

Theresienstadt occupied a special position in Hitler's plans for the extermination of the Jewish race. It served as a distribution centre for the transport of Jews (its location at the heart of Europe prevented the construction of a proper extermination camp of the kind to be found in the remotest corners of Eastern Poland). The Gestapo sent prisoners not only from Prague but also from the entire Protectorate of Bohemia and Moravia.

Deportation trains from other countries also deposited their human cargo here. Through the gate surmounted by the cynical motto ARBEIT MACHT FREI (Work Liberates) passed thousands of Jewish prisoners from Poland, Austria, Belgium, the Netherlands, Italy, Russia, Latvia, Lithuania, Greece, Spain, Yugoslavia, France. Towards the end of the war, as the battle front closed in on Germany and camps such as Treblinka had to be dissolved in order to hide the traces of the brutal mass murders, internees of other concentration camps were brought to Theresienstadt. During the five years of its existence some 140,000 prisoners passed through the camp; over 30,000 died in the dense overcrowding of the ghetto itself and 88,000 were shipped on to the extermination camps, especially Auschwitz.

Transport convoys bringing new inhabitants arrived continuously in the camp. No fewer than 500 trains – in other words, an average of one every three days – came to a halt here between November 1941 and April 1945. Amongst the

largest contingents were the 40,000 Jews brought from Prague, 9,000 from Brno, 13,500 from Berlin, and 4,000 from Frankfurt.

When liberation finally came in May 1945, the Allies encountered thousands of emaciated, terrified prisoners. This statement of bald facts cannot convey the agonies they endured in their perpetual state of uncertainty and fear that the following day they, too, might be taken away. Today, their most poignant memorial lies not in words but in the national place of remembrance.

After World War II, Theresienstadt was resurrected as a Czech town, under its Czech name Terezín. It became a notable centre for the manufacture of furniture and knitwear. ∎

In the autumn of 1939, from his London exile, Beneš had established a Czechoslovak National Committee which was recognised by the Allies as a provisional government. Despite their support from Moscow, even the Czech communists under the leadership of Klement Gottwald recognised the legitimacy of this government in exile; in 1943 the Soviet Union concluded a treaty of friendship and assistance. They agreed on the rejection of the Munich Agreement and the expulsion of the Sudeten Germans.

The role of the Soviet Union was in any case crucial as the Western Allies had already agreed at the Yalta Conference that the rearrangement of political relationships within Czechoslovakia should take place under the aegis of Stalin, and that the country should be liberated by the Red Army. Accordingly, in 1945 the American troops who had liberated Plzeň and Western Bohemia retreated once more in the face of the advancing Russian forces.

The National President, Beneš, and the Prime Minister, Zdeněk Fierlinger, who had taken up office in Prague in May 1945, saw no reason for alarm. During the turmoil and tragedy of the previous years the Soviet Union had shown itself to be a loyal ally, and in any case the Russians were fellow Slavs. The population at large demonstrated their confidence in the communists by awarding them almost 38 percent of the votes during the last free elections in 1946. The communist Klement Gottwald was appointed leader of a coalition government. President Beneš defined the role of the new Czechoslovakia as a bridge between east and west.

The peace was deceptive: in February 1948 the communists seized power by means of an arranged putsch with staged demonstrations and strikes. The move was non-violent but highly effective. The non-communist ministers resigned from the government; Beneš also stepped down. Jan Masaryk, the son of the founder of the Czech state, had been foreign minister since 1945. On 10 March 1948 his body was found beneath the open window of the foreign ministry in Prague, and it was assumed he had killed himself in protest at the Stalinisation of his homeland.

Collapse of a utopia: During each year of its existence (from 9 May 1948 as a People's Democratic Republic, and from 1960 as the Socialist Republic), the inevitable failure of the utopian vision became increasingly evident. The country, once one of Central Europe's most prosperous bastions of tolerance, was transformed into a prison. The political climate was dominated by elaborate mock trials. All western influence was designated as evil by the communist ideologists. The Soviet Union was upheld as the only

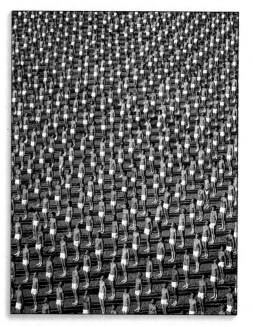

logical model for development; Marxist-Leninist doctrines were glorified as the all-embracing ultimate philosophy.

The country became the victim of intransigent socialist policies. Whilst thousands of citizens, especially the intellectuals, fled from the country once more – leading to an acute shortage of qualified doctors, teachers and scientists – the government embarked upon the enforced collectivisation of agriculture and the development of heavy industry without any proper regard for mankind or the environment.

The economy was subject to long-term planning policies, known as the Five-Year

Plans, and was under the direct guidance of the Central Committee. External trade became increasingly dependent upon the Soviet Union. In 1949 Czechoslovakia became a member of the Council for Mutual Economic Aid (COMECON); in 1955 it joined the Warsaw Pact.

Even after Stalin's death and the Twentieth Communist Party Conference in 1956, the situation within Czechoslovakia remained unchanged. The reign of terror inflicted by the leaders in Hradčany Castle was sur-

passed only on occasion by that of the rulers of the German Democratic Republic.

The Prague Spring: From the early 1960s it was public knowledge that the system was bankrupt; even within the party, voices of criticism could be heard, supported by writers, film makers and journalists, who ventured out of hiding despite threats of banishment and their repeated arrest. The Fourth Congress of the Czechoslovakian Writers'

Left, falling into line at the Spartacus Games. **Above**, Alexander Dubček (died 1992), pioneer of the Prague Spring and back on the scene in 1990 as president of the parliament.

Union in June 1967 marked a milestone along the road to the Prague Spring of 1968; for the first time a number of young writers dared to speak out openly in vehement protest. The lecture given by the dramatist Václav Havel, who was only 31 at the time, was greeted with wild enthusiasm.

In January 1968 the reform movement asserted itself. Alexander Dubček became the party leader and announced the new era of "socialism with a human face", respect for civic rights, protection for minorities and the urgently needed settlement of the Slovak problem. Oldřich Černík, a respected economist, began a comprehensive reform of the economy. The Prague Spring was seen by millions of Czechs as well as by citizens of other countries within eastern and western Europe as the last chance to put into political practice the true ideals of socialism.

The leaders of the Soviet Union and their puppets in Eastern Europe were alarmed; they feared the collapse of the Soviet national system and the loss of their own power. Brezhnev developed the concept that the Soviet path was the only path to real socialism. The Brezhnev Doctrine justified the invasion of Czechoslovakia by Warsaw Pact troops on 20 August 1968. The citizens struggled desperately; photos of old women and young students attempting to hold back the tanks with banners and slogans on Wenceslas Square were wired around the world. All to no avail – the hopes of an entire generation were crushed. Dubček was forced to retract his reform doctrines in Moscow; he returned to Prague a broken man and was replaced by the political hard-liner Gustav Husák.

The agony of Czech society was to continue for two more decades. In spite of the widespread resignation, many refused to give up; however, they now no longer demanded a reform of socialism, but a complete and unconditional democratisation of their country. With no organised support from the people, Czech civic rights campaigners such as Jiří Hájek, Jan Potočka and Václav Havel formed the Charter 77 in 1977, demonstrating that, even under a system which denied basic human rights, it was still possible to hold up one's head.

AN PALACH

TOMÁS

The year 1989 is without doubt one of the historic milestones of the 20th century, since within an incredibly short space of time a system which had embraced the whole of Eastern Europe for decades collapsed like a pack of cards. The conscious refusal of the Soviet government under Mikhail Gorbachev to use force to interfere in events permitted the countries of the Warsaw Pact to take their fate into their own hands again. Poland was the first to take advantage; in Hungary, too, the democratic process advanced at a rapid pace, and in East Germany the citizens rose in protest until the Berlin Wall – the most tangible symbol of the Iron Curtain – also fell.

The communist leaders of Czechoslovakia saw the disintegration happen before their very eyes, but they observed the tempestuous changes with apparent indifference, as if paralysed. The team was the same one which had been carried to power by Brezhnev's tanks. A peaceful demonstration began on 15 January 1989 on Wenceslas Square in memory of the self-immolation of the student Jan Palach in 1969. Police and army troops brutally separated the crowd. They returned at double and triple strength, and the demonstration continued until 19 January. Blows and arrests no longer frightened the citizens.

In June a petition entitled "A Few Sentences" was put into circulation, and thousands clamoured to add their names. Even now, however, the communists were not prepared to enter into discussions with the opposition, but preferred to maintain their approach in an attitude of unreal invincibility. The rejection of the last offer of talks was, it transpired, the final and crucial mistake of the ruling committee.

The peaceful student demonstration on 17 November 1989, in memory of the student Jan Opletal, who had been shot by the Nazis 50 years previously, triggered the course of events. Some 50,000 people took part; it was the largest mass demonstration since 1969. Although the protest march through Prague took place without incident, the police tried to prevent it by parking lorries across the route

Left, many revolutionary changes in the history of the country started out from Wenceslas Square.

and by driving cars in a threatening manner. The hated Red Beret units attacked the demonstrators with batons. After this first example of brutality against the younger generation, events got out of hand more rapidly than in any other Eastern European country. The opposition took matters seriously. Two days later it founded the Civic Forum Movement (Občanské fórum – OF), demanding the resignation of all members of the inner circle of the Central Committee of the Communist Party who had been involved in the intervention of 1968, and calling simultaneously for the immediate release of all political prisoners as well as a general strike. One day later the movement Public against Violence (Verejnost proti násilu – VPN) was founded in Bratislava.

Non-aggression wins through: In spite of much provocation, the democratic opposition honoured the rule of non-aggression. The resistance during those November days in 1989 went down in history as the "velvet revolution". For a whole week, 20–27 November, hundreds of thousands of citizens demonstrated in Wenceslas Square, demanding the resignation of the government. The Secretary General of the Central Committee, Milos Jakeš, was forced to resign on 24 November. Nonetheless a general strike throughout the country began on 27 November. Students were joined by actors, writers, artists and musicians.

On 29 November the general assembly of both chambers of the Federal Parliament passed a series of radical changes to the constitution. The lifting of the party dictate – which had originally been officially passed by the highest legal authority – was greeted with delight within the country and with respect abroad. It was a decisive moment for the continued progress of the peaceful revolution, because it paved the way for the necessary dialogue which was subsequently to develop over the following days and weeks in a new climate of free speech and increasing openness.

On 10 December the Prime Minister Marián Calfa, a Slovakian Communist, formed a new "Government of National Understanding". Gustav Husák resigned from his post as president and on 28 December the Federal Assembly elected Alexander Dubček as his successor. It was an office he had already filled during the Prague Spring, and for which he possessed not only the necessary moral authority but also the best qualifications as a representative of Slovakia, in accordance with the conditions of the federal constitution.

On 29 December the parliament met in an historic session in Hradčany Castle. After 41 years of communist rule, Václav Havel, until then a persecuted playwright and dissident, was elected by a predominantly communist parliament as the new representative of a democratically reformed Czechoslovakia. Havel was an immensely popular figure, and

in June 1990 he led Czechoslovakia into the first truly free elections since 1946.

The Civic Forum and the movement Public Against Violence in Slovakia received the endorsement of most of the electorate. But its leaders gradually drifted apart as the common enemy disappeared. The differences of opinion surfaced during debates on lustration, the "outing" of those who had held high office in the Communist Party or who had any connection with the secret police. It was meant not only to be an atonement by a handful for the rest of society, but also a practical measure to prevent tainted officials from holding any kind of public office for a period of five years.

Goodbye Czechoslovakia: The key question was how to achieve the economic reform that would lead to a free market. Throughout 1990 and early 1991, the great hope was foreign investment. When this failed to materialise on the scale required, an ambitious coupon scheme was introduced, giving every adult the chance to buy shares in the state firms being privatised.

The enormous success of the scheme boosted support for Václav Klaus, the country's finance minister and champion of the free market. The 1992 elections produced a clearer result than expected. Around 34 percent voted for Klaus's right-wing ODS Civic Democratic Party) and Vladimir Mečiar's HZDS (Movement for Democratic Slovakia). The electorate had chosen two strong leaders with conflicting views about the pace and scope of economic reform, with Klaus opting for fast-track privatisation. More importantly, in supporting Mečiar's HZDS, the people of Slovakia had signalled their approval for national independence. President Havel proposed a referendum but when this solution was rejected, he resigned, refusing to preside over the inevitable split.

At the beginning of December 1992, parliament passed the law providing for the dissolution of the country and from 1 January 1993 the state of Czechoslovakia ceased to exist.

Life after the "velvet divorce": In the new Czech Republic market reforms continued at breakneck speed under the abrasive but dynamic Klaus (with Havel as president). An ambitious privatisation programme was accompanied by a remarkably successful balancing of the budget, with an increase in exports, reduced inflation, low unemployment and impressive growth rates of around 5 percent in 1995. Such a uniformly upbeat picture could hardly fail to attract foreign investment and commentators began talking openly about an 'economic miracle'. The highpoint was reached towards the end of 1995 when the Czech Republic became the first post-communist state to join the Organisation for Economic Cooperation and Development (OECD), an important step on the road to the government's long-term goal of full membership of the European Union. However, there were already signs of trouble ahead.

Left, prisoners cast their vote in the first free elections of 1990. **Right**, their candidate.

The consumer boom of the early 1990s created a huge demand for Western goods and services at the expense of domestic suppliers, leading to a ballooning trade deficit. During the first half of 1996, as inflation showed signs of rising, ordinary Czech savers were hit by a spectacular wave of banking collapses, amid allegations of fraud and corruption. Unfortunately for the government, these worrying trends coincided with elections in which the Social Democrats, the main rivals to Klaus' ODS, quadrupled their number of seats, forcing the increasingly embattled premier to enter a coalition with two smaller parties. Since then the economic situation has deteriorated further, culminating in a 10 percent devaluation of the koruna, and the prospects of the Czech Republic meeting the criteria for EU entry by the target date of 2000 look questionable, to say the least.

Security was the major foreign policy goal of the Czech Republic in this period and the Klaus government saw membership of NATO as the best guarantee against foreign aggression. In March 1994 the Czechs signed up to the 'Partnership for Peace', a programme of military cooperation with the NATO countries. This was only a year after the Czechs had signed a Treaty of Friendship and Cooperation with Russia, which had already made its strong opposition to NATO expansion clear. Despite similar opposition voiced by Slovakia's premier, Mečiar, later dismissed as 'paranoid' by Václav Havel, it became clear that the Czech Republic was a likely candidate for inclusion in the first wave of new members. The Czechs, together with Poland and Hungary, were officially invited to join the club in June 1997.

Slovakia had also expressed a wish to join NATO but closer relations with Russia and the growing authoritarianism of the government were major obstacles to progress. Slovakia's economy had suffered in the early 1990s when the Czechoslovak government decided to reduce the production of military equipment and within a year of Slovakia's independence, unemployment was running at around 14 percent, more than three times the level in the Czech Republic. At the same time the Mečiar government was less committed to privatisation than its neighbour and its support for the arms industry was blatantly protectionist. Yet by the end of 1994 there were already signs of economic revival as GDP

increased by a healthy 5 per cent and the industrial sector also began to recover. In 1995 a strong and unexpected surge in exports contributed to a remarkable growth rate of 7 percent. However, progress in the economic sphere was impeded by growing political turmoil. Longstanding and increasingly bitter policy disagreements between the president, Michal Kováč, and the premier, Vladimir Mečiar, erupted into open warfare when Kováč's son was abducted in Bratislava and detained in Austria on embezzlement charges. Whether, as his enemies alleged, Mečiar was behind this attempt to discredit the president isn't clear, but the international community, led by the United States, was already con-

cerned about Mečiar's increasingly cavalier attitude to the democratic process. It was further outraged by the introduction, in 1996, of an anti-subversion law which could easily be used to curb freedom of expression and assembly. In May 1997 a new crisis erupted when the government announced it was removing a question on direct presidential elections from the referendum ballot on NATO membership. The opposition's call for a boycott was so successful that the vote was declared invalid. Given the present polarisation of Slovak society, it seems unlikely that the political climate will improve substantially until fresh elections are held in 1998.

The final division of Czechoslovakia into two completely separate republics was completed in January 1993. The divorce proceedings went smoothly although many feel that marriage could and should have been made to work. To others, who recognise that neither Czechs nor Slovaks had even considered living together in one state until the end of World War I, the failure to develop a common national identity despite common goals and common achievements comes as no surprise.

From the very outset, Czechoslovakia suffered from the fact that it was an artificial political unit welded together from fragments of the disintegrated Habsburg Empire. The last attempt of Czechs and Slovaks at forming a common state had been with the Kingdom of Greater Moravia more than 1,000 years ago. After its collapse, the Czech Lands and Slovakia essentially went their own separate ways, and their paths did not converge again until 1918. During all that time, the destiny of Slovakia was controlled by the Hungarians; even under the Habsburgs, Slovakia was counted as being part of Hungary. The industrial backbone of the Habsburg monarchy was formed by the twin Czech lands of Bohemia and Moravia; Slovakia was the poor neighbour.

The founding of the new nation in 1918 was a rushed affair; its leading lights – Masaryk, Beneš and General Štefánik – were all academics. Their political approach has been described, not unjustly, as the Professors' Revolution; something of this historic legacy no doubt played a role in the country's "velvet revolution" in 1989.

At the Writers' Congress in 1967, Milan Kundera asserted the responsibilities of the Czech intellectuals when he claimed that "Czech writers bear the burden of being for the entire nation" – a responsibility that Václav Havel accepted quite literally. Even the national revival during the 19th century was in the first instance a purely Czech, academic affair. The national tongue, Czech, had to be transformed from a despised rural dialect into a written language capable of doing justice to literary aspirations. Slovakia, however, had been subjected to Hungarian-

isation for so long that by the beginning of the 18th century the Slovak language had ceased to exist altogether. It was only under the influence of the Czech national revival that the Slovaks rediscovered their language; the awareness of an independent written culture started some 50 years later than in Bohemia and Moravia.

The Czech historian František Palacký, the "Father of the Fatherland", began his lengthy account of the country's history in 1836. The first volumes appeared under the title *The History of Bohemia*, and were written in German. The Czech edition followed in 1848, by which time the title had become *The History of the Czech People in Bohemia and Moravia*. Palacký exerted a considerable influence over the development of the Czech people during the 19th century, but he did not pay any attention at all to the Slovaks. To date, a Slovak version of Palacký has yet to appear on the scene.

A further example of Slovakia lagging behind can be seen in the National Theatre. The theatre in Prague was constructed between 1868 and 1881 with funds raised by the Czech people, who also paid for it to be rebuilt two years later after it was destroyed by fire. In contrast, until 1920 only German and Hungarian artists appeared in the National Theatre in Bratislava.

Reluctant partners: Disparities continued during and after the formation of Czechoslovakia. The Czechoslovak National Council was formed in 1916 by Czech and Slovak exiles in the US, but not until the Habsburg monarchy was collapsing did the Slovaks in America accept the ideas of Masaryk, and join in signing the Pittsburgh Convention on 31 May 1918. In the future republic of Czechoslovakia, Czechs and Slovaks were to be accorded equal individual rights.

After 1918, the Prague government tried to reinforce the Slovak education system and help the Slovaks develop their own intelligentsia. There were Czechs working in Slovak schools and colleges, in administration, in the judicial system and in other departments. Of course, this led to misunderstandings – the Slovaks felt first patronised and then oppressed by the Czechs. However, the Czechs also contributed to this misunderstanding. The Pittsburgh Convention stated that the Slovak people were to be equal partners in the new republic, but this was soon forgotten in Prague, and many Czechs came to look upon Slovakia as their colony.

Discontent in Slovakia found its expression in the programme of the Slovak separatists, the Slovak Populist Party. In March 1939, when the rest of Czechoslovakia was occupied by Hitler, the separatists felt that their moment in history had come. Under

resentation with its Czech counterpart in the Federal Assembly.

Spirit of free enterprise: It is easy to understand ordinary Czech and Slovak citizens who may feel rather bemused by all the dramatic changes that have taken place in their name. Despite the intrinsic differences between the two countries, many people, particularly Slovaks, fail to see any advantage to be gained from splitting up, in a Europe that is supposed to be edging closer together. Many look back to the days of the

Monsignor Jozef Tiso, they split off from the republic and, under Hitler's "protection", formed a supposedly independent fascist Slovak state, allied to Nazi Germany.

After the communists came to power in February 1948, Slovakia was subjected to a strictly centralised, Czech-dominated government. The constitution promulgated in July 1960 theoretically gave Slovakia equal rights with the Czech lands, and after 1969 the Slovak Socialist Republic had equal rep-

Preceding pages: lovers in arms on the Charles Bridge. <u>Above</u>, Northern Bohemian miners at the coal face.

First Republic, when Czechoslovakia possessed one of the most flourishing economies in Europe, with a well-qualified workforce, a solid foundation of medium-sized companies and highly developed industrial production in a variety of fields. One need only think of the Bat'a (pronounced: Batya) shoe manufacturing company. During the long years of state control, the name remained for Czechs and Slovaks alike a living memory of the golden years of free enterprise. Even today the many young people who are embracing free enterprise look for inspiration towards the shining example set by Bat'a. Although in 1949 the company's home town was renamed Gottwaldov by the communists, it is now once again known by its original name of Zlín.

Upholding traditions: Although the first empire founded within their borders was much older than, for example, the Holy Roman Empire of German Nations, the periods when Czechs and Slovaks lived under the rule of a king of their own are negligible compared with the many centuries of foreign domination. It was correspondingly difficult for the young republic to build up an awareness of its own historic traditions. The memories of the Hussite tradition had to be resuscitated during the 19th century. But this identification was only partly successful, for

heard every day on the radio. Moravian and Slovakian folk songs flooded the colleges, May Day parades, youth rallies and open-air concerts. Not only did jazz disappear completely from our country; it came to be seen as a symbol of Western capitalism and decadence. The young people no longer danced the tango or the boogie-woogie at parties; instead, they grasped each other by the shoulder and circled the floor in a round dance. The Communist Party was at pains to create a new lifestyle. It took as its credo Stalin's definition of the New Art: Socialist doctrine in national form. Only folklore was able to give this national form to our music, our dancing and our poetry."

despite massive criticism of the Church of Rome, Catholicism has remained a determining factor, particularly in Slovakia.

The socialist government became aware of a national vacuum and tried to fill it with patriotic traditions and folklore. National costumes suddenly reappeared in towns and rural areas where they had long since been forgotten. In his novel *The Joke,* Milan Kundera describes the ideological intentions behind this "revival": "Nobody had ever done more for folklore than the Communist government. It made vast sums of money available for the foundation of new ensembles. Violin and dulcimer were to be

The folkloric tradition was employed to serve the interests of socialism. Folklore festivals mushroomed, open-air museums were opened and new life was breathed into many an ancient village tradition. Writers laboured under the collective duty of creating a folk literature. An endless succession of folk song competitions was announced. Much of what was written during this period was later condemned as kitsch, but some of it had a lasting value.

Many artists who were later critical of the regime nevertheless found their first arena in the folklore movement. Under the guise of a folk song or fairy tale it was possible to give expression to many opinions which ran counter to the idealised views of the communist world. During the times when public lies were on every tongue, this critical strain within the folklore movement became one of the pillars of national identity and protest. These artists have lost none of their popularity.

The cultivation of national customs survived even without socialist subsidies. Eastern Moravia, with its big folklore festival in Stráznice, is one important centre in this respect; the region around Vychodna in Slovakia is another area where the traditional folk culture has been retained.

In July Slovakian ensembles gather with

Messing about on the water: Despite – or perhaps because of – the fact that they live so far from the sea, both Czechs and Slovaks have always had a special affiliation with water. Smetana's best-loved composition was dedicated to the River Vltava, and in summer the republic's rivers and lakes are abuzz with amateur sailors. The relatively unpolluted tributaries of the Vltava, Lužnice and Sázava rivers become the domain of canoeists and families in rubber dinghies, who coast along from landing stage to landing stage, gathering as dusk falls by the obligatory camp fire to toast *spekáček* (the traditional sausages).

Touring by boat is still one of the least expensive kinds of holiday, particularly rec-

their traditional instruments – the bagpipes (*gajdy*), the native fiddle and the dulcimer, pipe (*píšt'ala*) and the powerful shepherd's shawm (*fujara*). The dance groups regularly perform old dances such as the *Chorodový*, a communal dance for women, the *Kolo, Hajduch, Verbunk* and *Čardaš*, the polka and the *Odzemok*, the traditional shepherds' dance. A highlight of the festival is performance of the Janošík songs, which relate the exploits of the eponymous robber and folk hero from the time of the Turkish invasions.

Left, a serenade from the tower of the Old Town Hall in Prague. Above, learning ballet.

ommended for those who prefer the countryside to visiting historical and architectural sites. More ambitious canoeists will find that since the opening up of former military areas (for example in the Bohemian Forest), a number of more challenging watercourses have become available.

Although the major watercourses swell beyond the national borders into mighty rivers, within the Czech and Slovak republics they retain more modest proportions. Over the years the inhabitants have devoted considerable energies to the art of keeping their water within the country for as long as possible. For this reason, artificial lakes account for a large proportion of the water surface area. They serve a variety of purposes: some are used for fish farming, whilst others are reservoirs designed for flood protection or power generation.

Most impressive are the carp lakes of Southern Bohemia; these were excavated during the Middle Ages by engineers whose fame spread far and wide throughout Europe. Further important carp lakes are found in the lowlands of the Labe (Elbe) and in Southern Moravia. In late autumn they are fished with heavy-duty nets to provide the carp for the national Christmas dish. As Christmas Day approaches you will often see long queues waiting in front of barrels of fish placed at

Another reservoir on the Vltava, the picturesque Slapy Reservoir to the south of Prague, has become a favourite recreation area for the residents. Moored along its banks are houseboats, sailing yachts and simple rowing boats for fishing. Any visitor who has witnessed the bustling activity here on a hot summer weekend will immediately realise why the city centre seems populated only by tourists.

By the water, in the water, on the water – Czechs and Slovaks alike are in their element. That may at least partially explain why the joint Slovakian-Hungarian section of the vast Danube canalisation scheme, the controversial Gabčíkovo-Nagymaros project, has

street corners. For many people, Christmas Eve would be unthinkable without a baked carp (*smaženy kapr*).

The construction of reservoirs and dams for industrial purposes began during the First Republic. After World War II, increased energy demands led to the building of many more. The most important are the Lipno Dam on the upper reaches of the Vltava, the Orava Reservoir and the dam below Orlík Castle. The latter, which once stood sentinel on a rock – hence the name, which means "eagle's eyrie" – is now a moated castle. The foundations were reinforced with a thick layer of concrete against the waters.

met with far less opposition here than in Hungary or Austria.

Acid rain: The Czech national anthem waxes lyrical about the forests, which "tumble across the rocks". But despite the fact that one-third of the land is covered with woodland, any talk of the harmony between man and nature in this part of the world must be hedged with reservations. Acid rain, partly blown in from abroad and partly caused by the high sulphur levels in the brown coal reserves, has been responsible for appalling environmental damage, especially in Northern Bohemia. On many days of the year there is a smog warning in Teplice – once one of the most famous spas in Bohemia, where Goethe, Beethoven and Wagner took the waters. To the east of Chomutov the vast brown coal excavators have eradicated more than 100 villages. The historic town of Most, where coal mining began in 1613, was simply moved and rebuilt on another site: the venerable deaconry church had to be moved half a mile.

Refuge in the forests: However, if you approach from another direction, you may well gain very different first impressions. Entering the Czech Republic via the Bohemian Forest or Slovakia via the High Tatra, you can wander through immaculate woodland which casts into doubt the accuracy of a United Nations' study claiming that over 70 percent of the total forested regions of the Czech and Slovak republics are severely damaged. You will frequently encounter areas of untouched primeval forest – the best-known is the Boubín in the Bohemian Forest – in which time seems to have made little progress since the Middle Ages.

The nearer you are to the cities, the busier the forests seem. For city dwellers they provide a refuge from the stresses of everyday life. The desire to seek solace in nature is not just a modern phenomenon. The straitjacket of socialism and the steadily increasing housing shortage have only exacerbated a trend which started between the wars. In those days young anarchists disenchanted with conventional living formed groups and, equipped with little more than guitars and rucksacks, set off to pursue an alternative lifestyle in the countryside. Most of them came from the less prosperous walks of society; many of them were jobless. They built shacks in the forest which soon developed into little colonies. They saw themselves as the pioneers of a new, anti-bourgeois lifestyle, and their ideals, based on a return to nature and brotherly love, were popularised in songs, many of which are still sung today. They built up a sort of campfire romanticism which was the antithesis of the aggressive environment of the city.

Houses in the country: You will, however, find few traces of anarchy in the weekend colonies of today, for they have long since succumbed to the comforts of bourgeois

living. In the years immediately following World War II, the houses of the expelled Germans were appropriated; soon after that, the flight from the cities became a mass exodus, with the result that the government found itself obliged to intervene in the wild-cat development of the *chalupy* (farmhouses) and *chaty* (cottages) and to allocate specific areas for such settlements. The new owners erected prefabricated houses, so recent colonies tend to have a uniform appearance. Many areas have become so built up that planning policy for building weekend cottages has been severely restricted.

For many Czechs, their weekend *chata* forms the real centre of family life. Over the

years many families have transformed what was once their simple cottage into quite a comfortable dwelling, which they plan to retire to in due course. Mushrooms and blackberries grow in profusion in the nearby woods, meat and potatoes are brought from town, and beer is fetched in a tankard from the village tavern. Behind each house stands a large wooden barrel in which the owners collect the fruit to make their *slivovice* (Slivovitz), an eau-de-vie, which is drunk during the cold days of winter. The produce of such private stills is strictly illegal – but what would life be like without a little bit of anarchy here and there?

Left, a Slovakian knees-up. **Above**, a souvenir from the past: punks show off their Socialist Youth Organisation passes.

Following the collapse of the Habsburg Empire in 1918, the Treaty of Versailles allotted generous territories to the newly formed state of Czechoslovakia. It seemed as if the Czech and Slovak patriots' dream of independent nationhood had finally been fulfilled. But the very existence of the multinational state was threatened from the outset by the tensions between the politically dominant Czech majority and the sizeable ethnic minority groups.

Out of a total population of 13.6 million, barely half were actually Czech; in addition there were over 2 million Slovaks, 750,000 Hungarians living in Slovakia, some 100,000 Poles in the region bordering on Silesia and 500,000 Ukrainians and Carpatho-Ukrainians. The largest minority group comprised 3.2 million Germans living in Western and Northern Bohemia, Southern Moravia and the Carpathian mountains. To complicate matters still further, the racial melting pot was enriched by the presence of more than 100,000 Jews who had been living in the region for centuries.

The Czechs took advantage of their numerical superiority, whilst the minority groups, especially the so-called Sudeten Germans, made increasingly aggressive demands, which resulted in the collapse of the First Republic and the subsequent German invasion. Later, under the communists, the red flag of international brotherhood fluttering in the breeze served only to distract attention from the conflicts. In the 1990s both the Czech and Slovak republics are facing yet another crisis riddled with ethnic tensions and deep-rooted prejudice.

The Germans: Germans began settling in the region as long ago as the Middle Ages. The town of Olomouc (Olmütz), for example, grew up on the site of a colony of German merchants; in 1253 it was awarded a German municipal charter by King Otakar II. České Budějovice (Budweis) became world famous as a result of the *Budvar* beer

produced by the Municipal Brewery founded in 1794. The chequerboard layout of the Old Town displays the typical characteristics of a German town of the time. Bruntál (Freudenthal) was founded by settlers from Bavaria and Franconia; they came as farmers, summoned by the kings of Bohemia to improve the fertility of the barren soil. The free cities of Engelsberg, Herlitz and Würbenthal developed from German mining communities.

Traditionally, the Bavarian–Bohemian border region was an area of cultural interac-

tion rather than division. For example, the Bavarian-born master builders, the Dientzenhofer brothers, were apprenticed in Bohemia (Christoph and his son Kilian Ignaz were to become the masters of Prague baroque). During the 17th century, important South German baroque buildings were designed along the lines of the Jesuit church of St Ignatius in Prague. Today, many Czechs work in Franconia, and German shops have engaged Czech-speaking staff to cope with the influx of customers from the other side of the border.

But when it comes to a darker period in 20th-century history the Sudeten Germans

Left, German costume from Vyškov (Wischau) in Moravia. **Above**, S. J. Rapport, the Prague Chief Rabbi and scholar, around 1840 (Antonín Machek).

are understandably reluctant to enter into discussion. Instead, they prefer to idealise the "good old days" and are happiest when they can present themselves as a cheerful community who enjoy their brass bands, singing and dancing. It is therefore essential to consider the events which preceded their exile. During the 1930s the Sudeten Germans fixed their hopes firmly upon the German Reich; they spread the message of the "breakthrough to nationhood" and saw National Socialism as their salvation, for the Czechoslovak government had denied them any right of self-determination.

Following the Munich Agreement of September 1938, Czechoslovakia lost a consid-

mans began in 1945, shortly after the war ended. Overnight they were driven from their houses with only a minimum of personal possessions. According to reliable sources, over 200,000 died as a result of massacre, hunger, exhaustion or suicide.

Early in 1990, President Václav Havel of Czechoslovakia issued an official apology for his country's expulsion of the Germans. The Speaker of the Sudeten German Welfare and Cultural Association, Franz Neubauer, accepted the olive branch, although his stand was not shared by all Sudeten Germans. Now, at both national and regional level, cooperation is making rapid progress. Within the three-country triangle where the fron-

erable proportion of its industry and defensive power. Only six months later, Prague was occupied by the German army. Within the German Protectorate of Bohemia and Moravia, the former status of the ethnic groups was reversed. In line with the doctrines of the National Socialists, the Czech working class was to be Germanised, whilst the intelligentsia was to be repressed. From 1939 until the end of the war, all Czech universities, places of higher education and teacher training colleges were closed. As early as March 1939, over 5,000 individuals suspected of opposition were arrested.

The expulsion of 3 million Sudeten Ger-

tiers of Poland, the Czech Republic and Germany meet, the three towns of Jelenia Gora on the northern Polish side of the Krkonoše, Liberec (Reichenberg) in Northern Bohemia, and Zittau, in Upper Lusatia in Germany have formed a close bond. They have signed twinning agreements and organised an international conference on the Three-Country European Project. The will to cooperate is in evidence on a human, practical and political level.

The Hungarians: At the other side of former Czechoslovakia, there appears to be rather less harmony. The 600,000 strong Hungarian minority in Slovakia, which makes up 11 percent of the new state's population, is fearful that the rights of non-Slovaks will be overlooked in the wake of the resurgence of Slovak national consciousness. Now that the Czechs can no longer be blamed for Slovakia's ills, some feel the Hungarians will be the next scapegoats. For their part, Slovaks are afraid of demands for autonomy by ethnic Hungarians: a Hungarian enclave in the south of the country would be humiliating, particularly if it voted to join Hungary. Tensions have been heightened by the argument over the completion of the controversial Gabčíkovo dam project by the Slovaks, resulting in the displacement of ethnic Hungarians living along the effected stretch of the Danube.

their settlement areas in Eastern Slovakia, as well as in Ostrava in Moravia, the Northern Bohemian towns of Teplice and Most, and even in the Prague suburb of Zizkov, the *cikani*, as they are derogatorily referred to, are daily confronted with hate.

After the creation of the First Republic, President Masaryk encouraged many gypsies to move from Eastern Slovakia and settle in the industrial centres that were emerging at that time. Following the expulsion of the Sudeten Germans in 1945, a similar migration of gypsies occurred into that area, where labour was in great demand. Large communities of gypsies still live there today. Life is hard; many have no work and are

The gypsies: But at least the Hungarians, as well as the ethnic Ukrainians and Poles, can rely on the support of their respective mother countries. Not so the gypsies. They are a people without a state; for better or for worse their fortunes are totally dependent on the prevailing attitudes in the country in which they live. Since the revolution in 1989, life has become less tolerable for the approximately 1 million gypsies living within the boundaries of former Czechoslovakia. In

Left, Salzmanns Beer Hall in Liberec (Reichenberg) before World War II. **Above**, a gypsy family having a picnic.

forced to live in extremely basic conditions. Both Czechs and Slovaks claim that in areas inhabited by gypsies the crime rate is much higher than in the rest of the country. The authorities are attempting to counter this racial discrimination, although there is little evidence that any practical measures are being taken. Only a handful of social workers have been assigned to look after the fate of the thousands of gypsies who have sought refuge in the city of Prague.

The Jews: A modest plaque in the little village of Bánovce in Slovakia was the cause of a minor uproar during the autumn of 1990. Two weeks after its unveiling, Marian Čalfa, the local prime minister, had it removed because he was concerned about its effect on the reputation of Slovakia abroad. The plaque was in memory of the Slovakian Fascist Jozef Tiso, who in 1939 declared the independence of Slovakia as a "Protectorate" of the German Reich. Tiso had been involved in the extermination of the Jews, and by the autumn of 1942 had sent 58,000 Slovakian Jews to certain death. Of an original total of 135,000 Jews living in Slovakia, only one-third survived.

The removal of the memorial plaque in Bánovce nad Bravou was not the end of the story, however. Nationalistic attitudes to life and anti-Semitism are both deep-seated. During March 1991, 7,000 supporters of Tiso demonstrated for an independent Slovakia. Not only did they voice their demands for independence; in the presence of President Havel and Slovakian leaders, a crowd of thousands also chanted "We want no Jews!"

Gangs of nationalist skinheads continue to stalk the streets of cities like Bratislava, waving the Slovak flag and chanting their anti-Semitic and pro-Tiso slogans. For the few Jews, such actions revive fearful memories, for, apart from brief periods of harmony, they can look back on over 1,000 years of persecution. They have been forced repeatedly to be on the defensive against both rulers and mob. In 1096, Crusaders en route for the Holy Land massacred large numbers of Jews living in Prague and plundered their property. During the 11th century they were deprived of their civil rights and forced to earn their living as money-lenders. This represented a loss of social status for all of them, although for some it meant an improvement in their economic position. The city's oldest synagogue was burned down on the first occasion in 1142, and the Jews were permitted to make their homes only on the right bank of the Vltava.

Things eased under King Otakar II, who used his royal privileges to encourage Jews from Germany to settle in Prague. Nonetheless the position remained unstable for many centuries. Depending on the policies of the various kings – or, more precisely, upon their financial position – the Jews were the victims of stick-and-carrot tactics. In 1648 they were praised for their distinguished service in the defence of the country against Sweden; a few years later, under Maria Theresa,

they were exiled from Prague and subjected to unfair taxes. Emperor Joseph II, on the other hand, needed money and passed a decree of religious tolerance, allowing the Jews to build secular schools and requiring them to do military service.

Equality before the law was not achieved until after 1848. This finally led to closer links on a cultural level, and to the widespread adoption by Jews of the German language, traditions and way of life. Until the mid-20th century Jews formed the heart of the capital's liberal élite: writers, musicians and many of those connected with the theatre. A unique spirit of peaceful assimilation between the two cultures finally evolved.

Annihilation: When the German army invaded in March 1939, 56,000 Jews were living in the city. The "butcher" Adolf Eichmann took over the direction of the Central Office for Jewish Emigration. By the end of 1939, a total of 19,000 Jews had succeeded in escaping to Palestine, but the rest, some 40,000 from Prague alone, were transported to the concentration camp at Terezín (*see page 51*), and from there sent to the extermination camps.

The Nazi authorities planned to establish in Prague a Museum of the Former Jewish Race and brought valuable items there from synagogues all over the country, making it the most extensive collection of Jewish sacred items in the world. Historians who were entrusted with the work of cataloguing the items were executed before the end of the war and the collection was dispersed. But much of it remains, and under the auspices of the National Judaic Museum has found a home in Prague's Jewish Quarter (*see pages 144–5*). Inscriptions around the interior walls of the Pinkas Synagogue in Prague record the murder of 77,812 Jews within the space of half a decade.

During the short interval before the communists assumed power in 1948, the Jewish population increased rapidly. In Prague alone there were 11,000 Jews. But during the two decades which followed, half of them emigrated; anti-Semitism, actively encouraged by the authorities, continued. Now it is to be hoped that the Jews can resume their role in society without fear of discrimination.

Right, gypsies in the cities find it hard to procure accommodation and employment.

The fact that Czechoslovakia is no longer a single state will undoubtedly have an effect on the tourism trends in this part of central Europe. While the majority of visitors will continue to go to Prague and perhaps take the time to admire some of the magnificent castles and palaces within easy reach of the city, the fact that Slovakia has become a tourist destination in its own right will also make its capital, Bratislava, an increasingly popular centre. But whether travelling to the Czech Republic or Slovakia, the visitor should not forget that the countryside also has its appeal. The country folk themselves have remained friendly and hospitable, despite the vicissitudes of history.

Up until 1950, rural life was based on the traditional pattern, whereby local affairs were run by three people: the chairman of the parish council, the parish priest and the head teacher of the local school. The communists soon put an end to all that. Small communities came under the control of a central village. The bulk of investment was concentrated here, leaving the established structures of the outlying communities to decay. The top posts in the local authorities were no longer occupied by respected local citizens, but by unknown officials with good party connections.

Only in a few regions were priests able to maintain their influence on the population; notably in Slovakia and Southern Moravia. Religious education was, in any case, banned everywhere. Evidence of the declining influence of the church in rural areas can be found in the depressing state of repair of so many of the country's magnificent religious buildings, and the fact that one seldom sees young people in the congregations.

The influence of the village teacher has also disappeared. Under the communists school timetables were completely changed and acquired a new bias towards the technical professions. Hundreds of small schools were closed, with the result that many children in rural areas have long journeys each day to the central community school in the larger villages or towns.

Paradise lost: Under the communists, Czechoslovak agriculture was amongst the most advanced in Eastern Europe, with better than average yields. But the environmental costs of this achievement have been immense. Forty years ago the countryside of Czechoslovakia resembled a multi-coloured patchwork quilt. Narrow strips of tilled land were sown with golden corn, potatoes, hops,

flax or yellow flowering mustard. There were grassy hedgerows and meadows of wild flowers. Today, little remains of this agricultural pattern; valleys and hills are characterised by a dreary monoculture. In the First Republic the estates owned by the aristocracy and big landowners were redistributed in accordance with the new land reforms; the communists, however, combined existing parcels of land to form large fields, ploughing up the hedgerows as they went along.

Unlike in Poland, virtually all agriculture in Czechoslovakia was collectivised. One-third of the available land was farmed by national collectives; the rest was handed

Preceding pages: a Wallachian village in the Moravian-Silesian Beskids. Left, prize specimens from Southern Slovakia. Right, Slovakian farmer making hay.

over to the agricultural production cooperatives. The communists realised that it was essential to destroy all inherited ties with the land if they were to put an end to the dominant conservative ethic in rural areas. In accordance with Soviet practice, medium and large-sized farmers were designated as *kulaks* and evicted by force. The minority of small farmers who resisted this brutal expropriation were quickly made to see reason.

Although land is now supposed to be restored to the individuals from whom it was confiscated, most members of the various cooperatives show little interest in recovering their former farms. They receive a fixed wage and are able to supplement their in-

In search of a rural idyll: Despite the gloomy state of agriculture, the rural regions, with their pretty villages linked by tree-lined avenues, still enchant travellers. The country scenes recall paintings by Old Masters: ducks waddle across the road, dogs stretch out contentedly on warm cobblestones and hens scratch around in the ditches. To find the unspoilt backwaters you need to turn off the main road and drive slowly – not least because of the bad roads with their numerous bends, potholes and puddles.

Unfortunately many of the facades of the once splendid houses have decayed and the addition of ugly new houses does sometimes spoil the idyll. Traditional country houses

comes handsomely by means of their smallholdings. In any case, they have good cause to fear the dissolution of the cooperatives: the soil, exhausted by 40 years of irresponsible farming, is no longer capable of yielding a satisfactory harvest.

Environment-friendly farming is still in its infancy, and despite a concerted effort it will be many years before the land becomes fertile once again. There is also a shortage of appropriate technology; the antiquated but cumbersome farm machinery – heavy tractors and combine harvesters from the former Soviet Union and East Germany – are unsuitable for use on smaller farms.

are now built only in the foothills of the mountains, above all in Slovakia. In the less well-developed regions such as Southern Bohemia, famous for its baroque buildings, an individual style of rural architecture has developed. Paradoxically, the owners of weekend homes were the first to recognise the value of preserving the fine carpentry of many cottages and farmhouses; the villagers themselves have demolished many of the finest examples of domestic architecture, or ruined them with inappropriate extensions.

Travellers who want to discover the joys of country life, to explore myriad nooks and crannies, must be prepared to tolerate more than just bad roads. In former times every village boasted an array of restaurants and pubs; today there may well be only one – and that may be unable to serve a hot meal. One is lucky to be offered pork, cabbage and the typical Bohemian dumplings; in many cases the landlord can provide nothing more than sausages, cold meats or tinned goulash. Drinking is another matter, although this remains emphatically a masculine preserve. To this day, the presence of women within arm's length of the bar is frowned upon. There are surprisingly few small-scale family hotels and guest houses; the establishments which do exist mostly belong to the so-called consumer cooperatives. With the

cheered the Red Flag and the local bigwigs to the sound of dulcimer and brass bands. This cynical exploitation of local culture is the principal reason for the younger generation's rejection of their traditions. In some regions folklore is almost extinct, upheld only by semi-professional ensembles – not least because membership of these ensembles used to be one of the few ways of securing a trip to the West.

In the wine-growing areas of Moravia, in the Bohemian Forest, in the Tatra Mountains and along the Danube, an independent tradition has survived the embrace of Soviet-style socialism; and in some other regions a renaissance of old traditions is gaining impetus.

spread of privatisation it is hoped that the level of service will improve.

Villages and culture: The folklore of Bohemia, Moravia and Slovakia is equally fascinating, although not as prevalent as it used to be. From the 1950s folklore, "the people's culture", was unscrupulously used by the socialist state (*see page 62*) as a bulwark against the decadence of Western society. During the annual May Day processions, the villagers – dressed in traditional costumes –

Left, a farmer's wife sells fruit and vegetables. **Above**, a pleasant Sunday stroll at the foot of the High Tatra.

Here and there you will see the masques traditionally worn by villagers as they celebrate with due ceremony the arrival of spring or the beginning of the grape harvest.

One of the populist solutions of the communists was to turn many villages into towns. Many a village thus acquired an ostentatious "House of Culture". During winter these became the venue for balls, dances and cultural evenings in which "famous musicians from Prague" occasionally performed. It is hardly surprising that today district finance officers tear out their hair in despair at the high running costs of these sterile barracks; for some years now the rural population has tended to prefer an evening at home in front of the television to a dose of culture.

Family life: Just as was always the case, the kitchen incorporates the heart and soul of everyday life in the home. However, it has changed considerably in recent years. The old dressers have been replaced by fitted kitchens and the porcelain-tiled stoves have been abandoned in favour of gas cookers; plastic is the material of choice when it comes to everyday utensils, and the most important item of equipment is a large deep-freezer. Every summer it is filled with fruit, poultry, rabbits and pork.

Only in the evening does the family migrate to the living room, where a three-piece

suite, built-in shelving, a few pictures and sometimes a crucifix or a portrait of the Virgin Mary dominate the scene. Pride of place is occupied by the embodiment of prosperity, a colour television set.

Once upon a time, several generations would live together in the farmhouse; today, this is the exception rather than the rule. Young couples invariably try to escape as quickly as possible from the strict control of their parents by building their own house or moving into the nearby town. Once the children have left the house a whole storey often stands completely empty, and only when they and other relatives descend for holidays

and family celebrations will the former family home recover its old vitality, radiating warmth and comfort in spite of the characterless furnishings.

If you would like to see a house which is still furnished as it would have been in times gone by, you should try to see the inside of a cottage whose owners are town-dwellers. They are the ones who cherish and repair the old porcelain-tiled stoves, rescue hand-painted chests and cupboards, and spend good money on old cups, jugs, pots, butter churns and spinning wheels. Their yard is likely to be lovingly adorned with old cartwheels and even hand-made replicas of pre-war ploughs. It's all a bit contrived – a weekend refuge from the stress of everyday urban life and an attempt to recover an idealised golden past.

Town and country: Many children who grew up in villages moved to the city as soon as they were independent. A few of them joined the professional classes, becoming teachers, doctors and engineers. The majority, however, ended up in factories. Even today, the town exerts a magnetic pull on many country-dwellers, though most like to maintain some contact with their rural roots. Country life has its advantages: relatives supply them with fresh eggs, meat, vegetables and fruit, and the money thus saved can be spent on furnishings for the flat, cars or holidays. In many cases the parental home is regarded as a comfortable weekend *chata*.

The town-dwellers have quickly adapted to urban conditions. Most of the young people who have migrated to the city argue that nothing ever happened at home in the country, and that the town has more to offer. In recent years, however, the trend has been reversed. Increasing numbers of people are discovering the attractions of living in countryside within commuting distance of a town. They cite the clear air, the forests, the peace and quiet and the close-knit community as their reasons for preferring the country. Of course, the reality of country life isn't always so perfect, but anyone visiting the rural Czech and Slovak Republics can be sure that the old adage still holds true: "Every guest brings blessings upon the house".

<u>Above</u>, the belfry in Hrousek. <u>Right</u>, throughout the Czech Republic, pork is commonly served with cabbage and dumplings.

It was not until after the bloodless revolution of November 1989 that the population of the then Czechoslovakia was confronted with black-and-white evidence of what many of them had suspected for a long time: that they were living in what was, ecologically speaking, one of the most severely threatened countries in Europe. The Danube canalisation scheme for the power station at Gabčíkovo in Southern Slovakia, which has caused a major international outcry, is but one of the environmental catastrophes be-

school. For many years the black smoke belching from the factory chimneys was seen as a symbol of progress. If past trends continue, it is estimated that by the year 2000, air pollution will have destroyed or seriously damaged 70 percent of the forests in the Czech republic and 40 percent of those in Slovakia.

The main cause of air pollution lies in heat and power generation, which are heavily dependent upon fossil fuels and the associated release of oxides of sulphur, carbon and

queathed by the communists. The decision of the Slovaks to see the project through to completion demonstrates just how difficult it is to halt the trends of the past.

It could be pointed out that rivers have been harnessed in this part of the world ever since the Middle Ages. But such arguments cannot be used to justify the biggest environmental problem faced by the Czech and Slovak republics, namely air pollution. "The chimneys are smoking and a band of children is playing on a heap of sand. Life blossoms forth in a thousand things and grows in our hearts…" Thus ran one of the songs which Czechoslovakian children used to learn at

nitrogen as well as heavy metals. A particularly threatened area is northwest Bohemia, where pollution levels exceed all safety limits. Environmental experts describe the situation here as catastrophic. The region is the country's brown coal (lignite) mining centre; almost 70 percent of the total Czech production of this natural resource comes from local opencast seams. Most of the coal, which has a high sulphur content, is burned in the thermal power stations in the area. One-third of the total electricity generated in the Czech and Slovak republics comes from here. The industry has turned the district surrounding the town of Most into a barren lunar landscape and rehabilitation of the fields will take many years. The power stations lack adequate filters for the removal of excess sulphur, which means that local inhabitants constantly breathe in foul-smelling, poisonous fumes.

The sulphur emissions are also responsible for destroying forests on the mountain slopes of the Ore Mountains and the Krkonoše (Giant Mountains). Experts have estimated that the average life expectancy in the region is five years less than that of other areas within the Czech and Slovak republics. In some particularly endangered towns in northern Bohemia the authorities have distributed gas masks to children in the hope that at least some of the pollutants will be filtered out.

Northern Moravia occupies second place in the league of provinces severely at risk. Worst hit are the areas around Ostrava and Karviná. The Ostrava region is predominantly a manufacturing area, with heavy industry and hard coal mining. The worst air pollution comes from the iron foundries and the coke furnaces.

The third most polluted region in the Czech Republic is Prague. The concentration of industrial plant and exhaust fumes from the many antiquated vehicles has resulted in a pall of smog that hangs above the rooftops. Catalytic converters were made compulsory on newly registered cars in 1993, but in the opinion of many environmentalists this is not enough. Another serious problem is the pollution of the lakes and waterways. The River Elbe (Labe) is the dirtiest river in Europe. The towns and villages along its course are the main culprits, for many of them do not process their effluent.

Similar problems are faced by the Slovaks. The drive to transform what was traditionally an agricultural and deeply Catholic land into a modern industrial socialist state has also left its poisoned legacy. From the iron-ore works of Košice to the arms factories of Dubnica and Martin, the pall of pollution hangs in the air. As Slovakia confronts the reality of independence and the leadership struggles to maintain employment, there seems little chance that such carbuncles will soon disappear from the landscape.

While the modernisation of industrial complexes will depend on the ultimate success of economic reforms, there is no way that the republics will be able to meet the cost of the big clean-up on their own. The European Community will finance some environmental rescue programmes, and the United States and Switzerland have also promised assistance. A number of loans from the World

Bank and Scandinavian banks have been allocated for projects of this nature.

It is also hoped that money generated by the booming tourist industry will help finance environmental projects. With around 110 million visitors to the Czech Republic in 1996 alone, and a growing number of visitors to Slovakia, tourism has become a major resource. It would be misleading to give visitors the impression that the region is permanently veiled in smog and its countryside crossed by polluted, dying rivers. There remain vast areas of countryside, including broad virgin forests and pristine mountains, where nature can still be enjoyed.

Left, a tarnished idyll. **Above**, lignite mining near Most.

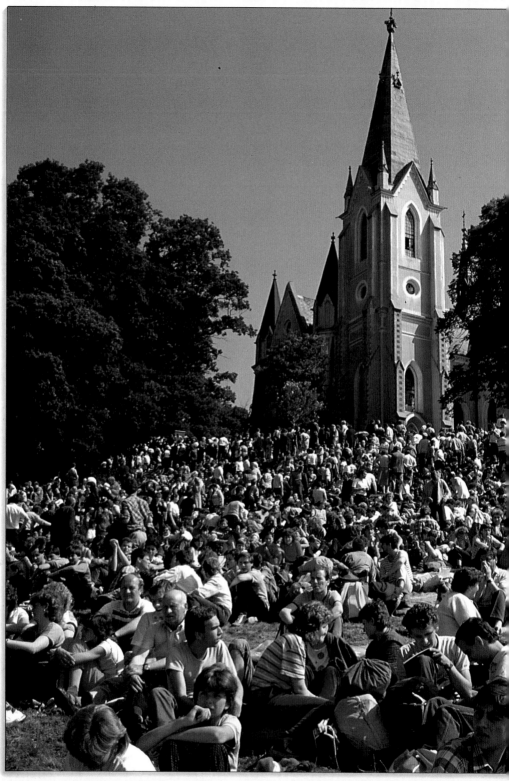

THE RELIGIOUS SPECTRUM

Pravda vítězí! – "Truth prevails!" In 1918, at the request of Czechoslovakia's founder President, Tomaš Masaryk, this old Hussite motto was incorporated into the emblem of the new republic. During the Prague Spring of 1968, it was written in bold on the banners hanging from the windows, demanding the end of Stalinism. Václav Havel had the same words emblazoned on his presidential standard, and while in prison as an opponent of the regime had even written a piece entitled: "Try to live in truth". Things may not have turned out quite as he hoped, but the search for the truth goes on.

Five hundred and seventy-five years after Jan Hus was burned at the stake as a heretic in Constance, the head of the Catholic Church visited the native country of the Bohemian religious reformer. On 21 April 1990 in Prague, Pope John Paul II celebrated mass before a congregation of more than half a million. But the pope only agreed in principle to a rehabilitation by the church of the Czech national patron. Although he praised his "spotless life" and his "endeavours for the education and moral improvement of the people", he indicated that it would be the task of experts to determine Hus's true importance in the history of the church.

The Catholics: The pope's journey through the newly democratic country was like a triumphal procession: in Velehrad, the place of pilgrimage in Moravia and the site of the grave of the Slavic apostle Methodius, he was rapturously received by 700,000 faithful followers. Church bells throughout the whole of Slovakia rang out when the papal jet landed at Bratislava airport.

As in the case of Poland, an appreciable proportion of the opposition to the communist regime was to be found concentrated in the ranks of the Catholic Church and its elderly but imperturbable representative, the then Archbishop of Prague, Cardinal Tomášek. But the Catholic Church sees itself faced with as many problems now as it did in the former socialist republic. The consequences of policies towards religion

Left, Levoča (Leutschau) in the High Tatra is the destination of a Holy Virgin pilgrimage.

during the socialist era are still much in evidence. The socialist state dissolved religious orders (with a few exceptions), sentencing large numbers of clergy to imprisonment in a series of mock trials. Access to theological college was strictly controlled; national salaries for priests were restricted to the bare minimum. Since the church of today is faced with a new range of important social tasks, the shortage of newly qualified young priests is especially problematic.

From 1977, an "underground church" developed alongside the official religious bodies. Lying outside the sphere of influence of the State and maintaining close contact with the activists of the opposition Charter 77

Many of the monastery buildings are not only in a desolate state of repair, but also house public facilities such as libraries and archives. Only a part of the ancient Czech Premonstratensian monastery of Želiv, for example, could be handed back: converted into a prison during the 1950s, the main abbey now houses a psychiatric clinic.

At least until it became clear that Czechoslovakia was going to split into two separate countries, the church was also confronted with the problems posed by the attitude of the Catholic clergy in Slovakia. While the Catholic bishops of Bohemia and Moravia – together with the Ecumenical Council of the Churches of Czechoslovakia – warned of the

group, it developed a range of spiritual and social welfare activities. Its members formed a congregation around a secretly ordained priest, it celebrated mass during "mountain walks" and similar events; illegal publications were distributed and theological courses organised. Today, the number of illegal priests is estimated at 260. The priests are considered to have been officially ordained, even though many of them are married. Their future position within the church has not yet been resolved.

A further problem is the return of confiscated church property, which is proving more difficult to realise than originally expected.

impending disintegration of the state, the Slovakian Bishops' Conference considered that the Slovaks had a perfectly legitimate right to self-determination. In contrast to Bohemia and Moravia, the proportion of practising Catholics in Slovakia is very high. It is difficult to say as yet whether the divorce from Slovakia will have any profound effect on the status of the Catholic Church in the Czech Republic.

The Hussites in history: Following the death of Jan Hus, revolution broke out in 1419 in Bohemia. The armies of Hussite zealots penetrated deep into the neighbouring countries, shattering the faith of the Christian Middle

Ages. Their theological negotiators attained a degree of religious recognition during the Council of Basle in 1433, in that they were granted what was called the lay chalice – in other words, the right to receive the Eucharist in the forms of both bread and wine. They acquired their name Utraquists from the Latin *utraque*, meaning "each of two".

But the Hussites failed to gain any political advantages from their military superiority. The moderate Utraquists, who had maintained amicable relations with the Roman Catholic Church, ultimately joined forces with the Czech Catholics and defeated the radical Taborites at the Battle of Lipany in 1434. For almost a century their modified

The present-day Czech and Slovakian Hussite Church has only indirect links with the old Hussite tradition, in that it claims to have created the idea of an independent national church. It was formed in 1920 as the natural result of the movement seeking independence from Rome under Masaryk's inspiration. During the First Republic it claimed some 750,000 members. Under the socialist regime it conformed largely to the orthodox party line and is consequently still seeking its own identity today.

On the occasion of his assuming office, the Hussites' new Patriarch, Vratislav Štěpánek, spoke of the "many sins" that had scarred the past and stated that the primary task for the

form of Catholicism was to form the basis of an independent Bohemian church.

Under the influence of the German Reformation, the majority of Utraquists subsequently allied themselves with the Protestants. Following the defeat of the Protestant forces in the Battle of the White Mountain in 1620, the Utraquists were outlawed in Bohemia and Catholicism became the only established state religion for almost 200 years.

Left, St Vitus is flanked by Charles IV and Wenceslas IV on the Bridge Tower in Prague. **Above**, Cardinal Tomášek on his way to mass in St Vitus' Cathedral, 1989.

future was the search for common ground with the Catholic Church. The most important theological elements of the Hussite church remain the Eucharist in both forms, the Apostolic Succession, as well as the right of a priest to enter into marriage and the ordination of women.

The Bohemian Brethren: The Unity of the Bohemian-Moravian Brethren (Unitas Fratrum) was founded in 1457 by Waldensians and a handful of Taborites. They aspired to a religious community based on the stories of the apostles; its pacifist and escapist tendencies originated from writings of Petz Chelčický (1380–1460). Until the expulsion of their last bishop, the educationalist Jan Amos Comenius (1592–1670) in 1628, the Unitas Fratum was subject to repeated persecution by the Catholic authorities. Some respite was gained by the establishment of links with the German Reformation; Lutherans, Calvinists and Brethren agreed on a common doctrine, the "Bohemian Confession" of 1557. This formed the basis for the Letter of Majesty of 1609, in which Rudolf II granted freedom of religious practice to non-Catholic sects within Bohemian territory.

But after the Catholics' victory in 1620, dissidents were faced with a choice between emigration or conversion to the state religion and Reformed communities in Bohemia and Moravia were amalgamated to form the (unified) Evangelical Church of the Bohemian Brethren.

In Slovakia the two denominations have remained separate to this day. In general, members of the Lutheran church tend to be Slovakians whilst Reformists are mostly Hungarian. During the communist era all attempts to forge links between Czech and Slovak Protestants were forbidden; today, however, the two communities emphasise their common historical links, particularly in the doctrines of Hus, Comenius and Luther.

Nowadays the Evangelical Church of the Bohemian Brethren is a popular church with

gion. Many paid only lip service to Catholicism and secretly remained faithful to their old beliefs. At the beginning of the 18th century, a small number of Brethren moved to nearby Lusatia, where they founded a new community in Herrnhut and embarked upon missionary campaigns throughout the world.

Joseph II's Edict of Tolerance in 1781 granted both Lutherans and Calvinists certain freedoms within Habsburg territory. The Unitas Fratrum, however, remained excluded from the new conditions. Freedom of worship was not granted to all sects until 1918, the year in which the Czechoslovak Republic was founded. In this year the Lutheran a Presbyterian constitution. Men and women have equal rights and privileges. The highest authority within the church is the General Synod. In the first democratic government after the fall of the communist regime the Chief Elder of the synod of the time, Josef Hromádka, was appointed the first Minister of Religion as well as deputy Prime Minister of Czechoslovakia.

The Orthodox Church: For as long as anyone can remember a dispute has raged in eastern Slovakia concerning church ownership. The protagonists are the Orthodox Church and the Greek Catholic Church (also known as the Uniate Church, since it was a product of the union with Rome in 1646). After World War II, the Orthodox and the Uniate Churches were forced to amalgamate here as in the Soviet Union and in Romania. Although it was considerably more extensive, in 1952 the entire property of the Uniate Church fell to the Orthodox community. In the aftermath of the Prague Spring the Greek Catholic doctrines were permitted once more, but it was not until 1990 that the Uniate Church was finally able to enjoy full reinstatement of its original privileges.

These historical developments have resulted in the Orthodox Church losing much of its original importance in Slovakia. The church, whose doctrines are based on the

teachings of the Slavic apostles Cyril and Methodius, suffers in particular from its failure to build its own churches and colleges. Today they are faced with the loss not only of their bishoprics but also their seminaries. In country areas, services are not infrequently held in the open air because church buildings were appropriated by the Uniates.

Religion in everyday life: As already indicated, there is a marked religious watershed

Left, Tábor, the town of the Hussites, named after the New Testament mountain of Christ's Transfiguration (Julius Marak). Above, Broumov Monastery.

separating the east from the west. In the Czech Republic religious or church-oriented social patterns are adopted by only a minority. In 1980, only 4 percent of couples in this region were married in church. Church baptisms represented only 13 percent and burials only 30 percent of the respective totals. In Eastern Slovakia, during the same period, 86 percent of all babies were baptised, 84 percent of all couples were married in church and 92 percent of those who died were buried according to the rites of the church. Today only 10 percent of the population of Bohemia claims membership of the Catholic Church; in Moravia the figure is 35 percent and in Slovakia over 50 percent.

One can only speculate as to the role which the church – or rather, the various churches – will play in future. Religious communities, like all other sections of society, must rearrange their priorities. It is one thing to overturn a system which has lost its credibility; it is another to develop a new, robust system which finds a consensus in society.

Mild atheism: Bearing in mind the wide media coverage of the Catholic Church during the first weeks following the Velvet Revolution, a number of voices were raised in warning against a new clericalism. As far as Bohemia is concerned, there seems to be no immediate danger of this. The citizens may well have a religious faith, but they are by no means zealots. You will find none of the arch-conservative Catholicism typical of Poland or even some areas of Slovakia. Bohemia is traditionally secular; perhaps it is here that the true legacy of the Hussites is found – in the sceptical approach to all doctrinal philosophies. On every street corner you will hear opinions such as "Anybody who supports a system as authoritarian as that of the Catholic Church cannot be a good democrat." One Prague theologian has recently spoken of a mood of "mild" atheism which has replaced the totalitarianism of the past years.

Demonstrating a deep understanding of popular feelings, Cardinal Vlk has been noticeably mild in his demands for the return of confiscated church property, for example church buildings being used as schools. In a region which has always presented pastoral difficulties for its clergy, a mood of premature rejoicing on the part of the church is the last thing required.

Smetana, Dvořák, Janáček: whenever anyone mentions Czech music, the names of the Big Three are uttered in a single breath. Smetana gave the world the most frequently performed Czech opera, *The Bartered Bride*, as well as celebrating the countryside and history of his native land in his music cycle Ma Vlást *(My Fatherland)*. Dvořák, on the other hand, was a master of the symphony, chamber music and oratorio; his compositions were rapturously received at home and abroad. Janáček took up the aims of Smetana and Dvořák and developed his own theory of the "speech melody", according to which the melodic form followed the tone patterns of speech. Janáček elevated this stylisation of speech melodies to one of the fundamentals of composition in his operas.

Compared with that of its neighbours, music in the Czech lands developed relatively late, although the beginnings of an independent musical tradition reach back to the Middle Ages. During the period of the Greater Moravian Kingdom, mass was celebrated in Slavic, not in Latin, and the Hussite Chorale influenced considerably the hymns of the German Reformation. During the baroque era the attempts at national assertion were nipped in the bud, and many musicians found themselves with no alternative but to leave and settle in another country. Among them was Johann Wenzel Stamitz, who composed at the court of the Elector Karl Theodor in Mannheim. He is regarded as one of the leading exponents of musical classicism, especially the sonata.

Vienna, a city long favoured by the muses, attracted numerous Czech composers. The virtuoso violinist and conductor Pavel Vranický came to live here – he was to be chosen by Beethoven to conduct the premiere of his First Symphony – as did Jan Leopold Koželuh who, for many years enjoyed a popularity equal to that of Mozart; and Jan Václav Hugo Voříček, the leading

representative of Czech musical classicism in Vienna.

While Vienna was welcoming Czech composers, Prague was enthusing over Mozart's *The Marriage of Figaro* and extending an invitation to its composer to visit their city. There he was commissioned to write an opera for the Nostitz Theatre (now the Estates Theatre). *Don Giovanni* premiered there in 1787 and Mozart became, and remained, Prague's most honoured adopted son.

Musical life in Bohemia was so rich that on

his journey through the country in the late-18th century the English traveller Charles Burney christened it the "Conservatoire of Europe". This wealth of musical talent was largely due to the many minor musicians, mostly church cantors, who found inspiration in the simple folk songs of their land as well as in the virtuoso compositions of the Italian masters. The most important among them was Jan Jakub Ryba whose perennially popular pastorale *Hej mistře!* (*The Bohemian Christmas*) is one of the most frequently performed compositions during the festive season.

Bedřich Smetana (1824–84) is the favourite

Preceding pages: a brass band in Mariánské Lázně (Marienbad). **Left**, music school for children with impaired sight in Prague. **Above**, Mozart loved Prague; here is his bust in the Villa Betramka.

composer of the Czech nation, although the works of his somewhat younger contemporary Dvořák are more frequently performed in international concert halls.

The careers of the two men were strangely linked. When Dvořák first arrived in Prague, Smetana left the city to try his luck in Gothenburg for five years. By the time he returned, Dvořák had already completed his first compositions. And when Dvořák returned to the Bohemian capital at the peak of his popularity after a triumphant visit to England, Smetana had just been committed to the city's mental asylum, where he died shortly afterwards.

One of Smetana's biggest preoccupations

was the development of an independent Czech popular opera, a matter which aroused great interest and debate, at a time when a sense of national identity was being forged. While the Czech old guard imagined it would be a pot-pourri of traditional melodies, the avant-garde Smetana demanded a fully developed dramatic style which would do musical justice to the newly discovered melodic patterns of the Czech language. He was accordingly scorned by his opponents as a "Wagnerian" or a "Germaniser", almost the equivalent of being charged with high treason.

And yet, Smetana was also granted a few happy hours in his musical life. In 1868, as the representative of all Czech artists, he laid the foundation stone of the National Theatre. The same year he conducted the premiere of his dramatic opera *Dalibor*. Though initially well received, the new work was performed only a few times and was not rediscovered until after the composer's death.

When the National Theatre finally opened in 1883, Smetana's opera *Libuše* was the first work to be performed there. Based on the legend of Princess Libuše, who inspired the foundation of Prague, it was a suitably stirring subject.

After a catastrophic first performance in 1866, Smetana's opera *The Bartered Bride* soon won the hearts of the Czech populace. It did not achieve an international breakthrough until after the composer's death, following a brilliant guest performance by the newly-formed Czech National Theatre in Vienna in 1892. Smetana himself had a far higher opinion of *Dalibor* than of his infinitely more successful comic opera. On the 100th performance of *The Bartered Bride* in May 1882, he said: "Actually, gentlemen, *The Bartered Bride* is really only a piece of nonsense which I allowed myself at the time. I composed it not out of ambition but in a spirit of contrariness, because after my *Brandenburgs* they all accused me of being a Wagnerian incapable of composing anything in the lighter national idiom."

Antonín Dvořák (1841–1904), the butcher's apprentice and self-styled "simple Czech musician", initially played second viola in Smetana's orchestra in Prague. He revered the older composer; the latter in his turn tried to support Dvořák's work as a composer. All the more incomprehensible to outsiders, therefore, was the conflict between the supporters of Smetana and Dvořák, which reached its climax in 1912 and left traces which are still evident today. Writing about the premiere of Dvořák's opera *Rusalka*, the ardent Smetana fan Zdeněk Nejedlý said: "Since we allow no other form of lyrical drama than musical drama, we must judge *Rusalka* to be flawed in its very inception, a failure." Nejedlý later became Minister of Culture and was largely responsible for the reaction against Dvořák's work in the 1950s.

Above, Antonín Dvořák composed the Symphony *From The New World*. **Right**, Bedřich Smetana is considered the Czech national composer.

SMETANA'S MOLDAU

From the Smetana Promenade on the right bank of the Vltava (Moldau), Prague presents itself to the visitor from its most attractive angle: the graceful masonry of the Charles Bridge spans the gleaming silver ribbon of water in front of the picturesque panorama of the churches and palaces of the Lesser Quarter, above which tower the massive bulk of the Castle and the Cathedral of St Vitus.

Today the Smetana Museum is housed in what used to be the municipal waterworks, near the former mills of the Old Town, a building complex which extends into the river itself. It is maintained by the Smetana Society, founded in Prague in 1931, and contains the composer's manuscripts and sponsors the publication and performance of his works.

Smetana loved to walk along the banks of the Vltava. He repeatedly found new ideas and inspiration for his compositions. A friend of his, Josef Srb-Debrnov, remembers:

"Most of the enchantingly emotional melodies in *The Bartered Bride* owe their creation to the evening moods on the Moldau Promenade opposite Hradcany Castle and the Lesser Quarter. The maestro would take a walk by the river here at dusk virtually every day, reading as he did the text sent to him piece by piece by Sabina, his librettist. The melodies flowed through his brain like a torrent. Returning to his apartment in the Palais Lazansky, he would sit down at his desk and make rough notes on manuscript paper of the ideas he had already worked out in his mind."

By the time he started to compose a grandiose musical monument to his beloved Vltava, Smetana was no longer able to enjoy his nightly walks along its banks. A rapidly worsening affliction of the hearing tract prevented him from listening to the river's song. Impoverished and derided by resentful critics he was ultimately forced to seek refuge in the country, in the hunting lodge of his son-in-law.

When *The Moldau* was given its concert premiere on 4 April 1875, the audience was ecstatic, but the composer himself was unable to hear a single tone. He had become completely deaf whilst working on the score.

The Moldau is the best-known and most frequently performed movement of the orchestral cycle *My Fatherland* (*Má Vlast*), in which Smetana's love of his Bohemian homeland and its people finds its most eloquent expression. The inspiration for the entire cycle, which Smetana wrote between 1874 and 1879, grew gradually over a period of many years. It is maintained that Smetana's earliest ideas about the subject started to crystalise some 20 years before the work was first performed.

The programme of the six cycles was sketched by Smetana himself: *Vyšehrad* tells of the heroic fights of the knights of old; in *The Moldau* the listener follows the river along its course from its source to the Vyšehrad Castle in Prague (the main theme is played by two oboes, symbolising the mountain springs, and repeated in rondo form in ever-changing variations before ending in a hymn-like E major passage). *Šarka* conjures up a

Bohemian myth with an Amazonian love story dominated by a stormy orchestral symphonic section; *From Bohemia's Meadows and Forests* is a succession of folkloric portraits, with peasants dancing the polka in the clearings and airs played on the horn recalling traditional melodies. *Tábor* recalls the tragic-heroic fate of the Hussites, whilst *Blaník* provides an optimistic final note to the entire cycle, echoing the hope that the warriors of the Lord will return victorious when the people's need is greatest.

Non-Czechs sometimes have difficulties with the patriotic symbolism of the two last cycles, but few people fail to succumb to the powerful emotions aroused by *The Moldau*. ■

Dvořák's success abroad was all the more controversial. He attracted musical fame beyond the boundaries of his native land, something Smetana was denied throughout his life. Dvořák's first triumph was in London, where his *Stabat Mater* was rapturously received, followed by New York, Berlin, Vienna and Budapest. He was helped in this by his older friend and patron Johannes Brahms, who not only invited Dvořák and his entire family to Vienna at his own expense, but also established his first contact with the Leipzig publisher Simrock and added a number of necessary corrections to the scores.

It was Dvořák's international reputation that brought him in 1891 the offer of directorship of the New York Conservatory. The three years which he spent in America resulted in his most popular orchestral score, *Symphony No. 9, From the New World*, the one most widely played on a worldwide basis. Its premiere in the Carnegie Hall in New York in 1893 was a runaway success. Dvořák wrote home: "The success of my symphony on 15 and 16 December was magnificent: the newspapers maintain that no other composer had ever enjoyed such a moment of triumph."

Critics emphasised the "American accent" of the themes. In this new work the Czech composer set an important trend for the development of an independent American national musical tradition. At the same time he helped the new music of his own country achieve world recognition.

Like Smetana, Dvořák rejected a direct transcription of folk melodies. His adaptation of folk songs always resulted in a completely new setting of the works. His cycle *Music from Moravia* (1875), which paved the way for his international recognition, demonstrates a sensitivity bordering on genius in his interpretation of Moravian folklore. The piano accompaniment is simple but often contains surprisingly sophisticated harmonic progressions which provide a perfect translation of the poetic lyrics.

Unlike the city-dweller Smetana, who was only driven to the country by the poverty of old age, Dvořák was a country-dweller who never felt quite at home in the city. While working in New York he remained, like his peasant forebears, an early riser. He did not go out after 6pm and spent his evenings playing cards with the family. During an entire year he visited the Metropolitan Opera only twice. Dvořák was always happiest at Vysoká, his country estate.

Dvořák left for posterity an impressive collection of compositions: 31 works of chamber music, 14 string quartets, 50 orchestral works and nine symphonies, including such works as the *Slavonic Dances*, whose wealth of catchy melodies has caused them to be condemned as merely light music by some composers, rather like Smetana's *Vltava* (*The Moldau*).

The distinguished musical tradition of Czechoslovakia did not end with the dawn of the 20th century. Leos Janácek (1854–1928) proved a worthy successor to Smetana and Dvořák. He composed, amongst other works, the world-famous operas *Jenufa, The Cunning Little Vixen*, and *Katja Kabanová*. Janácek was searching for new forms of expression, for a personal musical language, but he also intended his music to relay a message of common humanity, a proclamation of his humanistic ideal. Janácek founded the College of Music in Brno, and the annual autumn festival of classical and contemporary music focuses on his work.

Bohuslav Martinů, who lived in the US from 1940, also has a place in the country's modern musical history. Artistically speaking Martinů was an all-round genius who understood Impressionism as well as jazz. He was one of the first composers to incorporate elements of the latter in his works. His 400-plus compositions covered a remarkable range, comparable only with that of Mozart. He had a talent for mixing classical elements with avant-garde features to produce a completely new synthesis of sound. Two of his highly imaginative works, the ballet *Spaliček* and the opera *Juliette,* are still performed regularly today.

Music continues to play an important role in the lives of Czech and Slovak people. Prague in particular has a feast to offer music lovers, from performances at the State Opera House and symphony concerts in the Rudolfinum, to open-air summer concerts and the internationally famous Prague Spring Music Festival, as well as a lively tradition of street music.

Right, an open-air concert being performed on the Old Town Square, viewed from the tower of the Town Hall.

When anyone mentions Czech literature, most people tend to think in the first instance of *The Good Soldier Schweik*, the eponymous hero of the world-famous novel by Jaroslav Hašek who is often thought to represent the Czech national character. Václav Havel is well-known as a politician, but how many people can say they have read his dramas and diaries?

Bohemia's literary tradition: The origins of the literary tradition in the lands of the Bohemian crown stretch back as far as the 9th century. Seeing his kingdom of Greater Moravia threatened by the Franks, and as a kind of cultural offensive against the growing influence from the West, Prince Ratislav summoned the Slavic apostles from Byzantium. The learned brothers Cyril and Methodius who arrived in 863 invented the Glagolitic alphabet, based on the Slavonic dialect used in the area surrounding their native town, Salonika, and which was the foundation of the Old Slavonic language. The first book to be written in Old Slavonic was probably the Bible, but other Old Slavonic texts that can be assigned to this era are the 10th-century *Legends* about St Wenceslas (the Bohemian Prince Václav). The Old Slavonic language ceased to be used when Latin was introduced as the liturgical language of the country at the end of the 11th century. Cyril is also credited with inventing the cyrillic alphabet, although this may have been the work of his followers.

The historic foundations of Czech literature lie in the *Bohemian Chronicles*, the work of the Deacon Cosmas (died 1125). The Latin chronicle recounts the history of the land from the legendary times of the founding father, Čech, until the beginning of the 12th century. In the courts of the Přemyslid kings, encouragement was given to German literature, and the earliest preserved texts in Czech were only written in the latter part of the 13th century. During the reign of Charles IV (1347–78) learning and literature flourished in both German and Czech.

Left, Jan Amos Komenský (Comenius) (1592–1670) was one of the most important scholars of his time.

In the 15th century, the social and moral questions addressed by the Hussite Movement gave rise to a great deal of writing in the vernacular, in the form of treatises and hymns. Hus's own importance for Czech literature lay not only in his vernacular sermons and his letters; he also set about the reform of Czech orthography, which he laid out in the treatise *De orthographia Bohemica*.

One of the outstanding personalities in Czech literary history was the humanist Jan Amos Komenský (1592–1670), generally known by his Latin name Comenius. He was a teacher, writer and theologian whose influence spread across many countries. The son of Protestant parents, he studied in Heidelberg and became a preacher in the Community of Bohemian Brethren in 1616. He endeavoured to improve the lot of man (in preparation for the kingdom of heaven) through his reform of the educational system. Piety, virtue and learning were the cornerstones of his philosophy. His most famous work, *Orbis Sensualium Pictus* (The World in Pictures, 1654), was for many years the most widely used textbook in Germany.

The reforms of Emperor Joseph II, in particular the abolition of serfdom, prompted a period of national revival which marked the beginning of a new phase in Czech literature. The philologist and historian Josef Dobrovský, together with Josef Jungmann, produced philological works documenting the history of the language as well as a two-volume German–Czech dictionary. *May* (1836), the epic poem by the Romantic poet Karel Hynek Mácha, is regarded as one of the milestones in modern Czech poetry. Outstanding men of letters of this period, which reached its zenith in 1848, included the prose writer Božena Němcová, publicist and poet Karel Havlíček and dramatists Josef Kajetán Tyl and Václav Kliment Klicpera.

Tales of the Lesser Quarter: The transition from Romanticism to Realism was marked by Božena Němcová's novel *The Grandmother*, published in 1855. The Prague writer Jan Neruda (1834–91) achieved fame as the author of the *Tales of the Lesser Quarter* (1878), a collection of novellas and humorous, reflective sketches from the Malá Strana.

Pictures of Old Prague, a collection of short stories and imaginative pieces, transport the reader into late 19th-century Prague. The famous Chilean writer Pablo Neruda, the Nobel Laureate of 1971, adopted the surname as a mark of admiration and respect.

At the turn of the 20th century the classics of international literature dominated the literary scene. Numerous translations of literary works from other parts of the world, not least from the German classics, helped to raise the general level of education to a higher level and simultaneously paved the way for the integration of Czech into the broader European literary context. In those days a knowledge of German was a *sine qua non* in Bohemia, so many readers were able to claim first-hand knowledge of the works in question.

Prague as a literary centre: The Bohemian capital, moreover, had traditionally enjoyed a special position in European culture. Apart from the resident Czechs and Germans, a significant Jewish community had evolved, which also made an important contribution to literary history.

It is possible that some natives of Prague, such as Max Brod (who published the work of Franz Kafka against his will), or Franz Werfel, are still underestimated today. But even during his lifetime and despite his own uncertainties, there were a few who recognised Franz Kafka as a great writer. Kafka (1883–1924) was almost an exact contemporary of the perennially popular humorist and satirist Jaroslav Hašek (1883–1923), whose main work, *The Good Soldier Schweik*, is still the best-known book in the Czech language.

The Golden City on the Vltava was a centre of literary talent at many points in its history. At the beginning of this century, German and Czech enjoyed equal status as literary languages. A bohemian society similar to that of Paris established itself in the capital, gathering in coffee houses such as the legendary *Café Arco*.

Franz Kafka, a German-speaking Jew, was born on 3 July 1883 in Prague. He seldom left his native city and at the end of his short life was buried there, in the Straschnitz Cemetery. For 14 years Kafka worked as a legal clerk at the Workers' Accident Insurance Institution of the Kingdom of Bohemia, but he regarded his "scribblings" after hours as

his "only desire". His prose has turned Prague into a major literary landmark.

Although Kafka's diaries and letters fill over 3,000 pages, for many years little was known about his life. This had less to do with his own desire for privacy than with the political upheavals and repression – first the German occupation, then the communist regime – which prevented his work from being made public. In 1931, the Gestapo confiscated a large number of Kafka's manuscripts and these must be regarded as lost. The first Czech translations of his writings did not appear until 1957.

Most of the Prague houses Kafka lived in are still standing, including two which have

since become small museums: one in the Old Town Square, beside St Nicholas' Church, and his sister's house in Golden Lane.

In contrast to some of Prague's other German-speaking writers, Kafka actively sought contact with the Czech population and demonstrated openly his sympathy for the socialist cause; in later years he supported the idea of a socially-oriented Zionism.

Kafka's work remains controversial and the interpretations of his message are legion. In his posthumously published novels *The Trial* and *The Castle* he expresses the fears and alienation of 20th-century man by means of his dream-like visions. Of paramount importance in his imagination was a life-long struggle with the dominant figure of his father as well as the perpetual conflict inherent in his relationship with women, in particular Felice Bauer and Julie Wohryzek, both of whom were at one stage engaged to be married to him, as well as Milena Jesenská and Dora Dymant, with whom he spent the last year of his life in Berlin.

Norbert Fried, a German Jew, commented on the themes that preoccupied the authors of Prague: "The German-speaking authors of Prague often took as subject-matter the dark events of the time, bringing to life the split personalities. Whether they were Jews or not, they turned their attention to the Golem

and other legends and to the teachings of Rabbi Löw, or they wrote about the mysterious cabinet of curiosities of Rudolf II. During the 1920s the Jews probably sensed the dreadful fate which would befall them in 1938, whilst the non-Jews had a premonition of what they would face in 1945. Those who wrote in Czech, on the other hand, saw Prague only as the Golden City or the Matička ('Little Mother')." But Franz Kafka remarked that "The little mother has claws...!"

Left, Jan Neruda, the famous Prague story teller of the 19th century. **Above**, Egon Erwin Kisch, who made history as a "roving reporter".

The foundation of the independent Czechoslovak Republic in 1918 opened up new perspectives for the country's writers. Some of the greatest achievements of Czech literature date from the 1920s. Among them are the satirical plays of Karel Čapek, the son of a country doctor, who was a friend of the new republic's first president, T.G. Masaryk. Čapek's best works describe the problems of a centrally organised machine age. His play *RUR*, first performed in 1921, invented the word "robot", which has passed into international usage. The plot deals with the construction of a mechanical man which eventually overthrew its masters.

Also writing at this time was Jaroslav Seifert, who many years later, in 1984, was to become the first Czech writer to be awarded the Nobel Prize for Literature. Seifert was also a journalist and had been publishing poems since 1920. Until 1929 he was a supporter of the communists, but later became an ardent opponent of Stalinism.

Egon Erwin Kisch, a contemporary of Kafka, and like him a native of Prague, was the author of works of social criticism. He has gone down in literary history as the roving reporter, the title of his most famous work. Kisch travelled widely, fighting for the Republicans in the Spanish Civil War and writing about China, Australia and Mexico. He returned to Prague in 1945 and died in 1948.

The German occupation interrupted the history of Czech literature, although the works of Václav Řezáč did break new ground in the genre of the psychological novel. After the communist takeover in February 1948, Řezáč, like many of his contemporaries, declared his support for "Socialist Realism".

Until the beginning of the 1960s no works of any great significance were produced. Then political control relaxed slightly, and literature blossomed with the novels of Josef Škvorecký, Milan Kundera and Ludvík Vaculík, the short stories of Ivan Klima, Bohumil Hrabal and Arnošt Lustig and the plays of Václav Havel. Klima's collection of short stories, *My Merry Mornings,* is a wonderful evocation of life in Prague. Many of these works are now available in several languages.

For 20 years after the repression of the Prague Spring in 1968, three distinct literary traditions existed side by side: the "official" authors who were allowed to publish their works with the approval of the state and the party; the literature of Czech exiles, which had difficulty finding a new international audience; and the native *Samizdat*, the works of writers who continued to live in Czechoslovakia but whose writings were banned. Only small numbers of their books were printed and these relied on hand to hand distribution.

Perhaps the most successful of the exiled Czech authors was the prose writer Milan Kundera. Born in 1929, Kundera worked at the Prague Institute for Cinematographic Studies until the Soviet invasion of 1968. He subsequently lost his job, and his biting sa-

tirical novel on Stalinism, *The Joke,* was banned. He now lives in Paris, where he wrote his most famous work, *The Unbearable Lightness of Being.*

Pavel Kohout also played an active role in the reform movement of 1968. In company with many others he was forced to take cover during the next decade; after signing the Charter 77 demanding basic human rights he was driven into exile. His *Diary of a Counter-Revolutionary* describes clearly the determination of many artists not to give way in the face of wrong. Josef Skvorecky is another exiled writer who deserves mention. He went to Canada where he distinguished

himself by founding *68 Publishers*, which published the works of exiled authors, and wrote, among many other novels, *The Engineer of Human Souls,* which satirises the police state.

The most famous of all the writers banned after the failed Prague Spring of 1968 was the dramatist Václav Havel – also one of the first signatories of the Charter 77. Like many of his contemporaries Havel was imprisoned on occasions, and censorship forced him to do manual work to earn a living, but he continued to write.

Until his death in February 1997, Bouhimil Hrabel was widely regarded as the greatest Czech writer of his generation. His best known work, *Closely observed trains,* was made into an Oscar-winning film in 1967.

Slovak literature: The literature of Slovakia was closely interwoven with that of the Czechs until an independent language developed from the Slovakian dialects. After the disintegration of the kingdom of Greater Moravia, Slovakia became part of Hungary for a thousand years. As a result, its literature has strong Latin and Hungarian influences.

The most important names in Slovak literature before the creation of the Czechoslovak Republic in 1918 were the national revolutionary, writer and politician Ľudovit Štúr (1815–56), who is credited with creating the literary Slovak language; and the poet Pavol Orságh Hviezdoslav (1849–1921), who also gained fame as a skilled translator.

After 1918, conditions for the development of an independent Slovakian literature improved dramatically, and the newly acquired freedom was put to good use by a variety of literary trends, ranging from poetic symbolism to decidedly proletarian literature, and categorised by the all-enveloping term "Slovak Modern". The most important group of writers advocating social revolution, including the influential Laco Novomeský, established itself around the newspaper *Dav* (Mass) whose Socialist Realism after 1948 became the official doctrine. It remains to be seen how Slovak literature will develop, but it is something that all those interested in international contemporary writing will watch with interest.

Above, Franz Kafka and his fiancée Felice Bauer. Right, a famous depiction of "The Good Soldier Schweik".

JAROSLAV HAŠEK

Like his contemporary Franz Kafka, Jaroslav Hašek, who was born on 30 April 1883, lived to be just 40 years old. Hašek worked as a bank clerk, but by the age of 17 he had begun to write his first satirical articles for local newspapers. By the time he was 21, he had become the editor of a number of anarchist publications.

Drafted into the Austro-Hungarian Army, Hašek allowed himself to be captured by the Russians during World War I. While in Russia he joined the Czech liberation army, but then fell into the ranks of the Bolsheviks, for whom he wrote communist propaganda. Returning to Prague, he devoted himself to writing. His world-famous novel *The Good Soldier Schweik*, a masterful and wonderfully humorous satire on military life, was published in 1921. Brought to the attention of the international public by the Austrian writer Max Brod, it first appeared in English in 1930.

Hašek was a compulsive and accomplished hoaxer and practical joker who hated pomposity and authority. In many ways, the story of Schweik, a scrounger, liar and undisciplined drunkard, largely reflects Hašek's own eventful life, which ended in a haze of alcoholic apathy (he often only wrote in order to pay his drinking debts). Hašek drew a great deal of inspiration from the world of Prague taverns, where he noted down many a beery truism for use in his works.

Particularly famous is the scene in *The Good Soldier Schweik* where Schweik says to his fellow soldiers: "When the war is over you'll see me in my cups in the Chalice again." It guaranteed immortality for the tavern U Kalicha (The Chalice) and provided Prague with a meeting place for locals and visitors hoping to find wit and literary conversation. The venerable Chalice ("with blackened oak panelling and brass hinges on the bar") also formed the central stage in Berthold Brecht's comedy *Schweik in World War II*.

Readers the world over have laughed at the sly dog trader who took advantage of World War I to gain personal freedom "through idiotic senselessness and a clown's mask". Literary critics never tire of pointing out that the hero is not a prototype, to be found anywhere at any time. Schweik is the product of a highly specific milieu and a particular period – that of the Austria of the last century. That is why he has become living history. F. E. Weiskopf, who lived in Prague at the same time as Hasek, insists that Schweik is an "historical" rather than a fictional character:

"He could only arise in that period of narrow-mindedness, carelessness, good-natured treachery, anachronistic absolutism and national suppression which characterized the Danube monarchy of those days. He could only become the laughable, foolishly artful hero he was in wartime, in this era in which the rotten carcass of state lay in its death throes. And ultimately it was the mischievous, fatalistic sabotage of a Schweik which destroyed the state itself."

The combination in Schweik's character of genuine and feigned denseness, of the apathy and submissiveness of the little man, with artful cunning, slyness and cynicism, was rejected by

Czech intellectuals as being damaging to the national idea of what it meant to be Czech.

Brecht, on the other hand, maintains that it is not the little man himself who is to blame, but the circumstances in which he lived. In his play, the chorus insists that:

The times are changing.
The grandiose plans of the powerful
are coming at last to a halt.
And they will walk on like bloody fighting cocks.
The times are changing.
And no force can alter the fact.

A memorial plaque marks Hašek's birthplace in Školská street in the Novy Město. ∎

As long ago as the Middle Ages the Czechs could boast the beginnings of a national theatre in their native language, but its true roots lie in the period of national revival which began in the late 18th century. The first dramatic performance in Czech took place in Prague in 1771 – although the actors were German, and unable to pronounce the hitherto despised language properly. In a way it was the Theatre of the Absurd, long before the latter actually made its entrance in theatrical history.

At the end of the 18th century, the first major national play was the dramatisation of *Oldrich and Bozena*, an 11th-century legend. Almost 200 years later, in 1967, the same plot was presented once more, brought up to date by Frantisek Hrubin. The message is simple: Oldrich, a Czech prince, chooses as his wife a girl of humble origins. The prince is portrayed as a wise and just ruler, who shares the poverty and troubles of his people. This is a timeless theme, and one that appeals particularly to those who have more than their share of suffering. In this case, the audience could immediately identify Oldrich, the benevolent ruler as an exact opposite to their own repressive leaders.

In 1781 Count Anton Nostitz, one of the city's leading figures, founded the Nostitz Theatre, a lovely, neo-classical building which is now called the Estates Theatre. It opened with *Emilia Galotti*, one of the best known works of Gotthold Lessing, a German dramatist who died that same year. The play, written some nine years earlier, is a tragedy with a strong social theme, which delighted the German-speaking upper classes.

Real stage history was written, however, with the first performance of Mozart's *Don Giovanni* (1787), which went on from here to conquer the opera houses of the world. Not always appreciated in his native Austria, Mozart had been received with open arms by the people of Prague, and is still regarded as a favoured adopted son, although he spent relatively short periods in the city.

Czech players briefly won permission to stage plays in their own language in the Nostitz Theatre, but soon were forced to move out to a little wooden theatre, called The Bouda, in the Horse Market (now Wenceslas Square).

For the time being, the Nostitz was to remain the preserve of the wealthy, German-speaking citizens of Prague, although it was later to play a part in the history of Czech nationalism. It was here, in 1834, that a musical comedy by Josef Kajetán Tyl (1801–56), entitled *Fidlovačka*, introduced the song

"Where is my native land?" which became the Czech national anthem.

Two hundred years ago, ordinary people flocked in droves to the theatre and formed an enthusiastic audience – thankful to be able to see a play written in their own language, even if it was in the humble little Bouda. This enthusiasm was the beginning of the Czech national passion for all things theatrical, which reached its architectural climax in the construction of the National Theatre, funded by public subscriptions. Opened in 1881, the building almost immediately burned down, and was promptly rebuilt, also with money raised from the willing public, so keen were

Left, Milan Sládek, *The Whale*. <u>Above</u>, Boris Hybner, mime artist.

the people of Prague to have a theatre to call their own.

The magnificent building was designed by Josef Zítek, and the rebuilding was largely the work of Josek Schulz, who also designed the National Museum. The theatre was a symbol of nationalist aspirations and opened, appropriately, with a performance of Smetana's opera *Libuše,* based on the legend of the princess who married a humble farmhand and inspired him to found the city of Prague and the Přemyslid dynasty.

The foundation of the first Czechoslovak Republic in 1918 saw a second upturn in the fortunes of the Czech and Slovak theatre. (The Slovakian National Theatre was founded

Robots, Čapek first uses the word *robot* – one of the few Czech words which have entered the international vocabulary. The robots in his play acquire human emotions and then rebel against their overbearing masters – a theme which would not have been popular under the Soviet regime several decades later.

In the 1930s, it was the D-34 Ensemble, founded by Emil Frantisek Burian, and the aptly named Liberated Theatre (*Osvobozené divadlo*)which breathed fresh life into the Czech theatrical scene with their satirical and musical productions.

The war years, under the German occupation, were a naturally dark time for the Czech

in 1919: until then, only German and Hungarian works had been performed in Bratislava's main theatre.) The most important dramatist of the time was undoubtedly Karel Čapek. His brother Josef, an outstanding caricaturist who is remembered for a series of drawings entitled *The Dictator's Boots*, which he created at the time when Hitler was in the ascendant, was also a prose writer, and was mostly responsible for the production of Karel's plays.

Some of the most successful examples of their work are *The Insect Play, The White Illness* and *The Mother.* In his futuristic play *RUR,* which stands for Rossum's Universal

theatre. Hopes of a bright new dawn when the war ended were soon dashed, as the communist regime favoured socialist realism above genuine artistic expression. During these years, however, a number of small theatres opened up in the capital, breathing fresh life into the musty atmosphere which prevailed.

Most important among them were the *Divadlo Na zábradlí* (Theatre by the Railings), *Semafor, Rokoko*, the *Cinoherní klub* (The Actors' Club), and the *Divadlo za branou* (Theatre behind the Gate).They engendered a new spirit of optimism and excitement, but this was to be harshly crushed by the Soviet intervention during the Prague Spring of 1968.

The absurdity of the situation in which Czech theatre found itself during the past two decades was the fact that its most significant writers – Václav Havel and Pavel Kohout – were only able to arrange performances of their works abroad. When, in 1975, an amateur group in České Budějovice (Budweis) attempted to present one of Havel's plays, all the tickets were bought up by the local security police. The only people able to enjoy an evening of subversive drama were the local functionaries of the communist party.

Havel himself began his theatrical career as an assistant stage manager at the ABC

and Mrozek, thus paving the way for the Czech Theatre of the Absurd.

In 1963, the theatre was the stage for the premiere of Havel's first full-length play *The Garden Party,* which also established the author's international reputation. In 1965 the Theatre by the Railings presented a guest performance of the play – in Czech – in West Berlin. It was not long before it was being performed in theatres all over the world. The play represented an undisguised challenge to the socialist ideology of the time and made the authorities aware that both Havel and the Theatre by the Railings needed to be kept under observation.

Havel's most frequently performed play, a

Theatre, before moving as a dramatist to what was to become his home base, the Theatre by the Railings (*Divadlo Na zábradlí*). It had been founded in 1958 as the first small, alternative venue in Prague and quickly progressed to the position of one of the city's most respected experimental stages. Its artistic director, Jan Grossmann, presented productions by international dramatists such as Beckett, Ionesco, Arrabal, Jarry

Left, the facade of Prague's Estates Theatre by night. **Above**, performance of Smetana's world-famous opera *The Bartered Bride* in Prague's National Theatre.

one-act work called *Audience*, was based on his own experiences when, forbidden by the regime to publish his plays, he was forced to earn his living in a brewery – one of many manual jobs which the writer, and many others in his position, took on during the years of censorship.

While working at the *Na zábradlí* Havel met Boris Hybner, a young mime artist. Together with Bohumil Hrabal (later nominated for the Nobel Prize for literature) they formed their own highly subversive mime company. The dark humour and scruffy appearance of the three men led one newspaper to dub them "the three black beetles of

Prague". Hybner went on to found the Reduta theatre, which opened a few months after the Soviet invasion in 1968. It became known as a focus of political protest but inevitably it was soon closed down. Hybner continued working in Prague when he could, and now runs the **Studio Gag** mime theatre.

Hybner had been inspired by the popular mime artist, Ladíslav Fialka, whose imagination and inimitable style influenced a whole generation and helped make Prague a world centre for this form of theatre.

The kind of avant-garde theatre presented by these "alternative" dramatists, actors and directors of the 1960s represented a risk to the communist regime, especially after 1968, a forcible closure of the fringe scene would have brought in its wake.

Now that the ghost of the Cold War has been exorcised, and the countries of Eastern Europe have been opened up to the West, Czech theatre stands on the threshold of a completely new era. The first step was a radical change in cultural policy and the break-up of the large theatrical companies, which were generously subsidised by the regime as long as they toed the party line. Painful as this discharge of excess ballast may have been, it is a healthy development. Many private theatrical enterprises are mushrooming, ranging in output from conventional, musicals and operettas tailored to the

when the social climate became noticeably colder. Ewald Schorm, a producer with an established reputation in the film world, was able to steer *Na zábradlí* through the cultural-political problems of the era by mixing a repertoire of classics (Strindberg, Beaumarchais, Jonson, Ostrovsky, Goethe, Ibsen) with contemporary plays (Hrabal, Albee, Steigerwald). This helped prevent an enforced closure of the Czech fringe theatre, which was in everyone's interests: actors and dramatists could continue with their creative output, audiences could see high-quality, stimulating works, and the regime avoided the loss of face and reputation which

taste of tourists to totally avant-garde productions which attract a smaller audience.

It is a time to search for new authors as well, for the failure of the old system has robbed plays such as those by Václav Havel of their frame of reference, making them virtually unperformable. It is important for Czech theatre to now decide on a new subject matter.

The future certainly looks very hopeful. Prague has a number of small, forward-looking theatres including the Reduta and the Kolowrat. The Archa is dedicated to producing plays written by new, young Czech dramatists, while Czech and Slovak history and culture forms the basis of programmes put on by the Ungelt Theatre Club.

The established theatre, too, has a lot to offer. In 1991, after eight years of renovation, the Estates Theatre was reopened once more – naturally enough, to the strains of *Don Giovanni*. Its classical performances are a close second to those at the National Theatre, and its operatic performances rival those at the Prague State Opera. A glance at any newspaper or listings magazine in Prague demonstrates that Czech theatre is alive and doing extremely well, with a mixture of classical, middle-of-the-road and innovative offerings to suit all tastes.

Also waiting to be rediscovered are impor-

is typical of many of the little avant-garde stages throughout the former Czechoslovakia, evidence that enthusiasm for the theatre is not confined to Prague. Founded in 1974 in Prostějov in the Hána (hence the name) as an experimental stage, it moved seven years later to Brno. It is a typical writers' theatre which produces its own scripts. It is a small venue which sees its role as a cultural centre and its programme includes music and poetry readings as well as drama.

Two theatrical forms which are typically Czech, and are also interesting for visitors who do not understand the language, are black light theatre and puppet shows. The magic lantern (*laterna magika*) is the most

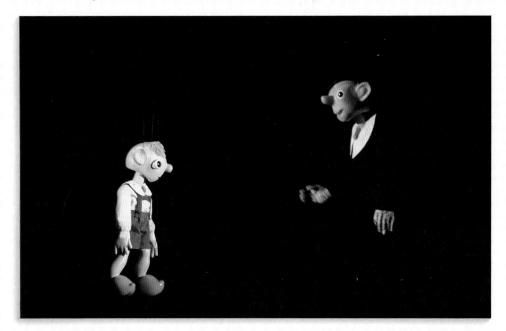

tant, long-neglected writers of the pre-war years. A step in this direction was taken by the little Há Theatre (*Ha Divadlo*) in Brno, with a new production of *The Human Tragicomedy* by Ladislav Klima (1878–1928). Klima was an existentialist, whose work was regarded by the socialist authorities as a shocking example of bourgeois decadence. Only during the brief flowering of the Prague Spring were any of his plays performed.

The development of the Ha Theatre itself

Left, a lavish performance of Puccini's *La Traviata*. **Above**, the puppet theatre Špejbel and Hurvínek.

popular of the former – so much so that it has a permanent home in the modern, glass **New Theatre** (opposite the National) which is now known by the troupe's name **Lanterna Magika** (*for more details, see page 173*).

Puppet Theatre has a long tradition in Czech culture (the Charles University in Prague offers a degree course in puppeteering and theatre design). Today the shows are popular with adults and children alike. The most ingenious productions, such as Orpheo and Euridice or Don Giovanni (complete with baroque-style marionettes) are presented by the National Marionette Theatre. (*See Travel Tips section for a full list of theatres.*)

"Homage to Prague" is the motto written in mosaic above the main entrance of the Municipal House, a monument to Prague's own brand of art nouveau architecture. The building was designed and built between 1906 and 1912 by the architects Osvald Polívka and Antonín Balšánek near the Powder Tower, on the site of the medieval royal palace and thus at the beginning of the traditional Royal Way. It was within its walls that the First Republic was proclaimed in 1918.

Conceived as a multi-purpose community centre with assembly chambers, ballrooms, exhibition halls and the magnificent Smetana Concert Hall, home of the Prague Symphony Orchestra, the Municipal House (Obecní Dům) has now reopened to the public after an extensive and painstaking restoration. The Brazerie Mozart and the Café Nouveau, will give visitors an idea of what the rest of the building is like but for the more curious there are regular guided tours through the Mayor's Chamber and other ceremonial rooms. Information about tours, concerts and exhibitions can be obtained from the foyer.

The most important Czech artists of the time were involved in the realisation of this city landmark. Karel Spillar provided the design for the mosaic by the entrance; the sculptures illustrating *Humiliation and Renaissance of the Nation* were the work of Ladislav Šaloun; Karel Novák produced the main decorative elements on the facade, including the light-bearing figures of Atlas gracing the balconies.

Particularly eye-catching are the large-scale allegorical portraits in the Primator Hall by Alfons Maria Mucha (1860–1939), the leading representative of the Prague Secessionists and one of the most popular of all the art nouveau artists. Mucha worked primarily as a painter and graphic artist, but was also active in arts and crafts. After studying in Vienna and Munich, in 1894 he moved to Paris, where he achieved artistic recognition

Preceding pages: the Mayor's Chamber in the Municipal House in the New Town, decorated by Alfons Mucha between 1906–11. Left, another Mucha masterpiece. Above, an art nouveau doorway.

almost overnight for the posters he designed for the actress Sarah Bernhardt. His sophisticated portraits of women – their hair and garlands of flowers elaborately entwined around their faces merging with the ornamentation of the background or the picture frame – set a new trend.

Jiří Mucha, the artist's son, describes his father's commercial success: "After the phenomenal success of the Sarah Bernhardt posters, which became sought-after collector's items as soon as they were published, the

printing firm of Champenois began to produce so-called 'panneaux'. They were really posters too, but without the advertising text. They were printed on good-quality paper or silk, and people either had them framed like pictures or used them to decorate screens. Within a short space of time, screens already decorated with these pictures were also being produced, and an entire chain of shops sold nothing but the works of Mucha, in every imaginable variation.

"The decorative panels were all characterised by the long, narrow shape typical of his theatre advertisements. Unfortunately they were not all well made. It was a question of whether my father himself carried out all the corrections. Sometimes the printers were in such a hurry that there was no time for this. In such cases you needed only to glance at the original to realise how many details of drawing or colour had been lost in the lithographic process."

Mucha's success seems to have come quite naturally. As his son comments: "It is typical of the paradoxes which were forever occuring in father's life that he achieved fame as a result of precisely that aspect of his work which happened to be most fashionable at the time. He was not really aware of this fact himself; in not a single one of his lectures or writings about art does he make even the

He was finally laid to rest in the Vyšehrad Cemetery, the pantheon of Czech artists.

There is no doubt that Czech art nouveau drew its greatest inspiration from Paris. Most Prague artists visited the French capital in addition to Vienna and Berlin, the other great artistic centres of the time. Nonetheless, art nouveau in Prague developed into an independent artistic form of expression, as witnessed by numerous architectural elements throughout the city. In the early years it represented a reaction against the contemporary predilection for over-emphasising historic forms in architecture.

The main trend-setter as regards the new range of forms was the Prague Academy of

briefest reference to the way in which he arrived at his style in those days…"

Exhibitions in Paris, Munich, Brussels, London and Prague followed. In 1904 Mucha travelled to America, where he worked for some time as stage designer and teacher at the Art Institute of Chicago. Shortly before the outbreak of World War I he returned to Prague, where he created his "Slavic Epic", a series of 20 monumental pictures dedicated to Slavic mythology.

In 1913 Mucha designed a magnificently colourful window depicting episodes from the lives of the Bohemian saints for the New Archbishop's Chapel in St Vitus' Cathedral.

Applied Art, which also achieved international acclaim with its contributions to the World Exhibitions in Paris (1900) and St Louis (1904). Using local folkloric elements, it developed a canon of expression which architects and craftsmen often followed down to the last detail. C. Klouček's ceramic and stucco ornamentation of facades was soon so widely copied that it was to become a characteristic of art nouveau buildings in towns all over Bohemia.

In architecture, Jan Kotěra, a pupil of the Viennese architect Otto Wagner, was one of the prime influences. He moved on from the originally naturalist conception towards a strong geometric and constructivist formal style. His most impressive works in Prague are the carefully restored Hotel Evropa and the Peterka House, with its elegantly ornamental facade, both on Wenceslas Square.

Apart from the sketches for the Municipal House, Osvald Polívka designed the house U Nováků (Vodičkova 36), the building housing the former Prague Insurance Company (Národní 7), the Bank of the Provinces (Na příkopě 20) and the New Town Hall on Mariánské náměstí.

The grandfather of Václav Havel designed and built the Lucerna Palace of Culture on Wenceslas Square as well as the family home on the Rašín Promenade.

architecture are the Koruna House on Wenceslas Square and the steel Palace of Congress in the Exhibition and Trades Fair Park. The Hotel Paříž (U obecního domu 1, immediately behind the Municipal House) was declared a national monument in 1984.

The Svatopluk Čech Bridge and the magnificent facades of Pařížka Street form a remarkable urban ensemble. The bridge was constructed by J. Koula in 1908. Although the shortest bridge in the city, it is certainly one of the most decorative.

The most outstanding sculptors of the era were Ladislav Šaloun, who was responsible for the vast monument to Jan Hus on the Old Town Square, which was unveiled on 6 July

With their new design for the main railway station (the Wilsonova) in 1980, architects Jan Šrámek and Alena Šrámková succeeded in integrating an historic building complex with a modern transport concept. The art nouveau building erected by J. Franta between 1901 and 1909 was remodelled around a massive ticket hall and departure area and linked to an underground railway without damaging the original fabric in any way .

Further impressive examples of art nouveau

Left, angel above a door in Celetná and the facade of the Hotel Evropa. **Above**, the dome of the Municipal House; decoration in "Carp Street".

1915 to mark the 500th anniversary of the death of the Bohemian reformer; and Stanislav Sucharda, who created the Palacký Monument on the bridge of the same name.

True art nouveau sought to establish a balance between man and nature by using artistic symbols to add a cosmic dimension to personal experience. The artist could fuse a complex living environment with an idealised creative sphere. The fact that he was attempting to achieve an ideal which has become topical again today may be just one reason why, in Prague, art nouveau has lost nothing of its original fascination almost 100 years later.

Since the opening of frontiers after the collapse of the Eastern bloc, protectionists and nature lovers in the Czech section of the Bohemian Forest, in Eastern Bavaria and the Mühlenviertel of Austria have been anxiously watching the fate of the previously inaccessible border regions in the three-country triangle northeast of Passau. The National Park area, made up of the Bavarian Forest and the Bohemian Forest (Šumava), now offers limitless opportunities for development. Memoranda and working papers are headed the *Green Roof of Europe, Intersilva*, the *Nature Park Region* or the *Euro-Region*. Institutions and interest groups are clamouring to win support for their proposals to use the tremendous natural potential of the area as the basis for an environment-friendly economic development. There has even been talk of an ecological model region.

The Czech Republic's creation of the Šumava National Park on 20 March 1991 fulfilled one of the important prerequisites for such a scheme. Together with the National Park of the Bavarian Forest in Germany, a total of 81,000 hectares (200,000 acres) of countryside now stands under the strictest protection laws. The area covered by the National Park includes the largest self-contained forest in Central Europe. It is also – uniquely in Europe – an area of over 80,000 hectares (198,000 acres) free of any major roads.

Unspoilt nature: The new Šumava National Park is just one of many areas within the country's boundaries where there are strict limitations on the way land is used. Reports about the severe environmental damage to the industrial areas, especially in Northern Bohemia, have tended to eclipse the fact that the Czech and Slovak republics form one of the few regions in Europe in which people will still be able to live in unspoilt natural surroundings in 10 years' time. It is also a land in which animals that have been long extinct in other countries – brown bears, wolves and lynxes – are still to be found in their natural habitat.

Despite their relatively small area, the topography of the Czech and Slovak republics is extremely varied. The upland regions include a wide range of scenery, attracting tourists from home and abroad. Cable cars and signposted footpaths lead up to the highest peaks and various recreational centres in the mountains. In order to limit the negative effects of intensive tourism, the authorities have drawn up a strict code of conduct gov-

erning visits to the national parks. For example, it is forbidden to leave the marked footpaths or to light fires or camp except within the specially designated areas.

National parks and nature parks are large areas of untouched or largely unspoilt countryside which are of scientific or general educational importance. Including as they do thousands of lakes and a well-developed network of signposted footpaths, they are rewarding for walkers and other nature lovers. There are tours to suit every taste. In some protected areas nature trails have been laid out (there were almost 100 of these in 1992), marked by a white square with a green

Preceding pages: a crisp morning in the High Tatra. Left, Slovakian paradise near Nová Ves. Above, canoeists can find ideal stretches in both republics.

stripe. Information boards provide details of local flora and fauna at regular intervals.

The seven national parks: Before 1987, six major areas had been declared national parks. Together with the 1,679 nature conservancy areas within the country, they cover an area of 17,272 sq km (6,666 sq miles) – in other words, 13 percent of the total land area. By comparison, the National Parks of the US cover an area of 65,000 sq km (25,000 sq miles) – 0.6 percent of the total land area. No country in central Europe can boast larger expanses of unspoilt natural habitats in which flora and fauna are preserved and studied in a scientific manner.

Although most of the national parks are

tains) in Northern Bohemia. The High Tatra National Park was founded in 1948 and joins the Polish Tatrzanski Narododowy National Park in the north. It covers an area of 770 sq km (300 sq miles); the protected area totals 510 sq km (200 sq miles). The Polish frontier is not open to traffic at this point. Nonetheless the twin national parks of the High Tatra are administered jointly by both countries.

The Vysoké Tatry (High Tatra) is the highest mountain chain in Slovakia; Mount Gerlachovský (2,655 metres/8,496 ft) and Mount Lomnický (2,632 metres/8,422 ft) are the highest peaks in the country. The topography of this alpine region, with its fissured craggy summits and picturesque

situated within Slovakia, it was in fact in the Czech lands that the very first attempts were made to preserve valuable natural habitats. As early as 1838 two nature conservation areas were set up here: the forest areas of Hojná Voda and Žofinský in Southern Bohemia. Twenty years later, the forest conservation area of Boubínský prales was added. After World War II a systematic programme was embarked upon to preserve typical scenery, archaeological sites and topographical formations.

The largest and most important national parks are the High Tatra National Park in Slovakia and the Krkonoše (Giant Moun-

mountain lakes, is typical of high-altitude landscapes and includes glacial valleys, moraines and more than 100 cirque lakes. It is ideal walking country and a popular skiing destination in winter, which means that it can be overcrowded at times.

The High Tatra forms the northernmost section of the 1,200-km (750-mile) arc of the Carpathian Mountains. During the Quaternary Era the mountains were largely covered by glaciers; the present topography is the result of glacial erosion. Robert Townson, a Scottish physicist and geographer, studied the region in detail and described it in his book *Journeys through Hungary in 1793*

(Slovakia belonged to Hungary at the time).

Brown bears and marmots: The national wildlife protection agency is a fairly recent innovation. The land within the boundaries of the National Parks is subject to fairly heavy tourist traffic (the Polish section of the High Tatra is a fully developed tourist region). Nonetheless, the importance of nature conservancy has been recognised and afforded a high priority.

There is already a ban on the construction of new hotels in the High Tatra, and in some areas there is a general ban on motor traffic. In July and August private cars are prohibited from using the roads to the holiday resorts from Poprad, the most important base

animals are hunted, but in the National Parks they are protected all the year round. For many years the chamois was considered a threatened species; nowadays they are more common. The chamois living in the High Tatra are a particular species only found here; the increase in tourism poses a threat to their habitat.

Amongst the birds indigenous to the area are pheasant, partridge, wild geese and a number of species of duck. They may be hunted, but rarer large birds, such as golden eagles, vultures, ospreys, storks, eagle-owls, bustards and capercaillies are protected.

The Krkonoše National Park was founded in 1963 and extends over an area of 385 sq

outside the National Park. The last stage of the journey must be undertaken by bus or train. On sunny days the sky here is a deep and clear blue.

The High Tatra is still the habitat of a large number of species which are extinct in most other European countries, or which are only able to survive in zoos. The mountains harbour brown bears, wolves, lynxes and wildcats (*felis silvestris*), marmots, otters, wild horses, martens and mink. Most of these

Left, this breed of chamois is unique to the High Tatra. Above, gathering hay in the Bohemian Forest National Park.

km (150 sq miles). The region bears traces of the ice sheets which once covered it. Corries, moraines and glacial valleys are evident, as are the remains of a more northerly flora (e.g. cloudberries). Characteristic species include monkshood, swallow-wort gentian, white hellebore, etc. The spruce trees planted during the 17th and 18th centuries have been badly damaged by pollution and acid rain. In one of the areas most badly affected by acid rain in the whole of Europe 10,000 hectares (25,000 acres) of pine forest are losing their needles. The stocks of beech are restricted to the lower slopes. The entire National Park area suffers from too many leisure visitors.

Slovakian paradise: The Slovenský raj National Park was established east of Poprad in 1988. The wild upland landscape extends over 140 sq km (54 sq miles) in an area which has been under a protection order since 1964. Wind, water and time have worn away the limestone plateau to form ravine-like gorges with waterfalls, cascades and karst. It is the habitat of many rare and protected plant and animal species.

The region has been made accessible to walkers and climbers by handrails, ladders and bridges (often consisting only of a tree trunk) where necessary. The main attractions of the park include the narrow defile at the rise of the River Hron and the Dobšina ice the Demänovské caves) which are accessible to tourists. The past few years have seen a number of hotels and chair lifts built and ski slopes prepared. Nonetheless, the eastern sections of the chain remain very peaceful and show few signs of human intervention. This is ideal walking country, since there are fewer steep gorges than in the High Tatra. Here, too, you may still meet bears, lynxes and wolves. Birds of prey are a frequent sight. You can also go fishing in the Čierny Vah River and in the large reservoir near Liptovský Mikuláš.

The Lesser Fatra National Park (Malá Fatra) in Western Slovakia occupies an area of 200 sq km (77 sq miles) in the northeastern

caves. For keen walkers, Slovenský raj is a true paradise.

The Lower Tatra forms the second-highest mountain chain in Slovakia, extending over a much larger area than the High Tatra. The long main ridge of the range, characterised by dense forest and bare, rounded mountain peaks, is no less than 80 km (50 miles) in length from east to west. It forms the heart of the Lower Tatra National Park (Národný Park Nizké Tatry), which covers a total area of 811 sq km (313 sq miles). The highest mountains are Mount Ďumbier (2,024 metres/6,477 ft) and Mount Chopok (2,024 metres/6,477 ft). There are dripstone caves (e.g.

section of the mountain range of the same name. The highest peaks soar up to 1,709 metres (5,469 ft). A variety of rock types are present, in particular granite, sandstone and dolomite. The park also contains an extremely varied selection of flora and fauna; among the plants are warmth-loving as well as high-altitude species. The lower slopes, interspersed with canyon-like gorges, are ideal walking territory.

Covering an area of only 21 sq km (8 sq miles), the Pieninsky Narodný Park is the smallest of the seven national parks. It comprises a limestone mountain range dissected by the deeply eroded valley of the River

Dunajec, which has become increasingly popular for rafting trips.

In addition to the seven National Parks, both the Czech and Slovak republics boast an impressive number of extensive conservation areas. The Beskid Conservation Area, for example, extends over an area of 1,160 sq km (450 sq miles) and includes the Moravian and Silesian Beskids, part of the Javorníky Mountains and the Vsetinské vrchy. The area is protected for its primeval forests and environmentally precious mountain meadows. Also of interest is the traditional architecture of the area.

Conflicting interests: As elsewhere in the world, a balance has to be struck between protecting wildlife and preserving the economic interests of the country, and each side has its energetic defenders. Slovakia in particular continues to suffer from governmental economic reform programmes. Attempts to limit armaments production and the export of weapons have already cost a large number of jobs. It must be tempting therefore to compensate for such loss by expanding and developing tourism, a course which would inevitably be at the expense of the habitats of rare animal and plant species. It is therefore remarkable that the Slovak authorities in the better developed tourist regions such as the High Tatra have refused to grant building permission for new hotels, and have placed rigid limitations on private transport.

A model national park region: As plans go ahead for the development of the joint National Park region comprising the Bavarian Forest and the Bohemian Forest (Šumava), it may prove possible to find a compromise between conflicting interests by preserving nature in cooperation with local residents. This is the idea behind the Biosphere Conservation Area, which originated in the proposal put forward in July 1991 by the environmental and nature protection agencies of the Czech Republic, Bavaria and Austria as "a united multi-national development concept to be agreed for the entire area". The authors see the "only chance for the Bohemian Forest and the Bavarian Forest in the preservation of the natural potential of the

entire region as the basis for an environmentally-oriented development within the framework of a model ecological region".

Part of the scheme would include the modernisation or revival of the railway system, and the encouragement of small and medium-sized businesses in an environmentally-conscious way, as well as developing tourist facilities in harmony with the National Park, the natural surroundings and history of the area. Major industrial projects and the promotion of through traffic and goods traffic by the improvement of the road network are thereby rejected.

The opinions of those directly affected are divided. Many village mayors are against the

conservation plan, and are determined to fight it with all the means at their disposal. "They want to send us back to the jungle so that people are forced to leave their homes once more." The opposite view is taken by Peter Pavlik, who was persecuted after the Prague Spring and subsequently found a new home in the depths of the Bohemian Forest. He has transformed a little farmhouse and goat shed into a cheerful restaurant. Just as he once wrote pamphlets against the Prague regime, so he now writes letters to German newspapers: "I beg you, help us to preserve our common natural heritage; there is nothing like it left in Europe!"

Left, strict rules apply to all visitors to the national parks and nature reserves. **Right**, summit experience in the High Tatra.

After years of ideological isolation, the Czech Republic has now emerged as one of Europe's most fascinating travel destinations. While the larger cities are by now well used to the demands of the tourism boom – and four of the country's airports are being enlarged to meet the demands of international traffic – it often seems that life out in the country has stood still. But even here there are increasing signs of change; and it isn't only the facades, neglected for so many decades, that are suddenly being returned to their former glory.

The Czech Republic can look back on a long and eventful history and in recent years the state has made enormous efforts to preserve its rich cultural heritage. Many of the old town centres have been preserved as historical monuments, while Prague, Telč, Český Krumlov and Kutná Hora all feature on the UNESCO world heritage list. Scattered throughout the republic are more than 2,000 castles and chateaux, 200 of which are open to the public, while in Moravia the pilgrims' church of St John of Nepomuk at Ždár nad Aázavou, and the Lednice-Valtice chateau, have recently been added to the tally of preserved monuments. Nature lovers will be delighted to learn that 10 percent of all Czech territory is protected from development, including the three national parks: Krkonoše (Giant mountains), Šumava and the valley of the river Dyje, home to many rare species.

For a region with such a wealth of things to see, any description must be selective. The journey begins in the Czech Republic, in the historical Crown Lands of Bohemia, and its magnificent capital Prague. We continue by exploring some delightful destinations in Prague's environs and then follow a large arc from Southern Bohemia to Western Bohemia and its famous spa towns, and then to Northern Bohemia before travelling east of Prague into neighbouring Moravia. Having visited its capital, Brno, we head off into the countryside once more. Whichever route you take, you will not only encounter beautiful countryside filled with countless historical and architectural gems, but also lashings of the generous hospitality for which the Czech and people are rightly renowned.

In both the Czech Republic and Slovakia, many of the towns have a history of German as well as Slavic settlement. In this guide, therefore, some of the Slavic names are followed by their German versions in brackets.

Preceding pages: blooming barley; bucolic bouquet; the blue Beskids. **Left,** the dream of a romantic holiday comes true.

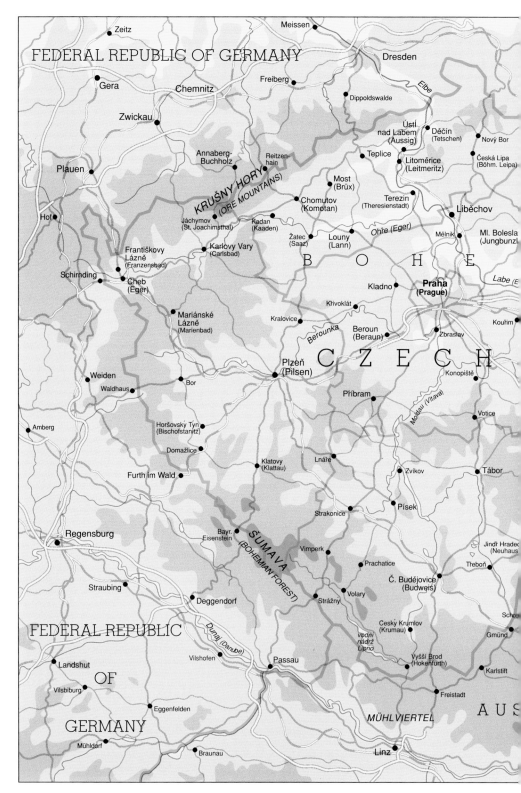

The Czech Republic

48 km / 30 miles

rlitz
Lwówek Śl.
Jawor

Wrocław
(Breslau)

Kluczbork

Jelenia
Góra

Frýlant
(Friedland)

Brzeg

Liberec
(Reichenberg)

Walbrzych

Swidníca

POLAND

Opole
(Oppeln)

Jablonec
n.Nis
(Gablonz)

Vrchlabí
(Hohenelbe)

KRKONOŠE
(GIANT MOUNTAINS)

Trutnov
(Trautenau)

Adršpach
(Adersbach)

Odra (Oder)

Turnov
(Turnau)

Klodzko
(Glatz)

Paczkow

Prudnik

Jičín
(Jitschin)

Hořice

Náchod

Bystrzyca Kl.

Jeseník
(Freiwaldau)

I   A

Nové Město
n. Met.
(Neustadt)

Krnov

Racibórz

Hradec Králové
(Königgrätz)

Poděbrady

Mladkov

Bruntál
(Freuden-
thal)

Opava
(Troppau)

Ostrava
(Ostrau)

Pardubice

Šumperk
(Mährisch
Schönberg)

Kutná Hora
(Kuttenberg)

Chrudim

E   P U B L I C

Mohelnice

Šternberk

Fulnek

Mor. Třebová
(Mährisch
Trübau)

N. Jičín
(Neutitschein)

Havl. Brod
(Deutsch Brod)

Žd'ár nad
Sázavou
(Saar)

Olomouc
(Olmütz)

Prostějov
(Prossnitz)

Přerov
(Peräu)

Hranice

Val. Meziříčí

Jihlava
(Iglau)

Blansko

M   O   R   A   V   I   A

Zlín

Třebíč

Brno
(Brünn)

Slavkov
(Austerlitz)

Morava (March)

Telč

Mor. Budějovice

Pohořelice

Staré Město

Uh. Hradiště

Žarosice

Znojmo
(Zaim)

Trenčín
(Treutschin)

Trenč.
Teplice

Waidhofen

Dyje (Thaya)

Mikulov
(Nikolsburg)

Hodonin

Horn

Břeclav
(Lundenburg)

S   L   O   V   A   K   I   A

ettl

Wilfersdorf

Jablonica

MALÉ KARPATY
(LESSER CARPATHIANS)

Piešt'any
(Pistyau)

RIA

Stockerau

Trnava
(Tyrnau)

Nitra
(Neutra)

St. Pölten

Vienna

Devín

131

Viewed from the Castle Hill, the historical centre clings to the gently curving bend in the Vltava, its rooftops reflecting the golden patina of the midday sun. Its banks seem to be only just held together by the filigrane constructions of its bridges: on the one side the Lesser Quarter and on the other the Old Town.

Anybody who gazes over Prague from the parapets of Hradčany Castle must surely consider it to be one of the most fortunate of all European cities; fortunate because its skyline was never touched by the ravages of war and because its essential appearance was never scarred by the addition of any modern eyesores. After years of painstaking restoration, important architectural ensembles such as the Old Town Square have now been returned to their former glory. Today, Prague is a living architectural museum, vividly documenting succeeding phases of development, from its Romanesque origins, its mighty Gothic churches and monasteries, to the baroque palaces and the magnificent art nouveau boulevards of the "foundation years" laid out towards the end of the last century.

Every year in May, the memory of Prague's most famous composers, Mozart, Smetana and Dvořak, whose names are so closely linked with the history of the city, is resurrected when the elegant concert halls, churches and palaces open their doors for the Prague Spring Festival. It is a time when great international ensembles perform in the city, as well as renowned native orchestras, such as the Czech Philharmonic or the famous National String Quartet. But good music can be heard in Prague all the year round: from jazz to rock to opera, all musical tastes are catered for.

The daily life of Prague is best experienced in its pubs. And it doesn't have to be the full-to-bursting U Flekuor U Tomáše, whose reputation is somewhat better than merited; or even the Chalice (U Kalicha), the local of Jaroslav Hašek's *Good Soldier Schweik*. No, the best beer, the most fortifying dumplings and the juciest goulash continue to be served in more cosy, hidden establishments.

Where does the city's pulse beat? Is it in its historical buildings around which big city and medieval atmospheres seem to fuse? Or in the magical squares, with their mysterious plays of light and shade, in which one might almost expect to bump into Rabbi Löw's monster, the Golem? And do the legendary days of Prague's writers and artists still exist? Or does the pulse of the city beat stronger today on the boulevard of Wenceslas Square with its shopping by day, and its bustling entertainment by night? The truth is that Prague is made up of so many different facets, and visitors must discover the city's secrets for themselves.

Preceding pages: a classic Prague scene: the Charles Bridge in the early morning. **Left**, no visit to Prague would be complete without a look at Hradčany; here the Matthias Gate.

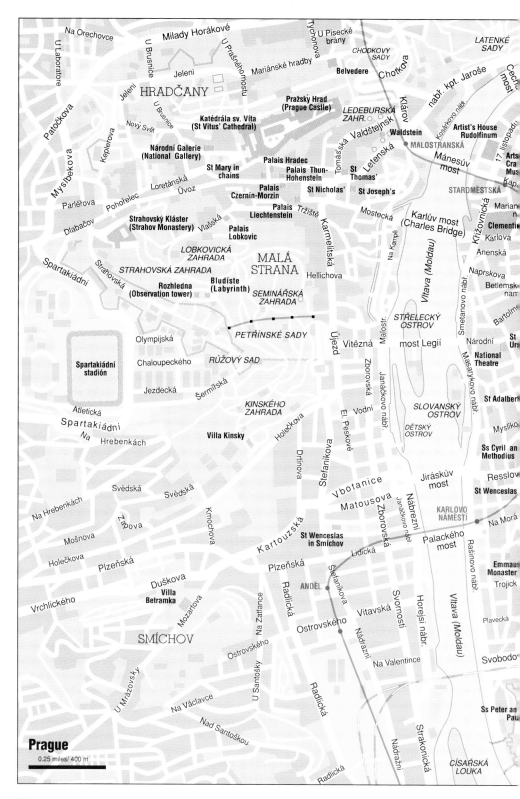

Prague

0.25 miles/ 400 m

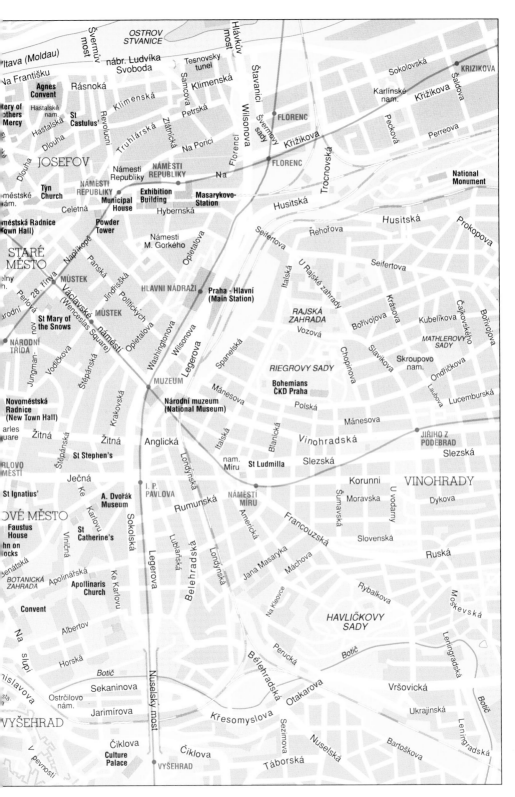

Vltava (Moldau)

Švermův most

Na Františku

OSTROV STVANICE

nábr. Ludvíka Svoboda

Hlávkův most

Tesnovsky tunel

Sokolovská

KRIZIKOVA

Agnes Convent

Rásnoká

Klimenská

Klimenská

Šaldova

Karlínské nam.

Křižikova

Křižikova

Samcova

Štvanici

Švermovy sady

Mery of others Mercy

Hastalské nam.

St Castulus'

Klimenská

Petrská

Wilsonova

Florenci

FLORENC

Peckova

Perreova

Hastalská

Dlouha

Revolucni

Truhlárská

Zlátnická

Na Porici

Na

Křižikova

FLORENC

Trocnovská

Dlouha

JOSEFOV

Námesti Republiky

NÁMESTI REPUBLIKY

Na

National Monument

Týn Church

NÁMESTI REPUBLIKY

Exhibition Building

Masarykovo-Station

Husitská

Husitská

Prokopova

městské ám.

Celetná

Municipal House

Hybernská

Řehořova

STARÉ MĚSTO

městská Radnice (own Hall)

Powder Tower

Námesti M. Gorkého

Opletalova

Seifertova

Seifertova

Italská

U Rajské zahrady

Seifertova

elny h.

Napříkope

Panská

Jindřišská

HLAVNÍ NÁDRAŽI

Praha - Hlavní (Main Station)

RAJSKÁ ZAHRADA

Krásova

Čajkovskeho

Bořivojova

MÚSTEK

Perlová

28 Ríjna

Václavské náměstí (Wenceslas Square)

Politických

Bořivojova

Kubelíkova

rodní

St Mary of the Snows

MÚSTEK

Opletalova

Wilsonova

Vozová

Chopinova

Slavikova

MATHLEROVY SADY

Ondřičkova

NÁRODNÍ TŘÍDA

Jungman-

Vodičkova

Štěpánská

Krakovská

Washingtonova

Legerova

Spanelska

MUZEUM

Mánesova

RIEGROVY SADY

Bohemians ČKD Praha

Skroupovo nam.

Laubova

Lucemburská

Novoměstská Radnice (New Town Hall)

Národní muzeum (National Museum)

Polská

Mánesova

arles uare

Žitná

Štěpánská

Žitná

Anglická

Italská

Blanická

Vinohradská

JIŘIHO Z PODEBRAD

Slezská

RLOVO MĚSTI

Ječná

St Stephen's

Londýnská

nam. Míru

St Ludmilla

Slezská

Korunni

VINOHRADY

St Ignatius'

Ke

A. Dvořák Museum

I. P. PAVLOVA

NÁMESTÍ MÍRU

Šumavská

Moravska

U vodamy

Dykova

VÉ MĚSTO

Faustus House

Karlovu

St Catherine's

Rumunská

Americká

Francouzská

Slovenská

Ruská

hn on ocks

Viničná

Sokolská

Lublaňská

Jana Masaryka

Máchova

enátská

BOTANICKÁ ZAHRADA

Apolinářská

Apollinaris Church

Ke Karlovu

Legerova

Belehradská

Londýnská

Na Kleovce

Rybalkova

Moskevská

Convent

Albertov

HAVLIČKOVY SADY

Leningradská

Na slupi

Horská

Perucká

Botič

Leningradská

íslavova

Botič

Sekaninova

Nuselský most

Bělehradská

Otakarova

Vršovická

Botič

sla. a

Ostrčilovo nám.

Jarimírova

Křesomyslova

Sezimova

Ukrajinská

Leningradská

VYŠEHRAD

Čiklova

Culture Palace

Čiklova

VYŠEHRAD

Táborská

Nuselská

Bartoškova

v pevnosti

PRAGUE'S OLD TOWN

The dividing line between the Staré Město and the Nové Město – the Old and the New Towns – lies at the far side of **Wenceslas Square**. To right and left, wide pedestrian thoroughfares follow the line of the medieval town wall dating from the time before Charles IV had the New Town built in a semicircle around the historic city centre.

The little street Na můstku leads straight to the heart of the bustling Old Town. After only a few paces visitors will come to a flea market – the traditional **St Gall Market** – to the left, which leads directly into the **Coal Market** one block further on. To the right, in the background, is the silhouette of the **Church of St Gall**. Originally Romanesque in style, the church was given its splendid baroque facade between 1690–1700. It marks the hub of the district as it was first planned in the 13th century.

One block further on again lies the **Estates Theatre**, scene of the premiere of Mozart's opera *Don Giovanni* on 29 October 1787. The theatre has been rebuilt several times; during the past few years it has been the object of a major restoration programme and was reopened to the public in 1991 – Mozart Year – naturally enough with a new performance of *Don Giovanni*. Mozart and Prague have reason enough to be grateful to each other. In The Three Golden Lions, a guest house on the nearby Coal Market, the composer prepared for the premiere. He also stayed several times in the Villa Bertramka – now the Mozart Museum – in Smíchov, the southern quarter of the city, where he was the guest of the Dušeks, a family of musicians. The citizens of Prague loved Mozart, and he felt at home and protected in the city. The Oscar-winning film *Amadeus* was largely filmed here and the props used in the film can still be seen in the Barrandov Film Studios outside the city.

The **Carolinum**, next door to the theatre, was originally a palace purchased by King Wenceslas IV from the Rotlev

family for the Charles University. When Charles IV decided to found the first university in the empire in 1348, it was his intention that it should serve the entire continent, or – as the Papal Bull confirming the foundation of the university stated – "for all inhabitants of the Kingdom and the surrounding countries, and for the students of all nations who shall flock to the aforementioned town". However, the noble concept of a universal establishment of learning proved difficult to put into practice. The masters of the university council were divided into four "nations" corresponding to the four points of the compass but, after the death of Charles IV, Jan Hus persuaded the new king to allocate the Bohemian nation three votes, thereby ensuring its majority within the administration. Such was their annoyance about this move that many foreign professors and students moved to other universities.

Across the centuries the university expanded to take over other buildings; all that remains of the original Gothic

Left, the House of the Stork on the Old Town Square. Right, sweet temptation.

college is an arbour and the magnificent oriel window created by the Parler School. The building is now used for official ceremonies.

The Old Town Square: The square forms the natural centre of the Old Town and the true heart of the city. Occupying pride of place in the middle is the massive **Monument to Jan Hus**. It was erected on 6 July 1915 to mark the 500th anniversary of the reformer's death. The surrounding buildings, dwarfed by the towers of the Týn Church, still form an imposing backdrop. At the base of the church towers lies the Týn School, which houses changing exhibitions.

You can go through the school, to enter the **Týn Church**, whose treasures include the oldest font in Prague (1414) and a series of baroque paintings, such as the main altarpiece *The Assumption* by the first great master of the Bohemian baroque, Karel Škréta (1610–74). The building, which was erected between 1365 and 1511 on the site of a small Romanesque church of St Mary, served the Hussites as their main place of worship until their crushing defeat by the Catholics at the Battle of the White Mountain in 1620.

Although the varied architectural styles of the surrounding houses blend harmoniously, one or two buildings are nonetheless outstanding. The first of them, **At the Sign of the White Unicorn**, is followed by the Týn School and the Gothic **Bell House**. The last in the row is the **Palais Kinsky**, whose fine facade reveals rococo elements. It was built between 1755 and 1765 by Anselmo Lurago according to the plans of the Bavarian architect Kilian Ignaz Dientzenhofer, who died in 1751. In the 19th century, it housed a German school which was attended by Franz Kafka. Today it is the home of the National Gallery's splendid collection of prints and drawings, and also houses temporary art exhibitions.

The smaller part of the square behind the Town Hall is dominated by the magnificent facade of the **Church of St Nicholas**. German merchants erected the first place of worship on this site

The astronomical clock was mounted on the Old Town Hall by Nikolaus von Kaaden in 1410.

during the 13th century; the present church was completed in 1735. Once again the architect was Kilian Ignaz Dientzenhofer who, together with his father Christoph, was in large part responsible for the city's baroque appearance (*see page 156*).

The **Town Hall** is now used only for ceremonial purposes. It is too small to house the administration of the city, especially as the North Wing was burned down in 1945 during the last days of German occupation; a memorial plaque recalls the event.

The building had formed the political hub of the capital since King John of Luxembourg granted the citizens rights of self-government in 1338. The chapel, council chamber and a number of other buildings in the western and northern corners were erected in rapid succession. In 1896 the corner house of U Minuty, adorned with antique and biblical murals, was absorbed into the complex. Among the tenants who were served notice to quit was the family of Franz Kafka. A photographic exhibition of his life story can be seen at U Radnice 5, the site of the house where he was born.

The most notable feature of the exterior is the amazing **astronomical clock**, dating from 1410 and situated to the right of the main late-Gothic portal. This wonderful contraption consists of two clock faces: the calendar, below, which moves on a day every time the clock (above) strikes midnight. The signs of the zodiac and the rural scenes depicting the months were painted by Josef Mánes in 1864. At the very top is the Procession of Apostles, which was only installed in the 19th century. Opposite the clock, No.26 has a fascinating exhibition of Czech glassware on the upper floor, and below, a forge where various glassblowing techniques are demonstrated to visitors.

The Southern Old Town: Leading off from U Minuty is the Malé náměstí, the **Little Square**, evocative of medieval Prague. Surrounding the fountain with its pretty Renaissance railings are a number of fine houses, each with its own history. In 1353 in No. 11, a Signore Agostino of Florence established

the first documented apothecary's shop in the city, and during the reign of Emperor Charles IV No. 1, which bears the twin names In Paradise and At the Sign of the Angel, was the home of a herbalist from Florence.

Most spectacular is the **Rott House** (No. 3), whose cellar was once the lower floor of a Romanesque town house. The first Czech Bible was printed here in 1488; at the turn of the century the new owner, an ironmonger, had the building renovated, painting the facade with the original sign – three white roses – and a selection of his wares.

Past the bend in the Karlova ul., on the right-hand side of the Husova, is the **Clam Gallas Palais**, a beautifully restored nobleman's house. The building, dating from the high baroque period, now serves as a home to the town's archives. Despite the cramped location, the facade is very impressive; it is framed by two decorative portals comprising pairs of Titans apparently bearing the weight of the entire world in general and the building in particular.

In the opposite direction, going south, Husova Street leads to the **House of the Lords of Kunštát and Poděbrady**, whose entrance lies in Retezova No. 3, and which is devoted to George of Poděbrady, the only king of Bohemia to be elected by the people. The palais retains its Romanesque features, especially the simple barrel-vaulted rooms on the ground floor and in the cellar.

Further to the left stands **St Aegidius**, the severe Gothic church of the Dominican friars. In marked contrast to its unadorned exterior, the hall church is magnificently appointed inside. Baroque paintings displaying a masterful command of perspective and colour adorn the vaulted ceiling.

Taking the third turning on the right off Husova, you will come to the **Bethlehem Chapel**. One of the most important shrines of the Czech people, its simplicity serves as a memorial to the inflammatory sermons of Jan Hus, who used this chapel to fulminate against bigotry and love of splendour. Other great religious reformers also preached here, including Hus's contemporary and fellow rebel Jakobellus von Mies (Jakoubek ze Stříbra), who introduced the administration of the communion in both forms, and much later (1521), the radical Thomas Münzer.

The focal point in the chapel is the pulpit rather than the altar. The walls were used to illustrate the preacher's message in large letters and pictures before a congregation of up to 3,000 of the faithful. Ironically, after the defeat of the Hussites, the church passed into Jesuit hands; in 1786 it was completely gutted, but from 1950–54 was painstakingly rebuilt in the original style to serve as a national monument.

The **Preacher's House** next door is also open to the public; it contains an exhibition documenting the life and works of the great reformer. On the west side of the square, surrounding a picturesque courtyard, is the well-stocked **Ethnological Museum**. Naprstkova leads to the River Vltava, where – on the far side of the promenade – a little café in front of the **Smetana Museum** offers

The historical core of the Old Town is dominated by the Týn Church.

the best-known view of the Charles Bridge and Hradčany Castle. The museum displays exhibits illustrating the life and works of the famous Czech composer (*see page 93*).

Beyond the former millhouses is the **Old Town Bridge Tower** and the **square of the Crusaders of the Red Star**. This remarkable fraternity was originally charged with the defence of the bridge and enjoyed high esteem within the city; between 1561 and 1694 the leaders of the order were ex officio the Archbishops of Prague. Their Church of St Francis, with its magnificently painted dome, was no doubt designed to vie with the pomp and circumstance of the Jesuits' Clementinum nearby.

A visit to the exhibition of jewelled monstrances and other exquisite items from the knights' treasury also includes an opportunity to view the medieval crypt and a surviving span of the 12th century Judith Bridge. The monument to Charles IV, standing outside the church was erected to commemorate the 500th anniversary of the founding of the university and portrays allegorical representations of the first four faculties at the feet of the founder.

On the far side soars the baroque facade of the **Church of St Saviour**. It forms a part of the sprawling **Clementinum**, which is scarcely noticed by most passers-by despite its size – probably because the nearby Charles Bridge diverts their attention. It may be overlooked now, but the importance of the college established by the Jesuits after they were summoned to Bohemia in 1556 cannot be denied, for it became the bastion of the Counter-Reformation in the Hussite capital.

The Society of Jesus took over a former Dominican monastery and a 2-hectare (5-acre) plot of land, which they were determined to transform into a first-class educational establishment with a school, library, printing works and theatre. Their university was soon granted the right to award doctorates and thus gained equal status with the Hussite Charles University. In 1622, after the Catholic victory on the White

Coffee houses: a venerable Prague institution.

Mountain, it was able to absorb the troublesome competition and remained for many years the only university in the Czech capital. Today the Clementinum houses a number of libraries, including the **National Library**; the magnificent rooms can be visited upon request.

Josefov, the Jewish Quarter: Considering the small number of Jews now living in Prague, it is hard to comprehend how enormously important their role in the economic and cultural development of the city used to be. According to records, the first Jewish community was founded here in 1091. In 1255 King Otakar II granted the Jewish Privilege, thus guaranteeing Jews security within the law for the first time. In return, thanks to their success as craftsmen and traders, Jewish people provided the king with a considerable income from the taxes that they paid.

Their relationship with the authorities constantly alternated between acceptance and hatred, and they frequently suffered at the hands of Prague's citizens. But the most terrible persecution was perpetrated by Hitler, as part of his "final solution". He intended to create a "museum of an extinct race" in Prague, and it was only because of this cynical plan that the synagogues and cemeteries were not destroyed.

The heart of the **Josefov** – named after the tolerant Habsburg emperor Joseph who described the Jews as a "useful element" – grew up after 1250 around the Old-New Synagogue. In 1382 Wenceslas IV pronounced the district a protected ghetto.

Behind the Clementinum, the Platnéřská leads almost back to the Old Town Square. Shortly before this point you can turn left into the Maiselova and left again opposite the Old-New Synagogue into the U starého hřbitova to the **Jewish Cemetery**, where weathered gravestones stand under gnarled trees. At the **tomb of Rabbi Löw**, pious Jews honour one of their great teachers who, during the 16th century, the Golden Age of the Jewish community, directed a Talmudic school in Prague. Students of literature know the rabbi better as the creator of the Golem, the artificial creature which he brought to life by mysterious magical practices, but which turned against its master.

At the entrance to the cemetery is the **Klaus Synagogue**, in which old manuscripts and prints are displayed. Adjoining the synagogue is a hall of remembrance containing a moving collection of drawings by Jewish children in the concentration camp at Terezín. On the opposite side of the cemetery is the Pinkas Synagogue. Now open as a memorial, its walls are painted with the names of the 77,297 Bohemian and Moravian Jews who perished in the Holocaust.

The **Old-New Synagogue** is Europe's oldest Jewish place of worship still in use today. Begun in 1270, the building has an elaborate brick gable and demonstrates unmistakable evidence of the severe Cistercian Gothic style, although a number of elements were purposely altered in order to avoid too much resemblance to the symbolism of the Christian church. Inside, the roof covering the main area is supported by twin col-

The old Jewish Cemetery was laid out at the beginning of the 15th century.

umns; only men were allowed access to this part of the synagogue, where readings from the Torah took place. The galleries were added during the 17th century in order to permit women to participate in the acts of worship.

Opposite is the baroque-style **Jewish Town Hall**. Eyes are drawn to the gable with its unusual clock adorned with Hebraic symbols: strangely but correctly, the hands turn anti-clockwise. The building still performs its function as the headquarters of Prague's Jewish community; it also houses a kosher restaurant called Shalom.

The building at the back houses the **High Synagogue**, so named because of its location on the second floor. Adjoining it is a little park flanked by 19th-century houses with imposing facades and a wealth of ornamental detail.

On the left, by contrast, the Cubist facade of the Inter-Continental hotel strikes a creative note on a functional modern building.

Returning to the Old Town Square, it is pleasant to stroll along **Pařížká** (Paris Street). This was created over a century ago within the framework of a restoration programme to alleviate insanitary conditions in the Josefov. Its magnificent art nouveau facades make it the most spectacular street in the entire city.

Between the square and the Powder Tower: From the earliest days of the city's history Celetná was an important trading street. Even though its buildings were frequently rebuilt in accordance with the tastes and fashions of the times (the predominant accent today is baroque), the visitor will be able to discern a number of medieval elements, such as the groin vaulting of No. 2, the **Sixt House** and the wooden roof trusses of No. 3 (The Three Kings).

On the left-hand side, immediately behind the Týn Church, the Štupartská leads down to the **Church of St James**. This was originally built by the Minorites during the reign of Charles IV, but it was later the subject of a particularly successful rebuilding in the baroque style. The expressive reliefs of the facade and the alteration of the interior to

The rococo staircase in the Clam Gallas Palais is the work of M.B. Braun (c. 1730).

create a theatrical setting provide a fine stage for the frequent concerts held on the ornamental and powerful organ, dating from 1705.

Returning to Celetná, you can continue your exploration of the city along a stretch of the former Royal Way. At the very beginning, almost by the junction with the square, you will find the **Egon Erwin Kisch Café**, named in memory of the German-Jewish writer who became famous during the 1920s as a roving reporter. Examples of his works can be found in the two bookshops on the left-hand side of the road, or in one of the second-hand shops under the arcades.

A little further on, where an alley joins the main road from the right, stands the corner house known as **The Black Madonna**. Its Rondo-Cubist style lends the little square a distinctive note and demonstrates that even in 1912 it was possible to renovate and build anew in the modern idiom without destroying the optical harmony of an entire district.

The end of Celetná is dominated by the **Powder Tower**. In 1475, King Vladislav Jagiello had a fortified building erected beside his royal residence, on the site of a defensive gate which had marked the boundary of the Old Town since the 13th century. Badly damaged by the Prussians during the Seven Years' War, it was rebuilt in neo-Gothic style at the end of the 19th century. It was during the 18th century, when it was used as a powder magazine, that the tower acquired its present name.

Next door – where the former royal court was situated – stands the **Municipal House** (Obecní dům). The architects Antonín Balšánek and Osvald Polívka produced the preliminary designs for this art nouveau building in 1903 and work was completed in 1911. Designed to provide, in the words of its founders, 'dignified and elegant rooms where Czech society can conduct itself with splendid bearing', the Municipal House was conceived as a cultural as well as a civic centre.

The best Czech artists of the period were called on to contribute to the lavish interiors which are sumptuously decorated with inlaid floors, stained glass windows, wrought iron work and panels of wood and marble. Conducted tours of the art nouveau splendours of Alfons Mucha's Mayor's Chamber and other rooms (*see page 111*) are organised from the Cultural and Information Centre in the foyer.

Immediately behind the Municipal House is another notable building, this one dating from 1907: the **Hotel Paříž** which displays a pleasing mixture of neo-Gothic and art nouveau styles.

The St Agnes Convent: This oasis of tranquillity lies on the banks of the Vltava, off the beaten tourist track yet only a few minutes' walk from the Powder Tower. After years of restoration work, the convent, the oldest Gothic building complex in Prague, was reopened to the public in 1980. It merits a visit, especially on account of its museum of 19th-century Czech art.

St Agnes was the sister of King Wenceslas I of Bohemia, but instead of agreeing to a dynastic marriage she took the veil. She founded the **Convent of St Clare** in 1233 and even became the abbess for a short while. A few years later a Minorite Priory was added, but in 1420, during the turbulent Hussite Wars, the entire complex was abandoned. In 1782 it relinquished all pretence of being a convent as a result of the process of secularisation.

The cloister is adorned with plain early-Gothic vaulting and simple capitals, but unusually fine and expressive stone carvings are found in the **Chapter Room** and the adjoining Church of St Saviour to the right. The archway is decorated with five crowned heads on each side – men to the right and women to the left. This may indicate that the Přemyslid dynasty extended and used the convent and church as their family chapel and burial place. In the magnificent choir, you will find an elaborate niche where the foundress of the convent was probably going to be buried. The **Church of St Francis** is an earlier building, but only the choir has remained more or less intact. Today, freshly restored, it is regularly used as the setting for concerts and lectures.

The Powder Tower is one of the city's main landmarks.

THE LESSER QUARTER AND HRADČANY

On the other side of the Vltava, Prague reveals a very different character from that of the bourgeois Old Town. In the vicinity of the river, the Malá Strana (Lesser Quarter) was previously the home of skilled workers, carters and fishermen; even today, it is a quarter inhabited mostly by working people, students and pensioners. Dominating the area is the residential district on the slopes of Hradčany, where the magnificent palazzi of the aristocracy rise amid wealthy monasteries and churches. Towering above it all is the imperial cathedral and the castle – the seat of the rulers of Prague for over 1,000 years.

The **Charles Bridge** remains the main link between the two halves of the city even today. In contrast to the thundering traffic on the other bridges, the Karlův most is an oasis of calm. Charles IV had the fine stone bridge constructed by his master builder Peter Parler. There had been a stone bridge here before, the Judith Bridge, constructed during the latter half of the 12th century and named after the wife of King Vladislav I. But, like its wooden predecessors, it could no longer stand the force of the Vltava and collapsed in 1342.

Charles then wanted to create a permanent link between the two settlements on opposite sides of the river, which in those days were frequently at loggerheads with each other. Begun in 1357, the bridge itself represents the central section of the "Royal Way", along which in medieval times the sovereign walked to his coronation. Today, the Karlův most is a favourite meeting place for half of Prague – local citizens and visitors alike.

Straddling its eastern end is the mighty **Old Town Bridge Tower**, the last work that Peter Parler bequeathed the city. In spite of its slender form and invitingly high archway it was originally designed for defensive purposes, proving its worth in 1648 when the Swedes spent two weeks vainly trying to capture the Old Town. The west side of the tower was

Preceding pages: at Hradčany – the Archbishop's Palace and St Vitus' Cathedral. **Left**, a view down St Vitus' nave. **Right**, the Charles Bridge connects the Old Town with the Lesser Quarter.

destroyed, but on the Old Town side the gallery of sculptures has survived, including that of the national patron saint. St Vitus is portrayed protecting the bridge between two kings – Charles IV and Wenceslas IV.

Most of the 30 statues of the saints which now dominate the bridge were added during the baroque period, although the ensemble was only completed in 1928 with the statue of St Cyril and St Methodius. The earliest statue (1683), on the northern central pillar, is that of St John Nepomuk, who was tortured then thrown into the Vltava by Wenceslas IV because he spoke out against the latter's religious policies. A pious legend maintains that the king's wrath had been aroused by Nepomuk's brave refusal to break the sanctity of the confessional by betraying the secrets of the queen.

Upstream from the bridge, the dramatic weir vividly evokes Smetana's symphonic poem *The Moldau*. Ahead and to the right, the view is dominated by the Cathedral of St Vitus, crowning

the summit of Castle Hill, and at the end of the bridge the Malá Strana is framed between the two **Lesser Quarter Bridge Towers**. The northern tower was built at the same time as the Charles Bridge, but the southern one is a remnant of the old Judith Bridge.

After passing under the arch, carry on along Mostecká (Bridge Street) before turning left into the Lázeňská. Continuing past the former hotels, The Spa and The Golden Unicorn (where Beethoven once stayed), you will soon reach the oldest place of worship in the Lesser Quarter, the **Church of Our Lady in Chains**, dating from the 12th century. The massive facade combines both Romanesque and Gothic elements. The adjoining Velkopřevoské nám. is bordered by elegant palazzi; the **Maltese Grand Prior's Palace** houses a delightful collection of historical musical instruments.

During the last decade of communist rule, the palace garden and the island of **Kampa** next door, accessible via a small bridge over the Čertovká Channel, be-

came the favourite meeting place for the flower children of Prague. They left behind lovingly executed murals in the district of the city known as Little Venice on account of its water mills and gardens. The most famous mural, which still draws visitors, is that of John Lennon. Improvised rock concerts used to be held here before an impassive audience of policemen and secret police informers.

Retracing your steps, cross the **Maltese Square**, site of the noble **Palais Nostiz**, which is now the home of the Dutch Embassy. Turning into Karmelitská, where the Vrtbovská Palace at No. 25 is notable primarily for its baroque terraced garden, the route returns to Mostecká.

Ever since the 10th century the **Lesser Quarter Square** (Malostranské náměstí) has been the focal point of the busy settlement under Hradčany Castle. It used to be the site where the daily market was held, and the meeting place of trading associations.

The Jesuits transformed the predominantly bourgeois air of this town centre. Exactly as they did when building the Clementinum on the other side of the Vltava, they purchased a large tract of land, had all its buildings razed to the ground – an entire street, two churches and a cemetery – and started building the massive **Church of St Nicholas**. It is regarded as the masterpiece of Christoph and Kilian Ignaz Dientzenhofer, and its monumental baroque architecture is a lesson in history. Every detail – from the powerful ceiling frescoes to the forbidding statues of the four Fathers of the Church to the elaborately decorated pulpit – expresses the power and absolute authority of the victorious Catholic Church. A comparison with the simple and austere Bethlehem Chapel, in which the heretic Jan Hus preached his sermons, clearly illustrates the full significance of the Counter-Reformation in this Protestant country.

In the immediate vicinity, in Letenská, which opens onto the square on the northern side, stand the **Monastery and Church of St Thomas**. The foundation and construction of the Augustinians'

A veteran of the times looks on.

Gothic basilica dates from the 13th century, and Kilian Ignaz Dientzenhofer gave the church its present appearance, including its imposing facade and the bright interior. The former town hall (No. 21) was the administrative centre of the Malá Strana until the creation of Metropolitan Prague. It is now a cultural centre, **Malostranská beseda**, a popular venue for jazz and rock music.

Neruda Street (Nerudova) is lined with Renaissance, baroque and neoclassical palazzi reflecting the prosperity of the nobility, who chose to build their residences on the approach road to the castle. There are some delightful house signs, especially The Three Violins (No. 12), The Golden Goblet (No. 16), The Golden Horseshoe (No. 33), The Black Madonna (No. 36) and The Two Suns (No. 37). The latter was the home of the poet Jan Neruda (1834–91), the author of the *Tales of the Lesser Quarter*.

Along the lower section, at No. 5, stands the imposing **Palais Czernin-Morzin** on the left, dating from 1714, with an impressive doorway and a bal-cony supported by statues of Moors. Built at about the same time was the **Palais Thun-Hohenstein**, diagonally opposite at No. 20. Next door are the **Church and Monastery of St Cajetan**, creating an architectural unity typical of the closing years of the 17th century. At its upper end, the Nerudova gives way to a romantic stairway leading to the castle. To the left, the Loretánská leads out to the Loreto Shrine and the district Nový Svět.

The Santa Casa: Loreto is a place of pilgrimage in Italy. It was believed that angels transported the sacred home of the Virgin Mary from the Promised Land to Loreto in the 13th century. When the Catholic Habsburgs tried during the Counter-Reformation to convert their Hussite subjects back to the "true faith", they used the pious legend to serve their cause. They had replicas of the Santa Casa built throughout the land. The best known and most attractive of these is the **Loreto of Prague** (1626–1750). Unlike the simple original, the shrine became, across the centuries, an entire

The Lesser Quarter and St Nicholas viewed from the castle.

complex consisting of various buildings with a chapel, cloisters several storeys high, and the Church of the Nativity. Dominating the group is the early baroque tower, into which a carillon, which chimes every hour, was built in 1694. The Loreto's main attraction is the **treasure chamber**, in which are stored the precious votive gifts presented by pious pilgrims to the statue of the Virgin Mary.

The castle quarter: Nový Svět (New World) is a picturesque alley leading off Loreto Square. For many centuries it was the poorest district of the Hradčany quarter. Today, however, the tiny, lovingly restored cottages with their doll's-house windows and tiny front gardens have made it a popular residential area for local artists.

For a long time, the **Castle Square** (Hradčanské nám), enclosed by magnificent buildings, formed an independent community, albeit under the control of the lords of the castle. Beside the stairs leading up from the Nerudova, the former town hall, dating from 1598, is adorned with both the imperial and municipal coats of arms. The southern side of the square is dominated by the stucco facade of the **Schwarzenberg Palace**, with its distinctive *sgraffito* patterns. Completed in 1563, it is regarded as one of the finest examples of Bohemian Renaissance, and today houses the **Museum of Military History**. Beside the castle entrance, the **Archbishop's Palace** adds an additional note of architectural splendour. Only visitors who happen to arrive on Maundy Thursday will be permitted to view the exquisite **French Gobelin Tapestries** and other treasures, for there is no public access for the rest of the year. The **Sternberg Palais** behind contains the National Gallery's priceless collection of European paintings dating from the 14th–20th century.

Hradčany Castle: Prague Castle is over 1,000 years old; the first Czech rulers, the Přemyslids, established their main residence here, on a strategic site dominating the ford over the Vltava. Since then, succeeding generations of rulers **The Castle Steps.**

have enlarged the complex with chapels, palaces, defensive structures and residential buildings.

A tour of Hradčany Castle begins in front of the **Matthias Gate** in the first courtyard, the most recent of the three. To the right, a flight of steps leads up to the former Throne Room; today this is where state receptions are held.

The second courtyard, with its beautiful baroque fountain, is more extensive. To the right is the **Chapel of the Holy Cross** built by Anselmo Lurago in 1753. The **cathedral treasure**, including reliquaries, monstrances, crucifixes, and mementos of Bohemian saints and kings, has been on view here since 1961.

Hard left, in the northwest corner, is the **Castle Gallery**, which since 1964 has housed rediscovered works of art collected by the Habsburgs in the 16th and 17th century; above this are the **Spanish Room** and **Emperor Rudolf's Gallery**. Rudolf II, the last ruler to bring imperial glamour to Prague, was an eccentric collector. To the wry amusement of his contemporaries, he showed no interest in politics, but assembled a curious collection of artefacts, including stuffed exotic animals, alchemists' tools and objects for use in shamanistic rituals. Although this remarkable collection was dispersed by war and plundering, and at one stage largely removed to Vienna, what remains is still well-worth seeing.

Through the north gate of the second courtyard, a causeway leads across the old moat directly to the attractively landscaped **Royal Gardens**, known today as the Presidential Gardens, open only at weekends. Head straight for the beautiful Renaissance **Belvedere**. In front of the building stands the so-called Singing Fountain, from which there is an attractive view of the magnificent cathedral across the moat, now transformed into a deer enclosure.

The Cathedral: The **Cathedral of St Vitus**, a Gothic basilica 124 metres (405 ft) long and 60 metres (196 ft) wide, was begun in 1344 on the instructions of Charles IV. The first of his inspired architects, Matthew of Arras, was →*158*

A smile from the Lesser Quarter.

MASTER BUILDERS

Charles IV, the scion of the Přemyslids who attained the imperial crown in 1355, transformed the city on the Vltava into the political and cultural centre of his vast empire. Under Charles, Prague was dubbed the "Mother of all cities", and the Gothic Prague that is admired by visitors today, bears his stamp. The Charles University, the New Town clustered around Wenceslas Square and Charles Square, the Charles Bridge, and – towering above all – the Cathedral of St Vitus – were all part of Charles' legacy.

Peter Parler: On 1356 Peter Parler was summoned to work on the Cathedral of St Vitus as the successor to Matthew of Arras. In choosing the young Parler, Charles provided Prague with a master builder of genius, entirely equal to the task of reflecting his imperialist aspirations. Parler came from a German family of builders and sculptors who made a significant contribution to the development of Central European Gothic art and architecture. The family

name, Parler, stems from Parlier or Polier, the title of the second-in-command of a team of builders. As their master's trademark, the family used an angle bar in the form of an S-rune interrupted in two places.

Peter Parler, the undisputed supreme master builder of the family, was born in 1330 in Schwäbisch Gmünd and buried in 1399 in St Vitus' Cathedral. Charles IV recognised Peter's exceptional talent when he saw him working on the church of the Holy Cross in his home town. The young architect's task in Prague was to prove the most important of his career: the completion of the Gothic cathedral in the Bohemian capital, which in 1344 had been elevated to the rank of archiepiscopal see. The new church was to serve as both coronation cathedral and royal burial place.

Peter Parler's genius can best be appreciated in the Golden Portal and in his design of the chancel. The monumental fan vaulting was the first of its kind in Central Europe and became the model for all German vaulted roofs until the end of the Gothic era. Parler assumed sole responsibility for the completion of the main building begun by his predecessor; by allowing light to flood through the upper walls he created a powerful contrast to the relatively dark lower section of the nave. A further trend was set by the cuboid shape of the building, which arose from the juxtaposition of the smaller units representing the various storeys. The angling of the transept towards the imperial palace provided a powerful link between the sacred and secular worlds.

The Old Town Bridge Tower, built for defence as well as ornament, is one of the loveliest and least corrupted examples of this building-block principle. Marking the entrance to the Charles Bridge, it has a rib-vaulted viewing gallery, and a collection of sculptured figures which include St Wenceslas and St Vitus.

Peter Parler's seminal influence in the field of sculpture is also demonstrated in the row of busts in the cathedral triforium which represent an important stage in the development of medieval portraiture.

Parler was also responsible for the All Saints' Chapel in Hradčany Castle, the chancel of the Church of St Bartholomew in Kolín and the Church of St Barbara in Kutná Hora, which contains one of the

St Wenceslas in the cathedral, by Peter Parler.

loveliest examples of fan vaulting in existence.

The Dientzenhofers: By the time the Dientzenhofers, the second of the great German families of builders, made their artistic mark on Prague, the importance of the former metropolis had degenerated into that of a provincial backwater in the shadow of Vienna. While the magnificence of the monumental Gothic buildings reflected the glory of the reign of Charles IV, the baroque splendour of a later age stood in crass contrast to the cultural and economic decline that the country had suffered since the disastrous Battle of the White Mountain in 1620. The architectural excesses of the baroque era lent the city an illusion of new vitality, but at the same time they testified in stone to the triumph of the Habsburg Counter-Reformation. This impression still persists today, when you walk alongside the wall of the Jesuit Clementinum, which seems to tower over the former Royal Way between Charles Street and the Charles Bridge like a massive fortress.

That the powerful ensembles of baroque Prague should be regarded as an architectural triumph is due in no small measure to the influence of the Dientzenhofer family. Born in the village of Aibling in Upper Bavaria, the five brothers moved to Prague in order to study contemporary architecture. Four of them left the city over the years in order to return to South Germany, where they left their mark on a number of important sacred buildings, but **Christoph Dientzenhofer** (1655–1722) lived the rest of his life in Bohemia, becoming known, with Fischer von Erlach, as one of the fathers of late German baroque. He was influenced by the Italian architect Guarini, and flowing curved facades blend with the traditional Bavarian pilaster system in his churches. Examples of Christoph Dientzenhofer's architectural skill can be found all over Bohemia. His supreme masterpiece is considered to be the church of St Nicholas in the Lesser Quarter of Prague, which he designed with his son **Kilian Ignaz Dientzenhofer** (1689–1751).

St Nicholas', the church commissioned by the Jesuits, was a perfect piece of collaborative work, by the Dientzenhofers. The father was responsible for the nave, and the son for the choir and the dome. This jewel of baroque architecture took almost 60 years

to complete; it is one of the masterpieces of the era, and its silhouette dominates the skyline of the Lesser Quarter to this day. Both Dientzenhofers died before it was finished, leaving the work in the hands of Anselmo Lurgo.

The younger Dientzenhofer was born in Prague and is regarded as one of the leading architects of late baroque, eclipsing even his father. Although he was responsible for a large number of secular buildings (e.g. the Villa Amerika, now the Dvořák Museum, and the Palais Kinsky in Staroměstské nám.) Dientzenhofer the Younger's main interest lay in churches. Whilst his father favoured a longitudinal plan, Kilian Ignaz preferred a centralised building, which he laid out in the form of a double shell. This principle can be seen in the twin-towered centralised design of the church of St John Nepomuk on the Rock in the Nové Mesto. He was also responsible for the reconstruction of the Church of St Thomas, after it was struck by lightning in 1723; and for another St Nicholas', this one in Staroměstské nám., as well as the Church of St Mary Magdalene in Karlsbad (Karlovy Vary). ■

The dome of St Nicholas was the work of Kilian Ignaz Dientzenhofer.

trained in the French Gothic school and his basic design for the cathedral reflects this background. After his death, Peter Parler and his sons continued the work, but gave the building their own individual stamp.

Since it is impossible to step back and admire the facade from a distance, the visitor can only take it in as a steeply vertical wall. Consequently, entering the vast nave can be disorientating. There are no mysterious shafts of light as in other great cathedrals, for the original glass was replaced by modern panes. At first glance, too, the cathedral seems to lack a unity of style – partly because of the numerous extensions and additions across the centuries, the last being as recently as 1929, and partly because the church was planned from not only as a place of worship but also as a coronation church, mausoleum and destination of national pilgrimage.

The statues on the triforium record the important figures associated with the cathedral, ranging from Charles IV to more contemporary personalities.

The magnificent **Chapel of St Wenceslas,** in the south transept, is dedicated to the life and works of the saint. Two arches further on, in the chapel of the Holy Cross, a staircase descends to remnants of the early medieval building, and to the Royal Crypt, with the sarcophagus of Charles IV.

Don't forget to glance upwards to admire the lozenges adorning the roof of the choir, the work of architect Peter Parler. His extraordinary skills are also evident on the south side of the choir, where the interplay of columns and struts and the remarkable complexity of the tracery are especially impressive.

Unusual in both position and execution is the **Golden Door** and the remarkable entrance hall on the south flank. It is the main entrance to the cathedral and it was through here that monarchs passed en route to their coronation. A monarch's journey was not a long one, as the **Royal Palace** lay directly opposite. The visitor enters the majestic **Vladislav Hall** via the Riders' Staircase, made wide enough for rulers and guests to

The Royal Way on the Lesser Quarter side starts in Bridge Street (Mostecká ul.).

enter the room on horseback for tournaments. The intricate vaulting, spanning the whole width of the hall, makes it one of the most remarkable architectural achievements of the late Gothic era in central Europe.

The **Bohemian Chancellery** was situated in the adjoining rooms. On 23 May 1618, the furious citizens of Bohemia entered the room of the imperial governors Martinic and Slavata and threw them, and their secretary, out of the window. Although they all survived the 15-metre (50-foot) drop into the moat, this Second Defenestration of Prague sparked off the Thirty Years' War.

Opposite the eastern choir lies the Romanesque **St George's Basilica**. Despite extensions and rebuilding schemes during Renaissance and baroque times, the church has retained its original early medieval appearance and, following a recent renovation, has been restored to its former glory. The adjoining convent houses a rich collection of Czech Gothic and Baroque art. Behind the cathedral, the late-Gothic castle for-

tifications are dominated by the massive **Mihulka Tower**. It contains, amongst other curiosities, an alchemist's workshop.

Circumnavigating St George's and then turning uphill to the left, the route continues into **Golden Lane**, also known as **Goldmakers' Alley**, with antique shops, book shops and even a pub. The tiny houses, tucked into the arches of the battlements, have been the homes of craftsmen, goldsmiths and tailors for four centuries, conveniently situated to serve their exalted neighbours. Franz Kafka lived for a short while at No. 22, and the tiny museum there is usually packed with visitors.

From here, continue downhill, past the former burgrave's office – now the Children's House – to the **Palais Lobkovic**, housing exhibitions on Czech history. Through the East Gate, in the shadow of the **Black Tower**, is a terrace with a panoramic view. From here, you can descend the Old Castle Steps.

Down below, the route turns right and then right again into a second alley, the

Blossom in the Strahov Park.

Letenská. The first section runs alongside a blank wall, until a gateway suddenly provides access to the lovely gardens of the **Palais Waldstein** (also called **Wallenstein**). This was the very first baroque palace in Prague, built by the legendary general Albrecht von Wallenstein (1581–1634).

The massive building, is not open to the public, but the tranquil garden with its fountains and groups of statues is, and open-air concerts are sometimes held here. Unfortunately, when the Swedes conquered the Malá Strana and with it the palace of their former enemy, they removed the magnificent bronze figures by the Mannerist sculptor Adriaen de Vries. Nonetheless, some have been replaced by replicas, including the Laocoon group. The park extends as far as the Garden Room, where the unusual barrel-vaulted ceiling is decorated with illustrations of the Trojan War – an allegorical portrayal of Wallenstein's military zeal in the Thirty Years' War.

Waldstein Square (Valdšteijnské nám.) is dominated by the broad facade of the palace. Next door stands the **Palais Lebedour** (No. 3). Construction commenced in 1588, as the date carved above the doorway indicates, but the building assumed its present form during the 19th century. Other buildings of note in the square and in the adjacent Waldstein Street are the **Palais Pálffy** (No. 14), **Palais Kolovrat** (No. 110) and, at the far end, the **Palais Fürstenberg**. Virtually all received their elegant facades during the 18th century. Even more attractive are the gardens on the slopes of Castle Hill, designed by baroque landscape architects.

Sněmovní (Parliament Street) leads back to the Malostranské náměstí. At No. 4 is the **Palais Thun**, converted into the local parliament building in 1801. A memorial plaque recalls the fact that the first parliament of the Czechoslovak Republic met here on 14 November 1918 and officially deposed the Habsburg emperors.

Petrín Hill and Strahov Monastery: If you board the No. 22 tram by the

The Philosophers' Room in the Strahov Monastery Library.

National Theatre and travel across the Vltava as far as Hellichova, you will see, just opposite the tram stop, a signpost announcing the Lanova draha and indicating the way to the cable car up **Petřín Hill**.

This ancient cable car runs every 20 minutes, but it is far more pleasant to walk through the orchards and meadows. At the beginning the route passes a monument to the writer Jan Neruda; above the first cable car station, the rambling café terrace of the Vinárna Nebozízek offers a breathtaking panorama. On the summit of the hill are a number of interesting sights: the **Chapel of St Lawrence**, originally Romanesque but now almost entirely baroque, the **Labyrinth of Mirrors**, and the **Observation Tower** – a small-scale replica of the Eiffel Tower, which offers a remarkable view over the city. The tower and the labyrinth were both built for the Jubilee Exhibition of 1891.

Another important landmark lies only a few minutes' walk away. By passing through a baroque gateway, you can reach the **Strahov Monastery and Library**. The oldest buildings in this complex were completed after 1143, but completely destroyed by a fire in 1258. The wars of the following centuries also left their mark, with the result that very little remains of the original Romanesque building. Today the monastery is predominantly baroque in style, but it contains early Gothic and Renaissance elements. Only **St Mary's Church** retains traces of the Romanesque original.

The monastery library is one of the most beautiful and comprehensive historic libraries in Europe. The basis of the collection of over 130,000 volumes, including 2,500 first editions, was established by a perspicacious abbot in the middle of the 18th century. The secularisation under Emperor Joseph II led to the dissolution of a large number of monasteries, but Strahov was spared. The abbot took advantage of the dissolution to purchase a number of valuable collections. In 1945 the collection was enriched by the addition of works from other monasteries which were being closed down by the new regime.

Among the greatest treasures are the **Strahov Gospels**, dating from the 10th century (the book on display is only a replica: the original is in safe keeping), and a first edition of *De Revolutionibus Orbium Coelestium*, the work in which Copernicus first expounded his heliocentric theory of the universe in 1543.

The library's true fascination lies in the exquisite form of the two main rooms. The **Theologians' Hall**, with baroque frescoes in the stucco cartouches, is particularly attractive. Here you will find a small, barred shrine which contained books banned by the church's censors. In the middle of the room stand a number of valuable globes from the Netherlands, dating from the 17th century. The Theologians' Hall is currently undergoing renovation but is due to reopen in the near future. The **Philosophers' Hall** is notable for its rich gold inlay on the walnut cupboards and the elaborate ceiling frescoes depicting the harmony of philosophy, science and religion, by the rococo artist Anton Maulbertsch.

A typical amiable gesture from the late Pan Tau, alias Ota Simánek.

THE NEW TOWN

Wenceslas Square is not really a square and could hardly be called beautiful. It is rambling rather than intimate, a long shrill market place rather than a chic boulevard. But this is in keeping with its original purpose, for it was designed as a horse fair, and was intended to serve as the bustling axis of the Nové Město, the New Town, which Charles IV constructed in a semicircle surrounding the Old Town (Staré Město), which was bursting at the seams.

Although the New Town was founded 600 years ago, much of what we see today dates from the 19th and early 20th century, when elegant buildings mushroomed in place of the wooden shacks and dilapidated tenement blocks. Prague's revolutions, the great popular uprisings against despotism and foreign oppression, from the 15th-century Hussite Rebellion to the Velvet Revolution of November 1989, have all begun

here; at various times the square has been the stage for displays of national military strength, bitter defeats and jubilant victory parades.

The most prominent building on the square is the **National Museum**. It was constructed between 1885 and 1890 at the instigation of the Bohemian Patriotic Association. It was the Czechs' impressive answer to the nearby German Theatre (now the State Opera House) which had opened a few years previously to the strains of a Wagner opera. Another reminder of the proud era of Bohemian independence is the equestrian **Statue of St Wenceslas**, a massive monument erected in 1913.

Farther down, the square loses its civic character and turns into a lively shopping and pedestrian area. On the left-hand side is the modernist **Palais Alfa** (No. 28), built in 1928. One of the finest examples of art nouveau architecture in Prague is the **Peterka House** situated at the far end of Wenceslas Square. Architect Jan Kotěra built this private residence in just one year (1900).

On the other side of the square are the splendid art nouveau **Hotel Evropa**, the Zlatá Husa Hotel, and the Ambassador. The Evropa, dating from 1904, is a popular location for period films. Each floor of the hotel is decorated with floral motifs, mosaics and ornaments. The elegant café was recently renovated in the original style.

At the far end of the square, next to the row of hotels, stands the Palais Koruna. Constructed shortly before the war, its architecture demonstrates early constructivist elements combined with the decorative features of art nouveau.

Na příkopě (The Moat) is a lively pedestrian street, packed with strollers and shoppers. No. 10 is a magnificent baroque palace; it has a garden restaurant and serves as the venue for cultural events. The **Čedok Office** at No. 18 sells air and train tickets, and the **Prague Information Service** is next door, at No. 20. The former aristocratic town house at No. 22 is now a cultural centre with a restaurant and bistro.

Back on Wenceslas Square, the Alfa Passage leads to the **Church of Our Lady of the Snows**, founded in 1347. It was actually commissioned by Emperor Charles IV as a coronation cathedral, but as a result of the Wars of Religion which broke out a few years later, only the chancel was completed. The church became famous as the arena of the radical Hussites. In 1419, incited by their preacher Jan Želivský, they marched to the New Town Hall to demand the release of their brethren who were being held in prison, and threw two of the imperial councillors from a window.

Národní třída (the Street of the Nation) is, like Na příkopě, a wide and busy pedestrian area. On the right stands the modern department store K-Mart; to the left is the enchanting **Kanka House** (No. 16) and the baroque **Church of St Ursula** (No. 8), with fine frescoes and statues and a dynamic altar painting of the Assumption. The **Monastery Wine Bar** serves a fine selection of wines and specialities.

The end of the street is dominated by the **National Theatre**. Built on the banks

Catching Christmas carp on Wenceslas Square.

of the Vltava, this is a fine example of Czech neo-Renaissance architecture and embodies the national enthusiasm for culture in the second half of the 19th century. Funds to build the theatre were raised mainly by public contributions, and in 1883, the curtain was raised on a gala performance of Smetana's opera *Libuše* based on the myth of the founding of Prague. The adjacent New Theatre has now become the home of the **Laterna Magika** and has taken the company's name (*see page 173*).

Slavic Island (Slovanský ostrov), which lies below the theatre, is so called because it was the venue of the first Slavic Congress in 1848. It is now the site of a popular garden restaurant and cultural events are held here during the evening. The **Mánes House of Fine Art** on the banks of the river is interesting: the building itself reveals the influence of the Bauhaus movement, and exhibitions are organised inside by the Artists' Association. There is also an attractive café with a splendid view of the river.

In Jiráskovo náměstí, beside the Jiraskuv Bridge, a controversial new building, the work of American architect Frank Gehry, draws brickbats and bouquets in roughly equal measure. From the square, the Resslova ul. leads away from the Vltava. At the second crossroads stands the Romanesque **Church of St Wenceslas**, a Hussite place of worship. Diagonally opposite, the exuberant baroque facade of the **Church of SS Cyril and Methodius** was the scene of a tragic incident in the summer of 1942. The conspirators responsible for the assassination of the hated Reichsprotector Reinhard "the hangman" Heydrich hid in the crypt (now open to the public), but were betrayed to the SS, who surrounded the entire block. The conspirators on guard in the nave held out for two hours before being killed; those remaining in the crypt shot themselves before the Germans reached them. In reprisal, the Nazis destroyed the village of Lidice, 25km (16 miles) from Prague, shooting all the men and sending the women and children to concentration camps.

Charles Square was planned as the hub of the New City from its inception. Today it is dominated by the mighty **Church of St Ignatius** which served as the headquarters of the Jesuits from 1677. The stately **New Town Hall**, where the Hussite Revolution began in 1419, occupies the northern end of the square. The Town Hall remained the political hub of the New Town until 1784, when the four constituent towns which made up Prague at that time were joined together to form a single administrative unit.

To the south lies the **Faust House**, which has been associated with alchemists ever since the 14th century. Though transformed during the baroque era, the present building actually dates from the 16th century, when it was owned by an Englishman Edward Kelley, who served as alchemist to Rudolf II. It became associated with the legend of Faust in the 18th-century, when Count Ferdinand Mladota conducted chemical experiments here, which aroused great suspicion.

A few paces further on stands the

A chimney sweep plies his trade.

Church of St John on the Rock. An extravagant staircase leads up to the entrance, flanked by slightly protruding towers which curve away from the main axis of the building. Unfortunately, the church is often locked when services are not in progress.

The **Emmaus Monastery** (which is also known as the Slavonic Monastery) to the south of the square deserves even closer attention. Founded by Charles IV it came to play a significant political and religious role because mass was celebrated here according to the rites of the Old Slavonic Church – an obvious attempt on the part of crown and church to gain influence over the Orthodox Christians of Eastern Europe. Shortly before the end of World War II, many medieval works of art were destroyed when the monastery was bombed, but the fine cloisters, with frescoes dating from about 1360, are well worth seeing.

For visitors in need of refreshment, the **U Fleků**, situated in the Křemencova near the Town Hall, is the ideal choice. In summer a folk orchestra plays in the beer garden, but the pub atmosphere is equally convivial inside. One of Prague's most famous taverns, the U Fleků has been brewing its own dark beer since the 15th century. Although usually full of tourists in the summer months, it is well worth a visit.

Vyšehrad: Above the Vltava stand the ruins of **Vyšehrad Castle**. Legend has it that this was the home of Princess Libuše who prophesied the founding of the city. It became the political and religious centre of the country until the construction of Hradčany.

Apart from the tiny, Romanesque **St Martin's Rotunda**, there remains little evidence of the glorious early years. More interesting is the adjoining **cemetery**, where outstanding contributors to Czech cultural life and scientific advances lie buried, and where the **Slavin**, or tomb of honour, stands. Here the graves of composers Antonín Dvořák and Bedřich Smetana, as well as those of poets Karel Hynek Mácha and Karel Čapek, have become the goal of many admiring pilgrims.

The National Theatre and the Vltava Bridge.

NIGHTLIFE IN PRAGUE

Visitors setting out to discover the secret charms of Prague after nightfall will find the city an enchanting place. Bathed in the light of its old-fashioned street lamps, which lend it a veil of romance, it encourages long, lingering walks. At every corner one is tempted to pause in order to take in the breathtaking beauty of this historic capital.

The coffee house atmosphere: During a leisurely walk along Charles Street (Karlova), the visitor will discover numerous little bars and cafés with vaulted ceilings under whose arches aperitifs can be enjoyed before dinner. Across the Charles Bridge – during warm summer evenings a favourite rendezvous for lovers, musicians and tourists, and a place of entertainment in itself – you will find the Café de Colombia tucked away immediately behind the archway where they serve *blabla*, a brew of coffee laced with local schnapps whose warming properties are appreciated all year round. Locals and tourists rub shoulders in this small, hopelessly overcrowded room, but the atmosphere only gains from the enforced intimacy.

Visitors searching for a congenial place in which to while away the evening hours should investigate the many coffee houses, which serve wine, beer and other alcoholic drinks, as well as coffee. A number of cafés with exceptionally fine art nouveau décor also provide live music nightly – sometimes classical, sometimes jazz. They include the **Café Nouveau** (in the Municipal House), the **Evropa**, and the **Paříž** in the hotels of the same names. The coffee houses don't have quite the same atmosphere as they did at the turn of the century but they are still rather special. A current favourite with young American and English tourists is the Globe Coffee House and Bookstore, which stays open late and provides English language newspapers to browse through while you eat and drink.

Beer metropolis: Beer drinkers can have a field day in Prague with less effort than in virtually any other city in the world, for pubs and beer halls have a long, rich tradition here. The brew is known simply as *pivo* in all Slavonic languages – *černé pivo* is dark beer. A *pivnice* is an establishment in which one can do more than merely quench one's thirst; here, locals and visitors alike can sample a wide range of high-percentage brews accompanied by hearty Czech specialities.

There are more than 1,300 inns and taverns in Prague, and many of them can look back over a history spanning several centuries. Convivial traditional taverns include the **U Fleků** – a must on the itinerary of every visitor, the **U Pinkasů** – the first tavern in Prague to serve Pilsner as well as local lager, the **U Kalicha** (The Chalice) – a favourite haunt of the hero of Jaroslav Hašek's famous novel *The Good Soldier Schweik*, and the **U svatého Tomáše**, where beer has been brewed in the Gothic vaults for some 600 years. **U zlatého tygra** (The Golden Tiger) is another very popular drinking place, and one that is frequented by some well-known Czech writers.

Left, an open-air concert at the Waldstein Palace. **Right**, the Old Town Hall in the evening.

Wining and dining: If your idea of a good night out is lingering over a meal, there are plenty of places in Prague where you can do so. Gone are the days when queues formed outside restaurants unable to cope with the influx of tourists, or waiters turned you away when their dining rooms appeared half empty. Now you can choose between traditional Bohemian establishments and those serving international cuisine (there are several very good Italian ones); between the elegant and expensive or the small, cheap and friendly.

Even vegetarians are now being catered for, although they have to look a bit harder. Meat dishes do still predominate in most places, especially pork, game and goulash, and there are far more dumplings than fresh vegetables. But you can eat well, and even the more expensive restaurants are reasonable by most European city standards.

Wine bars (*vinárna*) are popular places to spend an evening, too, with the added advantage that some of them stay open until 2 or 3am (although many close at midnight). *Vinárna* range from places where you can drink a glass, or a bottle, of good Melnik or Moravian wine and have a snack, to newly-refurbished places which have become rather smart restaurants. It is usually easy to tell the difference before you step through the door, so the choice is yours. The Travel Tips section of this book gives a list of recommended restaurants and bars.

The cultural palette: Apart from the numerous bars, coffee houses, beer taverns, restaurants and wine bars in the city centre, Prague can also offer the visitor a remarkable wealth of cultural activities for a city of its size. Many churches, palaces and monasteries stage concerts, particularly during the summer months, when they are held at lunchtime and late afternoon as well as in the evening. Every day there is a huge choice of classical concerts which also provide an opportunity to see inside buildings which are otherwise closed to the public.

Many of these historic buildings provide a magnificent setting with fine acoustics. The Mirrored Chapel of the **Vltava illuminations.**

170

Clementinum, for example, the Martinů Hall in the Lichtenstein Palace, the House at the Stone Bell, the St Agnes Convent or the Great Hall in the Palais Waldstein.

Among the official music venues, the most important are the **State Opera House** (Státní Opera Praha), the **Estates Theatre** (Stavovskě divadlo) which stages both musical and drama performances, the impressive **Dvořák Hall** in the **Rudolfinum**, home of the Czech Philharmonic Orchestra. The Prague Symphony Orchestra was also based here while its permanent home, the splendid art nouveau **Smetana Hall** (Obecní dům) in the Municipal Hall, was being refurbished.

A pleasant way to spend a summer evening is at an open-air concert, and these can be found in a number of attractive settings: the gardens of the Palais Waldstein, in the Maltese Gardens in Malá Strana, and in the grounds dedicated to two of the three composers you are likely to hear most about in Prague – Antonín Dvořák and Wolfgang Amadeus Mozart (the third, of course, is Smetana). The Villa Amerika houses the Dvořák Museum, where concerts are held in the gardens; while the Villa Bertramka, where Mozart wrote *Don Giovanni,* also hosts outdoor recitals.

The theatre: Prague's numerous theatres also have something to offer everyone (*see Theatre chapter, page 103*). Until the Velvet Revolution in November 1989, the theatre represented far more than just a pleasant means of passing an evening; it was a medium which encouraged the development of revolutionary ideas and opposition to government doctrines.

It is no coincidence that Václav Havel, a poet and playwright who was a master of this subversive form of theatre, should have become the spokesman of the opposition and later president of the newly-liberated Czech Republic.

Foreign visitors who speak no Czech but are interested in the theatre can enjoy Boris Hybner's mime performances at the **Gag Studio** or Black Light shows from **Laterna Magika,** now in

Jazz with Milan Svoboda.

the Nova scéna (*see page 173*), or from the Divadlo Ta Fantastika.

Advance purchase of tickets is always recommended, whether you wish to attend a concert or a theatrical performance, as they sell out quite quickly.

Jazz and dance: Jazz enthusiasts, on the other hand, can risk a spontaneous visit to a concert. Prague has long been famous for its fine jazz. Among the best venues are the **Agharta Jazz Centrum**, the **Jazz Club Reduta**, the **Malostranská Beseda** and Jazz Club "U Stare Pani" in the hotel of the same name.

As far as rock and pop are concerned, clubs and other venues come and go, win and lose reputations with great speed; check the local listings magazines, refer to the *Prague Post,* or just accept the leaflets you will be handed in the streets. (*See the Travel Tips section at the end of the book for a list of recommended venues.*)

It soon becomes clear to visitors that Prague can offer a very varied programme of events. Things are a little more difficult if you prefer to go danc-

ing, or want entertainment which continues into the small hours. Prague is doing its best to keep up with other European capitals and a number of casinos and discos have sprung up in the city, but people accustomed to the flair and modernity of the nightspots of Western Europe will be disappointed.

Discos around Wenceslas Square should be avoided, or treated with caution, as they serve as popular pick-up spots for local prostitutes, of whom Prague has a huge number. Women going to these discos alone should be aware that they may receive unwelcome advances.

The city's casinos, new on the Prague night scene, are also haunts of the ubiquitous ladies of the night, escorted by foreign businessmen and a handful of locals with foreign currency to spare – usually taxi drivers and waiters, counted amongst the wealthiest people in the land since the tourist boom has taken off – as well as curious tourists and professional gamblers.

Around Wenceslas Square can be seen posters advertising strip-tease shows and similar seedy amusements. Often recommended is the **Alhambra Club** in the Ambassador Hotel; the programme, a mixture of buffoonery, music, variety and Black Theatre, is strangely old fashioned, and many people find it more soporific than entertaining. The Jalta Club and the Lucerna Bar offer similar shows, but are probably only worth visiting for their novelty value.

The gay scene in Prague is flourishing, with a number of clubs and bars. **Riviera**, a popular dance club, and the **Mercury Club**, with a nightly disco, are among the most accessible to foreign tourists.

Those who soon tire of bright lights and loud music, however, need only to retrace their steps to find on every corner the nightly enchantment of this loveliest of cities. In the silent alleys of the Old Town or the Lesser Quarter, the din of the discotheques gives way to the chiming of Prague's countless church bells, ringing out in gentle harmony the passing of the hours, and reminding you that it is time to go to bed.

A young flautist at a Christmas concert.

LATERNA MAGIKA

Under the socialist regime the theatre was regarded primarily as a service industry designed to provide the population with approved cultural entertainment. The authorities instituted a strict diet of traditional, realistic plays and conservative productions.

At the end of the 1950s, however, an experimental theatre group struck a completely new tone in Czech theatre. The ensemble – initially created by members of the National Theatre for the World Exhibition in Brussels, EXPO 58 – was known as the Laterna Magika. It aimed to present visitors to the Czech pavilion with a first-hand impression of life in the socialist republic, its art and its culture. Such was its success that the former cinema of the Adria Palace in Národní třída was placed at the troupe's disposal. It has since moved to the Nova scéna, Národní 40, which now bears its name. Laterna Magika has played to full houses virtually non-stop ever since, and has become one of the main tourist attractions in Prague. No doubt one reason for its success is that no knowledge of Czech is necessary in order to follow the performance.

The quaintly old-fashioned name "Magic Lantern" has been retained. The troupe's performance is based on a cinematic projection procedure in which the actors on stage become directly involved. Through a skilled combination of projections, movable screens and stage props, the players move between light and darkness, uniting film and theatre, mime and dance into one extraordinary stage experience. The disparate sections never have an independent role, but work together as a synchronised whole.

At the centre of the spectacle is the visual impression, the dialogue between stage and screen. The protagonists work with additional screens, on to which films or slides are projected. The often confusing actions of the performers on various levels of the stage in combination with the ever-changing projections give the audience the feeling of being transported to a world in which the laws of time and place have lost their meaning. The traditional theatre genres, such as tragedy and comedy, are fused into a drama of light and shadow which has entranced countless audiences, and left its mark on the development of international drama.

The performances of the Laterna Magika are among the most original on offer in the Czech capital. Programmes such as *The Magic Circus*, the *Tales of Hoffmann*, the *Odyssey* or the ballet *Minotaurus*, choreographed after a libretto by Dürrenmatt, have lost none of their fascination over the years. The founder of the Laterna Magika, producer Alfred Radok, suffered the same fate as many other artists and men of letters. In 1968 he was forced to flee the country. When he died in exile in Sweden in 1976, the media in his native country did not consider the fact worth mentioning.

As a theatre of illusion, Laterna Magika makes no attempt at a political statement, but it was nonetheless involved in the events of the Velvet Revolution. The Civic Forum established its first headquarters in the troupe's original theatre, and it was in the dressing room that Václav Havel wrote the appeal which ultimately forced Milos Jakeš to resign from the office of General Secretary of the Communist Party. ∎

Laterna Magika, the "Magic Lantern", in full swing.

TRIPS FROM PRAGUE

Every year, **Karlštejn Castle**, lying some 30 km (almost 20 miles) south-west of Prague on the railway line to Plzeň, is stormed by thousands of tourists in coaches, cars and trains. They achieve what their ancestors never managed, for the fortress, protected by massive walls and protruding cliffs, was impregnable to attackers.

But Charles IV did not have Karlštejn built as a military stronghold – strategically speaking, it would have served no useful purpose on this site. It was planned with the sole purpose of safeguarding the holy relics and coronation insignia of the kingdom. In medieval times these relics were of immense significance: they included two thorns from Jesus's crown, a fragment of the sponge soaked in vinegar offered to him on the Cross, a tooth of St John the Baptist and the arm of St Anne. To possess such treasures was seen as a sign of God's favour, a blessing for the emperor and his subjects. Even if Charles had felt no regard for this precious legacy personally, it would have been regarded as an unpardonable sin if they had not been used to further the greater glory of the emperor and the Holy Roman Empire.

Charles's collection of relics was presented once a year for public worship. On the Friday after Easter, the Day of the Holy Relics, the people flocked to the Karlštejn, and on 29 November, the anniversary of the death of Charles IV, Mass is still celebrated in the Chapel of the Cross, where the most precious items are preserved.

Visitors to Karlštejn Castle must join one of the official tours, which are conducted in various languages. It was built in the 14th century by Matthew of Arras and Peter Parler, but much of what we see today is a reconstruction, dating from the 19th century. You can reach the castle by road along the Berounka Valley, or – best of all – by one of the frequent slow trains from Prague's Smíchov Station. From Karlštejn Station the castle is a pleasant stroll across the river, through the village and uphill through the castle grounds. The tours begin in the **Imperial Palace**, before proceeding to St Mary's Tower, the Great Tower and, highest of all, the Chapel of the Cross.

The palace, which includes the **Great Hall**, the Audience Chamber and the private apartments of the sovereign and his wife, are lavishly appointed. The ornamentation of the rooms housing the relics, however, is almost beyond imagination. In the **Church of Our Lady**, Charles's court painter, Nikolaus Wurmser, portrayed the emperor with the sacred relics of the Passion beneath a heaven filled with an angelic host. The **chapel of St Catherine**, adorned with semi-precious stones, is where Charles IV spent days and nights in silent meditation. Above the door to the chapel is a portrait of the emperor with his second wife, Anna von Schweidnitz, carrying a massive cross.

The **Chapel of the Cross** itself is decorated with over 2,000 semi-precious stones. It is divided into two sec-

Preceding pages: Český Krumlov on the Vltava is dominated by its castle. **Left**, Karlštejn Castle. **Right**, scene from a folk festival in Jihlava (Iglau).

tions by a golden railing; the precious relics were preserved in the sanctuary, which only the emperor or the priests were allowed to enter. The walls are covered with over 100 paintings by Master Theoderic, dating from the mid-14th century; more relics are set into the picture frames. Owing to recent damage, this chapel is no longer open to the public for viewing.

After so much pomp and splendour, a walk in the attractive surroundings of the castle provides a welcome contrast. The Bohemian karst (limestone) on which it is built is the setting for a number of romantic lakes nestling in forests inhabited by a wide range of wildlife. In summer these lakes are popular with swimmers. The nearby caves of **Koněprusy** are also open to the public; in medieval times they were used as workshops by counterfeiters.

Massacre at Lidice: Twenty-five km (16 miles) to the west of Prague, off the main road to Slany, is the site of a World War II massacre carried out by the SS in retaliation for the assassination of the

Reichsprotector Reinhard "the hangman" Heydrich by members of the Czech resistance on 4 June 1942. It is believed that the SS received false information that Lidice had harboured the assassins.

On the night of 9 June, all 95 houses were burned to the ground. All 192 adult male occupants were shot on the spot; the women were taken to Ravensbrück concentration camp, where many of them were tortured to death. The 105 children were transported to Lodz, and many of them died in the gas chambers. After the war, a new village was built next to the ruins of the old. A rose garden was planted and the site became a memorial to the dead. The little museum to the left of the entrance shows films of the destruction and reconstruction of Lidice.

Mělník and its castle: During the 9th century the Slavic Pšovan dynasty constructed their castle where the Vltava flows into the Labe (Elbe), about 32 km (20 miles) north of Prague. Although to begin with this dynasty was the undisguised rival of the Přemyslids in Prague,

Grapes for fine white wine have grown on the slopes near Mělník for centuries.

the marriage of the heiress Ludmilla with the Přemyslid prince Bořivoj later united the twin territories. Thereafter the castle, which has since been rebuilt, served as a dowager residence for the princesses of Bohemia. The settlement grew into a flourishing trading centre; in 1274 Otakar II granted it royal privileges under the Decree of Magdeburg.

Under the direction of Charles IV vineyards were established on the slopes above the Elbe, after his coronation as Duke of Burgundy in 1365, from which he returned with vines and vintners. Not only was the red Burgundy-type wine popular at the imperial court, but it also brought considerable revenues to the town. The citizens, enjoying their new prosperity, sided with the moderate reformers during the Hussite rebellion and found themselves on the winning side at the end of the wars. As the hosts to three national Utraquist conferences between 1438 and 1442, the town enjoyed the special favour of George of Poděbrady, the leader of the faction, who rose to the position of king of Bohemia. Fortunes declined when his widow died in the Residence of Mělník.

Under a succession of further rulers the castle was rebuilt, fell into decay again and during the baroque era acquired its current character. The prestige it enjoyed in the Middle Ages never returned, however, for the new owners, the Princes of Lobkowitz, preferred to live in their residence in Prague. The town's growth gradually stagnated, although the viticulture continued to provide a good income.

The architecture of the castle reflects its historical development quite accurately. Each of the three main wings is characterised by a different style. In the west wing the Gothic influence is dominant, displaying a certain strictness of form; in the north, the Renaissance is clearly evident in the imaginative arcaded walks and ornamental facades, and in the south the opulence of the baroque style unfolds. The castle rooms, which have been refurbished in a variety of styles can be visited on an official tour. The extensive 13th century wine

Konopiště has an English style park with Italian-style ornaments.

cellars are also open (this tour includes tastings). The culmination of a tour should be a visit to the wine bar and restaurant, whose terrace offers a breathtaking panorama of the Elbe Valley. Opposite the entrance to the castle, the Church of SS Peter and Paul has a fascinating, if a little gruesome, charnel house in the crypt.

The town centre is extremely picturesque. The market place, with its fountain commemorating the grape harvest, is framed by a curving arc of arcaded town houses. The clock tower on the **Town Hall** and the **Church of the Fourteen Auxiliary Saints** complete the harmonious effect. On the far side of the square, a busy street leads down to the Prague Gate and the impressive remains of the town fortifications.

Konopiště Castle: The E56 leads in a southerly direction as far as Benešov, where you should turn off to the right towards **Konopiště** (about 40 km/25 miles southeast of Prague). The castle dates from the 13th century, and in 1423 – in the midst of war – the two Hussite factions negotiated over liturgical details here. The hostess was Widow Sternberg, who had joined the Hussites after her Catholic husband had fallen in battle. After plundering by the Swedish army during the Thirty Years' War, the entire complex – originally built in Gothic style – was rebuilt as a baroque residence. It was Archduke Franz Ferdinand, however – the heir to the Habsburg throne who was assassinated in Sarajevo in 1914 – who converted it into a fine private palace, which he proceeded to embellish with an extravagant collection of works of art.

Visitors are greeted by a solitary baroque gateway in front of the moat; the high walls are dominated by the **East Tower**. Worthy of particular note inside is the large banqueting hall, with two **Gobelin tapestries** from Paris, and the sketches made for Cervantes' *Don Quixote*. The smoking room, the library and the chapel on the second floor, as well as the countless hunting trophies adorning the corridors and staircases, bear witness to the sophisticated pleas-

The market place and town hall of Tábor.

ures of the lord of the castle and his guests. The vast castle grounds with their rose garden, ponds and game enclosures are partly open to visitors.

Tábor – bastion of the Hussites: Jan Hus and the Hussites have frequently cropped up in this guide, with Hus himself portrayed as a god-fearing reformer, an eloquent opponent of splendour and bigotry, and a social revolutionary. But in Prague – the Bethlehem Chapel and Jan Hus Memorial notwithstanding – evidence of his movement, which for centuries determined the history of the country, is rather hard to find.

It therefore makes sense to take a trip to **Tábor**, combining the excursion with a roam through the pretty countryside surrounding the capital. In Tábor, every stone recalls the Hussite era. The town itself lies some 90 km (56 miles) south of Prague, and is easily reached on the E56 trunk road towards České Budějovice (Budweis) and Linz.

Anyone familiar with the Bible will recall that, according to St Matthew, chapter 17, verses 1–9, Mount Tábor was the place of Christ's Transfiguration. The Hussites had this in mind when, in 1420, they gathered in their thousands near Kotnov Castle. It was five years after the execution of their teacher and a few months after their rebellion in Prague. Able-bodied men as well as women and children gathered to take up arms against the imperial army and fight against Catholic bigotry. The camp required fortifications, and from it grew the new town of Tábor. It was the starting point for a long campaign which culminated in the glorious victories at Vitkov in 1420 and Deutsch-Brod in 1422. However, after their brilliant leader, Jan Žižka, fell in 1424, a schism rent the movement in two – the moderate Utraquists and the radical Taborites. Divided, their strength inevitably waned. A crushing defeat for the Taborites at Lipany in 1434 finally put an end to their hopes and allowed George of Poděbrady to take power.

After the war Tábor grew into a busy town. Members of all Christian sects, including Catholics, were tolerated and

The Bohemians enjoy a good pint and also like their music.

the inhabitants coexisted peacefully as Bohemian Brethren, Waldensians and moderate Utraquists. The spirit of rebellion was still alive, however, and whenever the citizens of Bohemia revolted against serfdom and usury, the Taborite flag with its black background and red chalice would be seen fluttering among the rebel ranks. They were drawn into the defeat at the Battle of the White Mountain in 1620, after which they were forced to pay tribute to the Habsburgs.

Nonetheless, the little town still offers a fascinating glimpse of life in this stormy era. From the main road you should turn off to the right and park in the car park near the ruined castle. From here you can visit the mighty **Round Tower** and the **Bechin Gate**, which houses a small historical exhibition. The streets were deliberately made narrow and winding for defensive purposes. A fascinating tour of the cellars can be taken from the Town Museum. They climb up to **Žižka Square**, which – like most of the rest of the town – has cellars and subterranean passages, sentry posts

and storage areas. Since the Czech Nationalist movement in the 19th century discovered its precursors in the proud Taborites, the square has been dominated by a monumental statue of the leader of the Hussite legions.

Nearby are the **Roland Fountain** and two simple stone tables, at which Holy Communion used to be distributed. The lofty tower of the **Church of the Transfiguration** dates from Hussite times. It soars above the former Town Hall, now a museum to the Hussite movement, with its huge municipal coat of arms and a two-storey council chamber.

The Pražská ulice, which has a number of attractive Renaissance houses, starts in the southeast corner of the square. During the past few years the side streets have undergone their own miniature renaissance; artists have established studios here, and a number of new galleries, antique shops and bookshops have opened. The old town wall should also be seen: the northern section is still in good repair. From here you can enjoy a panorama across the **Jordán Reser-**

A field of dandelions.

182

voir. Created in 1492, it is the oldest construction of its kind in Bohemia.

East of Tábor: Halfway to Pelhřimov is **Kámen Castle**, and is well-worth a visit. It is no coincidence that it houses a **Motorcycle Museum**, for the International Motorcycle Federation was formed in 1904 in the inn Na panské in Pacov. In 1906 motorcycles roared along the so-called Pacovský okruh in the first ever motorcycle World Championships.

The architecture of **Pacov** (Patzau) blends with the hilly scenery. Where a stronghold and later a fortress once stood you can now see a Renaissance palace, its former defensive walls transformed into a magnificent promenade.

Pelhřimov (Pilgram) nestles by the River Bělá. The heart of the old town mirrors its history, with its Renaissance and baroque buildings (early-Gothic traces are still found under the facades). A few kilometres south of Road No 19 lies the village of **Včelnice**, with a glass foundry famous for the red glass known as Bohemian Garnet. An attraction here is the narrow-gauge railway, which replaced an earlier horse-drawn tram, linking the town of Kamenice nad Lipou with Obrataň in the north and Jindřichův Hradec in the south.

Southwest of Tábor: The spa town of **Bechyně** has a tradition of pottery making stretching back to the 15th century. It formed the basis of the town's present-day ceramics industry. Since 1884 Bechyně has been the home of a College of Ceramics, from which many famous Czech ceramic artists have graduated.

Following the River Luznice the route returns to the Vltava and the Orlík barrage, which is 60 km (37 miles) long. Dominating the central section of the lake, on the west bank, is **Orlík Castle**. Originally an early Gothic fortress, the castle was rebuilt on a number of occasions. Surrounded by an attractive garden, the castle contains furniture and memorabilia dating from the time of the Napoleonic Wars.

Another popular castle is that at **Zvíkov** in a romantic setting further south, at the confluence of the Otava and the Vltava rivers. **Písek**, some 20 km (12 miles) south has a colourful history. A stone bridge dating from 1265, the oldest in Bohemia, crosses the Otava at this point. It formed a part of the Golden Path, the trading route to Bavaria, the *raison d'être* for the town's foundation. The settlement prospered on the gold-rich sands of the river bed.

Strakonice is often wrongly described as being an exclusively industrial town. In fact, it has preserved many attractive medieval buildings and is the traditional setting for the International Bagpipe Festival. Strakonice achieved fame as the headquarters of the motorcycle company CZM, the fabric company Fezko, and a number of well-known producers of industrial machines.

To the north of the town is the moated castle of **Blatná**, an architectural jewel constructed at the end of the 14th century. Unfortunately it is closed for lengthy restoration. The town itself is famous for its rose plantations. Many new varieties were developed here, though the innovative five-petal rose was produced by the horticulturists of Rožmberk in Southern Bohemia.

A promising pub sign.

SOUTHERN BOHEMIA

The 19th-century Czech writer Jan Neruda described the town of **České Budějovice** (Budweis) at the confluence of the Vltava and the Malše as "Bohemia's Florence".

In 1265 the village, established by German settlers, received its town charter from Otakar II, and in 1358 Charles IV granted it staple rights. The discovery of silver deposits during the 16th century increased the wealth of the community and made it the economic and cultural centre of Southern Bohemia.

The old town was laid out on the rectangular grid pattern typical of German settlements; the site of the original walls and moat is now a broad belt of parkland. At the centre lies the **Žižka Square** (named after the Hussite leader), with the main streets radiating from its four corners. In spite of a certain amount of damage over the centuries, its medieval origins are still apparent. The pretty arcaded houses bordering the square have been meticulously restored. Only a few steps from the massive octagonal fountain, graced by a statue of Samson the lion-tamer, one of the paving stones (distinguished by a cross) marks the spot where, in 1478, the 10 men who murdered the local mayor were executed. Legend has it that anyone who steps upon the *bludný kámen*, the "madmen's stone", after 9pm will be led to hell.

Within the town itself, it is hard for visitors to lose their way. In the southwest, beyond the baroque **Town Hall** and the **Bishop's Palace** are the ruins of the town fortifications. In the west, the former **Dominican Monastery** lies on the defunct arm of the Vltava; it was founded by the King of Bohemia in 1265 and completed during the 14th century in Gothic style along with the **Church of Our Lady of Sacrifice**. Also of note nearby is the former arsenal, built in 1531, and the **Salt House**, the facade of which is liberally decorated with masques.

On the Hroznová to the north of the market place, make a point of visiting the former Masné krámy. The 16th-century "Meat Shops" have been converted into a restaurant and serve as a favourite rendezvous for experts and aficionados of the famous **Budvar**, the Budweis beer which is exported to 21 countries throughout the world. Suitably refreshed, one can continue to the **Kneisl House** in the northwest corner and the baroque **Church of St Nicholas**. Finally, climb the 360 steps of the Černá věz, the **Black Tower**, a free-standing belfry which soars above the rooftops and affords a bird's eye view of the other places of historical interest within the town.

The view unfolds as far as **Hluboká Castle** some 10 km (6 miles) away. The 13th-century former royal stronghold rises majestically from its rocky perch above the River Vltava. Its design has changed numerous times over the years. Today it resembles nothing so much as Windsor Castle. It is worth visiting for the collections of wood carvings, porcelain, tapestries, paintings and furniture collected by the imperial princes of

Left, the smoking room in Hluboká Castle north of České Budějovice (Budweis), one of the most-visited castles in the republic. Right, canoeing through the Bohemian Forest.

Schwarzenberg. The castle riding school and the elegant conservatory form the **Southern Bohemian Gallery of Art**, housing an exhibition of southern Bohemian Gothic and Flemish art. The permanent display is supplemented by regular travelling exhibitions, usually of a high standard.

The hunting lodge lying a mile or so to the southwest is also of interest; its attractive house and grounds contain a **Museum of Forestry and Hunting** as well as a zoo.

Třeboň and surroundings: Extensive woodland, meadows, peat bogs, artificial canals, ponds and lakes are characteristic of the countryside surrounding **Třeboň**. Many of the lakes were dug during the 16th century; the largest, covering an area of more than 500 hectares (1,200 acres), is **Rožmberk Lake** to the north of the town. The lakes made Třeboň the fishery centre of Bohemia, and the local carp are still considered a delicacy. Every three years, a non-stop carp angling competition is held over a period of three days. To the north of

Rožmberk Lake is the attractive **Svĕt Lake**, where you can hire a sailing boat or go for a trip on a steamer.

The healing powers of the peat moors were exploited during the last century in medicinal baths and sanatoria. The town fortifications, including the old town gates and walls, have largely survived and enclose a medieval town centre where many houses date from Gothic and Renaissance times. The rich variety of manuscripts and books in Rožmberk Castle archives has made them well-known throughout the literary world.

Also of interest is the village of **Chlum** near Treboň, famous for its glass-making; the blown and cut glass products are exported all over the world. The little town of **Jindřichův Hradec** is worth visiting, since attractive religious buildings and a large number of late-Gothic, Renaissance and baroque houses have been preserved. The medieval **castle** was enlarged in Renaissance style by Italian architects in the 16th century. The Gothic chapel of St George contains a cycle of frescoes depicting the

Communal fishing in one of the many lakes near Třeboň.

slaying of the dragon. Here, too, the skills of an ancient craft are practised: a local workshop still produces hand-made Gobelin tapestries.

The route from České Budějovice leads in a southeasterly direction along the Malše to **Trocnov**, the native town of the Hussite leader Jan Žižka. The former gamekeeper's house has been turned into a museum. Only a few miles further on lies the village of **Římov**, surrounded by a Way of the Cross marked with 25 little chapels decorated with exquisite wood carvings and sculptures. Near the village the valley has been dammed to create a reservoir serving two-thirds of Southern Bohemia. No bathing is allowed here, and for once the prohibition is accepted without demur as the area offers a large number of attractive alternatives.

The rooms in **Žumberk Fortress**, southeast of Trhové Sviny, containing the castle's original furniture, provide an evocative picture of what life must have been like in these ancient castles, when the flickering of pinewood torches

was the only illumination and open fires the only means of heat.

The village of **Nové Hrady**, near the Austrian border, was built during the 13th century. Particularly interesting is the exhibition of unusual black glass, known as hyalite, which was produced in the surrounding foundries.

Following the main road to the southwest of České Budějovice, the **Zlatá Koruna Monastery** (The Golden Crown) lies a few miles north of Český Krumlov.

The chief attractions of the monastery are the extensive library and the triple-naved basilica dating from the 14th century. Legend has it that the linden tree in growing in front of the monastery produces leaves in the shape of a hood, recalling the unfortunate Cistercian monks whom Žižka hanged from its branches after he had set fire to the monastery buildings. Přemysl Otakar II founded the religious community here in 1263 in order to protect his royal interests in the region against the incursions of the Vítkovci (Wittigo) family.

Český Krumlov: Český Krumlov (Krumau) has retained its medieval character better than any other town in Southern Bohemia. Every alleyway and hidden corner is an invitation to explore. The entire town has been declared a historic monument and, although restoration work during the past decades has made only slow progress, and some architectural treasures are still crying out for renovation, a leisurely exploration is recommended.

In 1240, the Vítkovci dynasty built their castle overlooking the Vltava. They were followed by three families of German nobles: the Rosenbergs (1302–1611), the Eggenbergs (1622–1717) and the Schwarzenbergs (1717–1945). The original fortress was rebuilt as an aristocratic palace, from which the lords of the castle administered their economic and political interests throughout Southern Bohemia. German colonists settled on the far side of the bend in the River Vltava and were awarded a town charter in 1274. Silver deposits in the nearby Bohemian Forest brought wealth to the noble rulers and diligent burghers alike; even when the mines were exhausted during the 16th century, the town was able to retain its prosperous air.

In the middle of the Old Town lies the Ring, bordered by charming Renaissance houses and the richly decorated **Town Hall**. To the south and west you can see sections of the original fortifications, topped by the slender tower of the **Church of St Vitus**. The latter contains Gothic wall paintings and an elaborate early baroque altar. Of particular interest in the east of the town are the Curate's House and the **Town Museum**. Forming part of the former Jesuit College (now in use as a hotel) is a theatre completed in 1613.

In the suburb of Latrán on the other side of the bridge across the Vltava is the **Convent of the Minorites and the Sisters of the Order of St Clare**. Both communities used the adjoining Corpus Christi church. A long-established brewery occupies a 16th-century arsenal. The **castle** sprawls high above the town – less extensive than Prague Castle, but

Sightseers in Česky Krumlov (Krumau).

no less attractive, thanks to its moat, now the home of a colony of bears. The Upper Castle was designed as a feudal residence. The **Hall of Masques** is decorated with wall paintings and the **Chinese Cabinet** contains a collection of exquisite porcelain from the Chang Dynasty. The massive tower belongs to the earliest period of the medieval castle, although the cap and arcade were not added until 1590.

A bridge flanked with statues of saints leads across to the baroque **Castle Theatre**, built in 1767. The castle gardens contain an open-air theatre with a revolving stage which hosts a wide range of imaginative productions during the summer season.

To the Lipno Reservoir: Like Rožmberk Castle, **Vyšší Brod Monastery** was founded by Vok von Rožmberk in the first half of the 13th century, along the trading route to Austria. The community soon prospered and expanded. Before World War I its estates comprised more than 4,000 hectares (100,000 acres). Part of the monastery was re-turned to the Cistercian order in 1990.

The road to the Lipno Dam on the Vltava passes through **Hořice na Šumavě**. This village was traditionally famous for its Passion Plays, performed by the local residents (largely of German extraction), which continued to be staged throughout the war years. The tradition broke down after the Germans were expelled, but now the community is endeavouring to revive it. The little medieval town of **Horní Planá** (Oberplan) lies directly on the shores of the lake. It is the birthplace of the poet and painter Adalbert Stifter (1805–68). The house where he was born now contains a small museum.

The **Lipno Reservoir** is 44 km (27½ miles) long and up to 16 km (10 miles) wide in places. A steamer service links the lakeshore communities of Lipno, Frymburk, Černá v Pošumaví and Horní Planá. For many years, a considerable stretch of the long strip of land between the lake and the Czech–Austrian border was fenced off with barbed wire, which enabled it to retain much of its wildlife.

Reflections of Jindřichův Hradec near the Austrian border.

A footpath leads from Nová Pec to the **Plešné Lake**, above which a monument to Adalbert Stifter stands on a high cliff.

Unspoilt nature in the Bohemian Forest: The Bohemian Forest (Šumava), especially the sections adjoining Germany and Austria, are less suited to a touring holiday than to a peaceful stay in unspoilt natural surroundings. The **Schwarzenberg Canal** is a remarkable construction dating from the end of the 18th century. In times past it served as a means of transporting felled logs; today it links the sleepy villages and isolated farmsteads of the Bohemian Forest. A yellowing postcard outside a wooden chapel near the border states: "This was once the flourishing village of Schwendreut, now gone with the wind. It was built upon a hill which used to be covered with dense forest and which the forest will now reclaim once more."

The Iron Curtain tolled the death-knell of the border regions. Now, with the creation of a national park spanning the frontiers, new life is blossoming in the area. For some years now it has attracted country lovers keen to save the lovely old farmhouses from decay. Thanks to them a number of the typical 17th-century wooden cottages are still standing, and the wooden chapel on the hillside near **Stožec** has been faithfully restored. In the Upper Vltava Valley you will notice encouraging signs of careful tourist development designed to attract visitors seeking peace and quiet in restful surroundings. Here you can wander at leisure through the forests (though some sections of the Bohemian Forest are under strict protection and not accessible to tourists).

South of Vimperk (Winterberg), at the foot of Mount Boubín (1,362 metres/ 4,358 ft), lies the **Boubínský Prales Forest**, a conservation area since 1933. Some of the trees here are 400 years old, and the rare flora and fauna of the region attract botanists and zoologists.

Zlatá stezka (The Golden Pass) was the name of the trading route from Bohemia to Bavaria. During the Middle Ages it brought considerable prosperity to the towns in the Bohemian Forest.

The highpoint of a trip for these country women.

Volary (Wallern), the best-known resort in the area, was founded by settlers from Tyrol. Even today you can see the occasional wooden chalet with sloping roofs weighted down with stones, which is so typical of alpine regions.

Vimperk (Winterberg), also along this route, is the gateway to the Bohemian Forest. In 1264 Přemysl Otakar built a fortress above the Volynka Valley to protect the trading route. The town is noted for its printing works, founded in 1484. It produced elaborately decorated missals, copies of the Koran and other books. Fine examples are on display in the municipal museum and the Bohemian Forest Gallery in the castle, along with an exhibition of cut glass characteristic of the region. Above Vimperk, the cross-country ski tracks lead to Zadov and Churánov, the winter sports centres of the Bohemian Forest.

All the old routes of the Golden Pass converge on the little town of **Prachatice** (Prachatiz), where luxury goods, cloth and weapons were stored until their sale or onward transport had been arranged.

The most important trading commodity was salt; until the 17th century the town was the biggest repository of salt in Bohemia. When the Habsburgs introduced a monopoly and diverted the salt routes through České Budějovice (Budweis) and Gmünd, Prachatice declined into an economic and cultural backwater. Remains of the 14th-century town walls are still standing today. There is also a Gothic church housing a number of treasures, and a Town Hall constructed in 1570 and reconstructed during the 19th century with elaborate sgraffito decorations. The grammar school on the market place was where Jan Hus, a native son of neighbouring **Husinec**, was educated.

At the end of the 16th century, Wilhelm von Rosenberg (Rožmberk) commissioned the Renaissance **Kratochvíle Castle** some 20 km (12 miles) from Prachatice. His brother, Peter Vok, embellished the property with a park, surrounded by a wall and bastion. Today the castle serves as an exhibition centre for Czech cartoon films.

The
Bohemian
Forest in
winter.

WESTERN BOHEMIA

The historical and cultural development of Bohemia mirrors that of its capital, Prague. The area has always been subject to both Slavic and German influences and this is particularly true of Western Bohemia. A journey through this scenically attractive region can be combined conveniently with a tour of the world-famous spa towns described in the next chapter.

Plzeň (Pilsen) is the second-largest town in Bohemia, with a population of 180,000. It is famous for the local beer, *Prazdroj* (Pilsner lager, *see page 198*). Plzeň rose to international importance soon after receiving its charter from King Wenceslas II in 1295. Lying at the confluence of four rivers – the Mže, the Radbuza, the Úhlava and the Úslava – and at the crossroads of four long-distance trading routes, the town rapidly established itself as a trading centre. In addition, the locally mined raw materials (kaolin, mineral ores and hard coal) helped to make it a flourishing centre for crafts and industry.

It was in Plzeň that the first Czech book, the *Kronika Trojánská*, was printed and published in 1468. From 1420, following the voluntary departure from the city of the Hussite military leader Jan Žižka, Plzeň was loyal to the Catholic emperors. To show his thanks, Emperor Sigismund relieved the town of all feudal dues; Plzeň thus acquired the privileges of a tax haven and entered a new era of economic prosperity. In 1599, when the plague was rampant in Prague, Emperor Rudolf II moved his official residence here for nine months. The entire court and all foreign representatives were forced to follow suit, and once more the town boomed.

The stormy period of industrialisation during the 19th century was accompanied by the expansion of Plzeň to a cultural centre for the surrounding region. The first theatre opened here in 1832, and today Plzeň has three major dramatic stages, including a Children's Theatre and a **Marionette Theatre** where Josef Skupa, creator of the legendary puppets Špejbel and Hurvínek (*see page 107*), once worked.

Plzeň is also the home of the famous Škoda Works, founded by the engineer and industrialist Emil von Škoda at the end of the 19th century. The enterprise grew from the modest base of a small machine factory to become one of Europe's greatest industrial complexes, known for its arms production in both world wars. The company was for decades the town's largest employer, and would probably have continued to expand according to the values of Western capitalism had the American troops under General Patton, who liberated the town in 1945, not subsequently withdrawn in accordance with an agreement with the Soviet army.

The Gothic heart of the city takes the form of a rectangular chessboard, with a large square, known today as the **Square of the Republic**, in the centre. The middle of the square is occupied by the early Gothic parish **Church of St Bartholomew**, whose spire (103 metres/

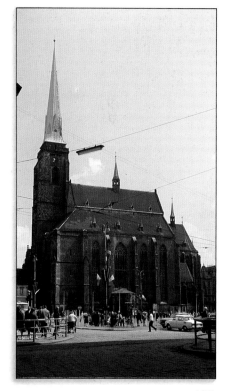

Preceding pages: the extensive Peace Square in Domažlice (Taus) in the Chodsko region. Left, the spa baths in Karlovy Vary. Right, the Church of St Bartholomew in Plzeň market place.

330 ft) is the tallest in Czech Republic. The interior is decorated with murals dating from before 1400. Dominating the high altar is a Gothic statue, the **Plzen Madonna**, completed in about 1390. With its flying buttresses and pendant keystone, the **Sternberg Chapel** on the southern side of the chancel is a typical example of late-Gothic architecture. The **Town Hall**, built in the Renaissance style between 1554 and 1558, is decorated with extravagant *sgraffito* ornaments, making it by far the most conspicuous building in the entire square. When Rudolf II came to the city, he resided in the **Emperor's House** next door.

House No. 234, opposite the main entrance to the church, dates from the Middle Ages. Since its renovation in 1770 it has been considered one of the finest baroque buildings in Bohemia. The architectural magnificence continues around the square and along the narrow alleys of the **Old Town**, where the facades of the houses are decorated with fine frescoes and sgraffito, the work

of Mikulá Ale, an esteemed Czech artist of the 19th century. In the midst of all this splendour, only the solitary **Plague Column,** erected in 1681, is a reminder that the residents of Plzeň did not escape the dreadful pestilence.

In the southeastern corner, the Franstiskanska ul. leads to the former monastery with its pretty **Chapel of St Barbara** and its late-Gothic frescoes illustrating the lives of the saints. In the northeast of the Old Town, by the Perlova, are the former butchers' stalls, recently converted into an exhibition hall and concert auditorium. The water tower nearby is 450 years old. A few yards further on, in the Veleslavinova ul., the **Museum of Beer Brewing** is also worth a visit, particularly as it is the only such museum in the country.

The environs of Plzeň: During the Middle Ages a community of Cistercian monks settled near **Plasy**, some 15 km (9 miles) north of Plzeň. They built a vast monastery complex, one of the largest in Bohemia. The most impressive building is the convent itself, which

The main square in Plzeň's old town is the largest town square in Bohemia.

196

was constructed on oak stilts because of the marshy conditions. The two-storey **Royal Chapel** is a particularly fine example of the Gothic masons' art.

Following the course of the Střela in an upstream direction, you will reach **Rabštejn nad Střelou**, the smallest town in Central Europe, with only 40 inhabitants. It perches on a rock above the swiftly flowing river, which is spanned by a magnificent 14th-century Gothic bridge. From the 13th century onwards a well-fortified castle protected this important crossing on the long-distance trading route to Saxony and Northern Europe; the remains of the stronghold can still be seen today.

The little town of **Manětín** lives up to its reputation as the best place to see baroque architecture in Western Bohemia. It lies some 30 km (19 miles) from Plzeň. The town grew up around a hunting lodge, which was totally destroyed by fire in 1712. During the 18th century, Manětín was given a complete facelift. Surrounding the palace – the work of the Italian architect Giovanni Santini

who was responsible for many such projects in Bohemia – are numerous examples of baroque sculpture. Also worth mentioning are the fine paintings by the Czech master of the baroque, Petr Brandl, which hang in the town's two churches.

Some 9 km (5 miles) southeast of Plzeň lie the ruins of the former **castle**, mentioned in records as early as 976. After the foundation of the town of New Pilsen, the site of the fortress was rechristened Old Pilsen; it later came to be known as **Starý Plzenec**. The castle was built by the Přemyslid dynasty as a cultural and administrative centre. Its fortifications included a 10-metre (32-ft) wall – a section of which is still standing today – and the oldest intact monument in the Czech Republic, the **Rotunda of St Peter**, which dates from the second half of the 10th century.

A few miles further on, rising on a hillside to the east of the village of Stáhlavy, stands **Kozel Palace**. This splendid classical-style building nestles in magnificent woodland; the main

The large salon in Kozel Castle near Plzeň.

PILSNER LAGER

F ew Czech products are as famous as its beer. The brewing tradition in Bohemia extends over many centuries – in Prague, the oldest written record of the brewer's art is found in a document dated 1082. And yet the capital does not produce the country's best beer; that honour is uncontestably held by Plzen (Pilsen).

Although the Prazdroj Brewery was founded as recently as 1842, the town's brewing tradition stretches back much further. When Plzen was founded in 1290, the town was granted the right to brew its own beer. Numerous exhibits in the Museum of Beer Brewing, which has been established in a late-Gothic malthouse in the Veleslavinova ul., testify to a thriving brewing industry here in the Middle Ages. Before the new Prazdroj brewery opened, beer was produced in various private houses scattered through the town.

Like every other beer, Pilsner is produced by heating ground malt with water and hops before allowing the liquor to ferment at low temperature by the addition of a special yeast, the *saccharomyces carlsbergensis*. Despite all this, the flavour of Pilsner lager remains unique and many attempts have been made to discover the secret. The water used in the brewing process clearly plays an important role in the determination of quality and taste; the local water is very soft and has an exceptionally low level of salinity. The secret of the beer's success lies in the preparation of the malt; only barley with a low protein content is used. But the characteristic taste and headiness of the beer is achieved by the addition of first-class, oast-dried hops from Zatec. All these basic ingredients have been employed in numerous foreign breweries but to date, not a single one has succeeded in producing an authentic-tasting Pilsner Urquell.

Another secret must lie in the cellars in which the beer ferments and matures. They were driven deep into the sandstone cliffs and extend over a distance of 9 km (5 miles). Throughout the year, they are maintained at a constant temperature of 1–2°C (33–35°F). The walls of the cellars in which the beer is kept for two to three months are coated with a fungus similar to penicillin. Many "spies" have tried to kidnap the fungus from the Plzen cellars in order to introduce it to the cellar walls of their own breweries. So far, nobody has been able to find a suitable habitat; sooner or later it always died.

Fourteen years after the brewery was set up, local lager was sold for the first time outside the country. The citizens of Vienna were the first to try Pilsner Urquell; by 1865, three-quarters of the brewery's total production was destined for export. From 1 October 1900, a "beer train" left Plzen daily for Vienna. Somewhat later, a similar train travelled regularly to Bremen; there the lager was loaded on to ships for transportation to America. Today the Prazdroj Brewery alone produces 1.3 million hectolitres (28.6 million gallons) of beer each year. If you visit the brewery in Prazdroj Street, which lies to the east of the inner city, you can study brewing techniques at your leisure. Having done so, you should treat yourself to a glass of the delicious brew in the adjoining bar. Be careful, though: the alcohol content of Pilsner lager is unusually high, and many visitors overestimate their capacity. ■ Who would say no?

Pilsner Urquell

section was completed between 1784 and 1789. Several years later a number of additions were made, following plans drawn up by the master architect Ignác Palliardi. Nowadays the palace houses an exhibition of 18th- and 19th-century art. It is worth making a short detour from here to see the **Empire Theatre**, which has been maintained in the original style.

From Plzeň to the German border: The E53 from Plzeň leads south to the little town of **Švihov**, where there is a magnificent moated castle built in a mixture of Gothic and Renaissance styles. It houses a comprehensive collection of medieval weapons.

The town of **Klatovy** (Klattau), a few miles further on, is known as the gateway to the Bohemian Forest. It is also famous as a horticultural centre specialising in the cultivation of carnations. The **Black Tower** soars to a height of almost 80 metres (256 ft) above the Renaissance-style Town Hall and the market square. Its airy gallery affords a wonderful view of the historic town walls and the surrounding hills. Those with a liking for the macabre can gaze at the mummified corpses of Jesuits in the catacombs beneath the early baroque Jesuit **Church of St Ignatius**. A veritable treat for the eyes is the so-called **White Tower**, a free-standing belfry belonging to the early Gothic **church of St Mary**.

Visitors should also take a look inside the former chemist's shop (*lékárna*) on the Town Square, which still contains its original, baroque shop fittings. In this it is unique, and is listed in the UNESCO catalogue of historic monuments.

The beautiful countryside of the central Bohemian Forest also deserves protection. Particularly attractive is the valley of the thundering **Vydra torrent**, which is 7 km (4 miles) long, and which lies a few miles southeast of Klatovy. Beyond Susice, where the river flows more quietly, stand the ruins of **Rábí Castle**, built in the mid-14th century to protect the local gold-panning industry. This, the most powerful ruined castle in Bohemia, was captured twice during

A bubbling stream deep in the Bohemian Forest.

the Hussite rebellions; it was later destroyed by fire and finally abandoned.

At the centre of the western section of the Bohemian Forest is **Železná Ruda**. The most interesting sight in this small town is a little church topped by the onion-shaped domes typical of high baroque architecture in the region. In the immediate vicinity is a ski circuit as well as a cable car to the summit of **Mount Pancíř** (1,214 metres/3,885 ft).

Shortly before the German border, the ancient trading road turns in a southwesterly direction towards the Bavarian towns of Furth im Wald and Regensburg, cutting through the **Chodsko** region. The Chods – the name is derived from the Slavic word for "patrols" – are a Slavic ethnic group whom the rulers of Bohemia allowed to settle in the district some 1,000 years ago. Their task was to defend the border and to offer protection to travellers and traders. They accomplished this with such efficiency that they were awarded special privileges, which they continued to enjoy until the region came under the rule of the Habsburgs after the Battle of the White Mountain in 1620.

To this day, on the weekend following 10 August, the Chods make their annual pilgrimage to the **Svatý Vavřinček** mountain, where they take part in an age-old festival of song, dance and bagpipe music. The Chods still wear their traditional costumes, and are also noted for their production of exquisite handicraft, particularly pottery and wood-carving.

The town of **Horšovský Týn** is another Chode settlement. It was protected by a mighty fortress, built during the second half of the 13th century. Some parts of the early Gothic castle are still standing. Following a devastating fire in the mid-16th century, the fortress was rebuilt in the style of a Renaissance palace. It is surrounded by an extensive landscaped park.

Domažlice (Taus), the capital of the Chodsko region, lies only a few miles from the German border crossing at Furth im Wald. The town was established around 1260 as a customs post.

The Chods celebrate their annual festival in Domažlice every August.

The fortifications are still visible in places; the **Lower Gate** (Dolní brána) leads directly on to the long, narrow market square of this pretty little town, fringed by attractive arcaded houses of various periods. A massive belfry rises up above the **deanery church**. Every evening, an ancient Chode trumpet melody rings out from its panoramic viewing platform.

The **castle** itself was built during the 13th century; it was later completely destroyed by fire and rebuilt in 1728. Of the original fortress, only the **Round Tower** remains today; it houses collections from the **Chodsko Regional Museum**. The **Jindřich Museum**, named after the well-known composer and expert in Chode folklore, provides an introduction to the particular character of the customs and culture of the area. There is also an interesting and comprehensive display illustrating the traditional craft of glass painting.

Visitors wishing to learn more about the folklore of the Chodsko should pay a visit to the surrounding villages.

Drazenov, Mrákov and **Újezd** are typical of the local architectural style; particularly attractive are the traditional Chode log cabins.

There is plenty to see on the E50, which runs in a westerly direction from Plzeň (most drivers move too fast to appreciate the sights and villages). The first town along the route is **Stříbro**, founded in 1240 in the vicinity of a silver mine. Parts of the late-Gothic fortifications are still visible, including a Gothic bridge with a Renaissance tower, and Renaissance-style houses – including the town hall – surrounding the market place.

It is worth making a short detour to the south to visit the important monastery at **Kladruby**; its cathedral is the work of the 18th-century architect Giovanni Santini.

A few miles before the border stands **Přimda**, originally built in Romanesque style during the 12th century as a lookout fortress. The little township nestling beneath the castle used to be inhabited by the Chods. **Tachov**, a former royal

The Bohemian Forest in autumn.

town, is considered to be the centre of the region. Remains of the medieval town wall and a good number of fine old houses testify to its illustrious past.

To northwestern Bohemia: From Stříbro you can turn north along the main road leading up to Cheb in the northwest of Bohemia, a route which provides access to the Bohemian spa towns which will be described in the following chapter.

Cheb (Eger), a lovely town on the bend in the river, always lay right in the firing line of two opposing cultures. The town bears traces of a turbulent history, originating in the 10th century when the Slavs built a stronghold on the rock overlooking the ford. Soon afterwards, German merchants settled around the fortress, founding the town of Egire which acquired market privileges in 1149. A young Swabian duke carried off and married Adelheid, the fair maid of the castle. In 1167, as the Emperor Frederick Barbarossa, he became ruler of the fortress and township, and embarked upon an ambitious scheme to enlarge its base. He held court here on

three occasions; his son often celebrated Christmas here, and even his grandson, the Emperor Frederick II, despite his preference for Apulia, summoned his vassals to this imperial palace on several occasions. **Cheb Castle**, therefore, is not only the oldest well-preserved building in the Czech Republic, it has also served as a stage for European history on various occasions.

The town has one more claim to fame – or notoriety. During the period when the country was subject to Habsburg rule, it fell into the hands of the Bohemians. Albrecht von Wallenstein, the brilliant general in charge of the imperial army stationed his troops in Cheb during the Thirty Years' War. In the interests of a united Germany, with himself as its supreme authority, he was considering the possibility of negotiating peace with Sweden – a course of action which would have saved many hundreds of thousands of lives and prevented the devastation of vast tracts of land. He demanded that his officers, who were under oath of loyalty to the emperor, swear

The old apothecary in Sušice.

202

allegiance to him personally. The emperor naturally saw this as an act of high treason and declared the general an outlaw. The Irish cavalry officer Walter Devereux led an attack on Wallenstein in February 1634; the general's troops were overpowered and Wallenstein himself was assassinated in his house by the market square.

Cheb today is a much quieter place. The market square is the focal point of this little town of some 20,000 inhabitants. Surrounding the square (named after King George of Poděbrady, the first Hussite sovereign of Bohemia), beneath the arcades of the half-timbered houses, are a number of pretty shops and cafés. Some of the buildings are particularly striking: the former **Town Hall**, a splendid example of baroque architecture, dominates the eastern side of the square. The **Schiller House** next door was where the famous German dramatist (1759–1805) stayed whilst gathering material and impressions for his famous *Wallenstein* trilogy. The **Hotel Hvězda** on the corner has a restaurant, bar and overnight accommodation.

The broad market place is graced by the Roland Fountain on the south side and the **Hercules Fountain** to the north. In the centre is the Spalícek, a collection of market stalls (formerly constructed of wood, which could be extended as required). Of special interest are the **Schirnding House** behind, with a high gable, and the **Gabler House**, which was originally Gothic in style. Tucked away at the top of the square is the **Municipal Museum** – the house in which Wallenstein was assassinated.

On the southwestern and northern periphery of the Old Town, comfortably reached on foot through the picturesque alleyways, lie five interesting churches. All were built by religious communities which took up residence in the town during the 13th century. To the south lie the Gothic **Church of Our Lady of the Ascension** and the baroque **Church of St Clare**; to the north are the churches of **St Wenceslas** and **St Nicholas**, the portal and towers of which display elements from the original Romanesque period. The latter was substantially altered by the master of the German baroque, Johann Balthasar Neumann, who was born in Cheb in 1687, and went on to design many outstanding secular and religious baroque buildings all over southern Germany. The **Church of St Bartholomew** lies directly on the River Ohře; from here it is only a few steps to the fortress.

The **Black Tower**, the massive keep of lava stone, is perched on steep cliffs overlooking the river dominating the Romanesque **castle complex**. The showpiece of the castle is the painstakingly restored two-storey **Romanesque chapel**. It looks unassuming enough from the outside, and the gloomy lower floor which housed the guards and servants confirms the initial impression. The airy upper floor, however, which was also reached by a wooden bridge from the palace proper, is a miniature gem of late-Romanesque architecture. Graceful columns with exquisitely carved capitals support the elegant ribbed vaulting of the ceiling – a fitting setting for the emperor and his retinue.

Fine residences line the market place in Cheb (Eger).

THE SPA TOWNS OF WESTERN BOHEMIA

Nowhere else in the country will tourists find their needs better catered to than in the spa towns of Western Bohemia. Not even Prague has greater experience in dealing with the requirements of the more demanding guest. In the spas, visitors can still immerse themselves in an atmosphere belonging to the long-vanished era of the Austrian empire. Since the Velvet Revolution of 1989, this has acquired even greater nostalgia value.

Sadly, the architectural sins of the more recent past are not so easily undone; here and there, grey concrete buildings characteristic of the communist period rise between the faded "imperial yellow" of the residences and sanatoria.

Karlovy Vary: Karlovy Vary, formerly Karlsbad (Charles' Spa), is the oldest of the Bohemian spa towns. Legend has it that Emperor Charles IV discovered the healing spring on which it is centred quite by chance, whilst chasing a stag on a royal hunting expedition from his nearby castle of Loket. The exhausted animal sprang from a cliff straight into a bubbling hot spring, with the baying hounds close on its heels. Despite the scalding temperature of the spring, the emperor's personal physician declared that it possessed healing properties. In 1349 Charles founded a settlement here; and in 1370 he granted the town its municipal charter.

But it wasn't until the latter part of the 17th century, following a period of devastating fires and damage during the period of Swedish occupation in the Thirty Years' War, that the town's golden age began. Under the generous patronage of the Habsburgs, Karlsbad rose to supremacy as the most elegant spa town in the world, offering every refinement essential for fashionable amusement at the time. Competitions and plays, gossip and political intrigue, exhibitionism and witty conversation were its hallmarks. Everyone wanted to be a part of the scene. The sins and vituperations of the nights of riotous drinking and extravagant parties were washed away by morning constitutionals and bathing in the healing waters.

Crowned heads, literary luminaries and great musicians were all attracted by this heady mixture. Peter the Great put in an appearance on two occasions – under the pretext of engaging in discussion with philosopher Gottfried Leibniz over the progress of science and art in Russia. Among the visitors to the spa were great men of letters such as Gogol, Goethe and Schiller, and composers including Bach and Wagner, but Karlsbad also attracted the new tycoons of Europe, who tended to stay in the high-altitude Sanatorium Imperial. Aristocratic visitors preferred the velvet-and-plush Grand Hotel belonging to the former confectioner Johann Georg Pupp. Even Karl Marx took the waters in Karlsbad; in fact, the town provided him with inspiration for several chapters of *Das Kapital*.

World history was also made in Karlsbad. Matters reached a head in 1819, when the frenzied times of the

French Revolution and the Napoleonic Wars gave way to the Congress of Vienna. The Austrian Chancellor, Prince von Metternich, invited representatives of those German states he considered to be "reliable" to join him in determining the Karlsbad Decrees. These represented a joint agreement to repress all attempts at greater civil liberty within Europe, an aim which would be achieved through the use of police informers and censorship. Metternich and his decrees were largely responsible for the tension that ultimately led to the European revolutions of 1848.

In the spa's heyday the journey to Karlsbad – by carriage through the Bohemian Forest and then down into the narrow Teplá Valley – was much more difficult than it is now. But at least there was no shortage of parking spaces, and the lords and ladies were not forced to abandon their carriages by the roadside. Today, vehicles are prohibited excluded from the historic spa district itself. The easiest approach is from the south; if you are lucky you may be able to leave your car by the bend in the Teplá, or even on the promenade by the river.

The row of stately buildings begins on the left bank of the river with the **Art Gallery** and a magnificent **casino**. Together with the **Parkhotel**, the **Grand Hotel Pupp** is impossible to overlook as it extends across several blocks along the esplanade. Its main entrance, much less conspicuous, is set back on a square where the Teplá takes a bend to the right. Behind the hotel, a cable car climbs some 200 metres (640 ft) to the **Friendship Heights** where there is an observation tower and the Restaurant Diana. The station half-way up is the starting point for a number of clearly marked walks such as the tranquil footpath to the Petrova Výšina (Peter's Heights) and the steep cliff known as Jelení skok (Stag's Leap), at the top of which a bronze chamois stands sentinel. From the numerous clearings in the woodland, the wanderer can enjoy a fine view of the town and the surrounding hills.

Returning to the valley, a favourite walk is along the Stará louka (Alte

Spa colonnade in Karlovy Vary.

Wiese), an avenue containing the most elegant and expensive shops in town. Particularly tempting is a factory outlet selling locally-manufactured Moser glass and porcelain; the factory's vases and dinner services are internationally known. Here, too, you can buy other typical souvenirs from Karlovy Vary, including Lázeňské oplatky (Karlsbader Oblaten) – wafers which have enjoyed popularity for over a century – and Becherovka, a brand of bitters prepared since 1805 from 19 different herbs, in accordance with a traditional recipe drawn up by the imperial count's personal physician, Dr Frobzig. The appropriate antidote in cases of excessive consumption is Karlsbad Salts, also locally produced and offered for sale in every shop. Beware, though, they are a powerful laxative.

On the opposite bank of the river, which can be reached comfortably by one of the many little footbridges, stands another famous hotel, the **Kaiserbad**, which was built before the turn of the century by Viennese architects in French Renaissance style. Nearby is the **Municipal Theatre**, built in 1886 and carrying on a theatrical tradition that has flourished in the town since 1602.

The promenade leads to the market place. It is to be hoped that future renovation work here will take into account the mistakes of the past, the most glaring examples of which are the hideous **Pump Rooms** opposite. The magnificent **Church of St Mary Magdalene** is well worth a visit; completed in 1736 on the orders of the Knights of the Cross, it is another fine example of the work of the Bavarian architect Kilian Ignaz Dientzenhofer. It invites comparison with his famous church of St John on the Rock in Prague.

The focal point of the spa town is the **Mill Colonnade**, built from 1871 to 1879 by Josef Zítek, who was also responsible for the National Theatre in Prague. Here you can sample one of the four thermal springs upon which the town's reputation rests. There is no need to extend the tour to include the other spa and medicinal bath complexes fur-

Drinking the curative waters.

ther to the north, unless you want to indulge in long-term therapy in what is the largest balneological establishment in the country. Instead, take the left-hand fork, which leads to the **Russian Church**, completed at the end of the last century. By following the steep incline up the Savodá třída – Park Road – bordered by towering, ancient trees and charming villas – you can quickly escape the noise and bustle of the promenade and look down over the spa quarter with its hotels and baths.

The basis of the treatment at Karlovy Vary is its 12 thermal springs, each possessing a high mineral content. They gush out of the earth at high pressure, at a rate of almost 3,000 litres (660 gallons) per minute. The best-known spring – Vrídlo, the bubbly one – produces more than 3 million litres (660,000 gallons) of water each day at a constant temperature of 73°C (163°F). The most important part of the cure is drinking the water, but the baths are also believed to be beneficial. In former times only baths were prescribed and the patients were obliged to lie in the water for two days and two nights without interruption. Today's cures are less rigorous, and treatments, whether they are for metabolic disorders, digestive complaints, chronic malfunction of the liver and gall bladder, infectious hepatitis, diabetes or gastric and duodenal ulcers, by no means preclude taking advantage of all the leisure facilities and attractions that this lively spa town provides.

Karlovy Vary also has plenty to offer on the cultural side. As well as theatre and opera performances, exhibitions and promenade concerts, the summer film festival (*see page 212*) provides exciting variety. The festival has established a notable reputation as a stage for young film-makers from Central and Eastern Europe; as such, it attracts increasingly large audiences.

Jáchymov: Jáchymov (Joachimsthal) lies in the foothills of the Ore Mountains (Erzgebirge), a few miles north of Karlovy Vary on the road to Chemnitz in Germany. The first settlement was founded here in 1516 following the dis-

The Café Elefant in Karlovy Vary.

covery of rich silver deposits; three years later, the town acquired a royal charter. The founder of Jáchymov, the Imperial Baron Schlick, was granted the privilege of minting the famous Joachimsthaler guilders, which were soon recognised as international currency, giving their name first to the *Thaler* – the silver coin formerly used throughout Germany and Austria – and ultimately to the leading monetary unit of the modern world, the dollar.

In the 16th century, Jáchymov, then with a population of some 20,000, was the largest town in Bohemia, after Prague. At times, as many as 1,000 miners were employed underground. After just over a century of intensive exploitation, however, the silver seams were exhausted; by 1671, even the mint had to close down. The little town, having lost its *raison d'être*, was given a new lease of life by the worldwide scientific revolution. For a while, the people of Jáchymov eked out an existence manufacturing porcelain and glass. The dyes were extracted from pitchblende, a waste product of silver mining.

But in 1896, the French physicist Antoine Becquerel discovered radioactivity in these mineral deposits. Shortly after that, the physicists Marie and Pierre Curie demonstrated the existence of the elements polonium and radium, which they were able to isolate from the heaps of waste. The town became the site of the first radium baths in the world. A small baker was the first to open a jerry-built bathing establishment. The next complex was more elaborate, and by 1906 Jáchymov was recognised as a medicinal spa town.

Today the little town's main source of income remains its medicinal baths and cures. The healing properties of the radioactive waters from the mines, which bubble forth from galleries more than 500 metres (1,600 ft) below the earth's surface at a pleasantly warm temperature, have been found particularly efficacious in the case of disorders of the locomotive and nervous systems and cardiovascular disease.

The spa buildings are concentrated in the south of the town, surrounded by woodland and lying some distance from the road. The **Radium Palace**, the magnificent spa rooms built in 1912 in the Secessionist style (a variation of art nouveau which began in Vienna and spread to Bohemia), contains a concert hall and a number of elegant restaurants. In the nearby park stands a fine monument to the scientific pioneer Marie Curie-Sklodowska, erected by the grateful citizens of Jáchymov. The modern spa rooms, the Akademik Běhounek, are named after one of Curie's pupils, and further testify to the town's economic expansion.

To the north, the **Old Town** marks the historic centre of the mining community. Characterised by its octagonal tower and terraced gables, the late-Gothic **Town Hall** dominates the central square. The long, narrow market place is bordered by a number of distinguished, well-preserved houses in a mixture of Gothic and Renaissance styles. Despite frequent renovation, the parish **Church of St Joachim** is worth a visit. The former mint behind the town

Marble elegance in the historic Grand Hotel Pupp.

FILM FESTIVAL

For two weeks in summer, usually in the month of July, the Film Festival brings an international flair to the little Bohemian spa town of Karlovy Vary. Since 1950 the festival has been held biennially, attracting film makers and cinema enthusiasts from all over the world. It is the second-oldest festival of its kind in Europe – younger than Venice, but founded before those of Cannes, Locarno and Berlin.

Paradoxically, the origins of the Karlovy Vary Festival lie in neighbouring Mariánské Lázně. Immediately after the Czech film industry was nationalised in 1946, the first festival was held there. Originally there was no element of competition, but in 1948 a jury, at first drawn just from within the country, began to judge the films that were shown. In 1950 the first international committee of judges was formed and the festival became linked to an annual theme.

During the early years the festival also included short films and cartoons, and for a while there was a special section for films from the Third World. The competition also introduced a new category for first films by young directors.

From the beginning, the Karlovy Vary Festival showed a strong bias towards films on social themes. At the same time, it offered cinematographers from socialist and developing countries the chance to present themselves on an international stage. The quality of the films chosen confirmed the value of the concept: among the prize-winning works were *Auschwitz*, by the Polish director Wanda Jakubowská (1948), *No Peace under the Olive Trees* by the Italian director Santini (1951), *The Children of Hiroshima* by Japan's Kanet Schindó (1954), the Soviet film classic *Nine Days in a Year* by Michail Romm, *Diary of a Lady's Maid* by Luis Buñuel (1964) and Antonio Saura's brilliant film version of Lorca's *Blood Wedding* (1980).

On the negative side, it was clear that the organisers were often guided by ideological rather than artistic motives in their choice of winning films. Nonetheless, the Karlovy Vary Film Festival was the only such event within the former Eastern bloc to achieve the highest international "A" rating.

The 27th festival in 1990 was held under very different conditions within Czechoslovakia. On this occasion, the organisers had moved away from the previous, rather pompous framework. Nevertheless, all the national film critics were unanimous that the festival had not gained in quality. Only the retrospective on Czech film production during the 1960s and some examples of the later works of Miloš Forman compensated for the lack of interesting new films.

In 1992, the festival was organised, as planned, as a showcase for contemporary European films, including previously unseen Czech productions. But the future of the festival is now uncertain as it faces unwelcome competition from the capital. Rival organisers held the first Golden Golem International Festival in Prague in June 1995. As this new festival is intended to run as an annual event, it may now spell the end of the road for the Karlovy Vary Film Festival. ■

**HENRY MILLER
CLAUDE CHABROL**
Jedno z najslávnejších diel svetovej erotickej literatúry sfilmované jedným z najvýznamnejších režisérov našej doby

Tiché dni v
CLICHY

Poster advertising Chabrol's *Quiet Days in Clichy*.

hall now houses a **Museum of Mining and Numismatics** and provides an interesting insight into local history. To gain the best overall view of the town, take the chair lift to the top of the **Klínovec** (1,244 metres/3,980 ft), the highest peak in the Ore Mountains and a spectacular vantage point.

Loket Castle, some 10 km (6 miles) southwest of Karlovy Vary on a minor road to Cheb, is a favourite destination for an outing and worth the detour. The royal fortress is built on a high cliff overlooking a bend in the River Ohře, which explains the appropriateness of its name: *loket* means elbow. The first documented reference to the stronghold was in 1239; the oldest section of the building still standing, a Romanesque-style rotunda, was probably built towards the end of the 12th century. The main tower is constructed of granite blocks; the gateways and the margrave's residence were added during the 14th century. Additional points of interest include an attractive collection of locally manufactured glass, porcelain and pewter. There is also the **Goethe Museum**. Protected by the castle, the settlement has survived until the present day, and the medieval houses grouped around the market square continue to charm visitors.

Frantíškový Lázně: Frantíškový Lázně (Franzensbad), lying a few miles north of Cheb (*see previous chapter*), is the odd one out among the spas of Western Bohemia, because the little town with its 24 icy mineral springs, was conceived in a unified style at the end of the 18th century. Taking the waters here, or undergoing a course of baths in the radioactive moorland mud, is beneficial in treating coronary and rheumatic disease and a wide variety of gynaecological complaints. Frantíškový Lázně has an international reputation.

The healing water comes from the Ohře, an acidic spring whose curative properties were well known even in the 16th century. It was a local physician, Dr Vinzenz Adler, who introduced the spa to an international public at the beginning of the 19th century. Emperor

Loket Castle; summer rapture.

Franz I of Austria discovered the benefits of the spring and gave his name to the newly-built town.

The town centre is laid out on a regular grid pattern and surrounded by spacious parks, containing the springs, spa rooms and baths. The Národní třída, or National Street, is bordered along its entire length by attractive turn-of-the-century houses, although the House of the Three Lilies at No. 10, one of the first boarding houses, is 100 years older. Standing off centre in the southwest corner is the Nám. mírů, the main square, with colonnade, meeting rooms, gas baths and the elegant **Frantisek Spring Pavilion**, which was built in 1832. Adjoining it on the west side, in **Dvořák Park**, is the Bath House I and the massive wooden pavilion housing two further springs, the **Luisin pramen** (Luisenquelle) and the **Studený pramen** (Kalter Sprudel).

In the vicinity are two Glauber's salt springs, the source of an efficacious laxative which, together with the spring water, constitutes one of the spa town's principal export commodities. The other springs are to the southeast near the **Hotel Imperial**, still one of the best addresses in town, which enjoys a splendid location and can be reached by a pleasant walk. To the north and east is the **Municipal Museum**, the theatre and the **Music Pavilion**, the setting for frequent promenade concerts.

Only 6 km (4 miles) from Františkový Lázně lies a bizarre landscape. The peat moor of **Soos-Hájek** has been declared a nature conservation area. Poisonous carbon dioxide issues from funnel-shaped hollows; the bubbling mud, like a landscape in a science-fiction film, recalls the volcanic origins of the region. This is even more in evidence in the nearby **Komorní Hůrka Nature Reserve**, where traces of the region's last volcanic eruption during the Quaternary Period can still be seen.

Mariánské Lázně Marienbad: Situated at a height of some (600 metres) 1,920 ft in a protective arc of wooded hills stretching to the north, west and east, **Mariánské Lázně** makes a good base

Františkovy Lázně (Franzensbad) has been a spa town since 1793.

for a tour through Western Bohemia, not only for its favourable geographical location but also for its well-developed tourist infrastructure.

One of Europe's most scenic spas, Mariánské Lázně's long list of famous visitors includes Edward VII, king of England from 1841 to 1910. The town possesses more than 40 mineral springs, whose highly saline waters are used for the treatment of bladder disorders, respiratory problems, heart ailments, rheumatism and blood and skin diseases.

The Premonstratensian monks from nearby **Teplá** must have been aware of the healing properties of the water when they established the village of Auschowitz near the springs in 1341, creating a sort of *dépendance* of their abbey, which lay some 13 km (8 miles) to the east. In 1710 the abbot had a pilgrims' lodge built to provide shelter for the steadily growing band of invalids who came in search of a cure. At the same time, the springs were tapped; the monks decanted the water into barrels which they sold for a handsome profit to prosperous cities and noblemen's estates. In 1749 an inventive apothecary at the abbey found a convenient way of cutting the transport costs by evaporating the water and marketing the much more convenient Teplá Salt.

The mineral baths were added a few decades later. The water from the Stinking Spring (Stinkquelle) – named for its high hydrogen sulphide content – proved particularly efficacious, and thankful patients dedicated votive pictures to the Virgin Mary. The spring's name was changed to Mary's Spring (Marienquelle), and in 1818 it became known officially as the Spa Town of the Austrian Monarchy, although it did not receive its town charter until 1868.

Mariánské Lázně is full of fascinating stories. In 1820, at the age of 74, Goethe drove over by coach from Karlovy Vary. He returned the following year, the constant companion of the charming Baroness Ulrike Levetzov, who was only 19 years old. Their relationship developed into a passionate romance, but when the potential mother-in-law re-

Ballroom dancing in Mariánské Lázně's main colonnade.

fused to give her consent to a marriage, Goethe withdrew and never visited the spas again.

Goethe was only the first of many writers and composers to be inspired by the springs of Mariánské Lázně. He was followed by Frédéric Chopin, Richard Wagner, Mark Twain and Henrik Ibsen. In 1833, the violinist Ludwig Spohr composed his romantic waltzes entitled *Memories of Marienbad*, and in the 1960s Alain Resnais made the film classic *Last Year in Marienbad*, which rapidly gained cult status.

A popular venue for international congresses and symposia, Mariánské Lázně has developed into the most comfortable and modern of all the spas, expanding far beyond its modest origins. Today the southern approach leads through several miles of uninspiring modern suburbs before the elegant spa district unfolds. On the left-hand side, the central avenue, **Hlavní třída** (formerly Kaiserstrasse), is bordered by a variety of shops, attractive restaurants and several large hotels. The hotels include the Bo-

hemia, which underwent renovation a few years ago and now combines art nouveau elegance with modern facilities and comfort.

On the right, the spa gardens extend towards the horizon across gentle hills. On its southern boundary stand two fine buildings dating from the turn of the century – the **New Baths** and the former pump rooms, now known as the **Casino** and used as a cultural centre. (The casino proper, with an excellent restaurant and bar, lies a good 300 metres (nearly 300 yards) further to the south, at the entrance to the spa district.) From here you pass the **Ambrožův pramen** (Ambrosiusquelle), the **Central Baths**, the **Mud Baths** and the **Mariin pramen** (Marienquelle).

Ascending the hill, the road passes the **Church of the Assumption** before reaching the spa promenade. The rotunda housing the **Křížový pramen** (Kreuzbrunnen) was built in 1818 when the town was first recognised as a spa. The cast-iron structure of the **New Colonnade** is fascinating both optically and

The Rudolf Spring in Mariánské Lázně.

technically. The filigree struts forming the framework of the finely proportioned **Promenade Hall** were produced by a Moravian foundry in 1884–89; they lend the open construction, with its lively ceiling frescoes, a wonderful light airiness. The computer-controlled **Singing Fountains** – a series of playful water sculptures immediately in front of the building, completed in 1988– cannot really compete

Climbing up to the next terrace, you reach the **Goethe House**. Today the neoclassical building serves as municipal museum. The square in front is dominated by the old-fashioned **Hotel Kavkaz**. Its rooms appeal to lovers of faded elegance who are prepared to ignore the dripping taps, musty carpets and warped window frames.

A stroll along the northern perimeter of the park will lead past a number of other hotels and bath houses and then back to the upper end of the Hlavní třída. It is worth checking the programme at the **Municipal Theatre**.

Nature-lovers will also find plenty to enjoy in the immediate neighbourhood of the town. There are many delightful woodland walks along a total of 70 km (40 miles) of signposted paths.

A few miles northwest of Mariánské Lázně lies **Lázně Kynžvart** (Bad Königswart), another little spa town, known for its therapeutic, iron-rich, acidic waters, and specialising in the treatment of childhood illnesses. The town, which came into the possession of the dukes of Metternich in 1630, is dominated by a massive castle.

In 1690, the dukes proceeded to erect a mighty baroque palace over the old castle walls. Chancellor Metternich (1773–1859) then had the building renovated in the Empire style at the beginning of the 19th century.

Goethe and Beethoven both stayed here. Today's visitors can enjoy the castle's valuable collections which include such diverse treasures as Egyptian mummies, and oriental and Gothic paintings, as well as a display of curiosities. The castle is surrounded by an extensive, landscaped park.

Goethe with Ulrike von Levetzov; he was 70, she was only 19.

NORTHERN BOHEMIA

Northern Bohemia is a region of great scenic beauty as well as a treasure chest of history and culture. It is an area famous for fruit, hops and wine, but it is also a mining district with smoking chimney stacks and factories. The observant traveller crossing the countryside on the southern slopes of the Ore Mountains (Erzgebirge) will stumble upon many contradictions.

Leaving behind the spa towns described in the previous chapter, the next stage of the tour strikes out from Karlovy Vary in a northeasterly direction towards **Klášterec nad Ohří** (Klösterle), on the River Ohře (Eger). This ancient little town was originally the possession of the Benedictine order; the Bohemian king Přemysl Otakar II later presented it to the aristocratic Cumperk family. The Renaissance **castle** acquired its pseudo-Gothic appearance after being gutted by fire in 1856. Today it houses an extensive porcelain collection with exhibits ranging from Chinese antiquities to contemporary items.

Another interesting town is **Kadaň**, on the Ohře. The medieval town square with its arcades, elaborate gabled roofs and stone portals is especially attractive. The **town hall,** with a Gothic tower and pretty oriel window, was rebuilt in the baroque style following a fire, as was the church opposite, also originally Gothic. On the southern slopes, overlooking the river, stands the former **monastery**, now the municipal archives. Apart from a large number of Gothic remains and baroque additions, it boasts cellar-like vaulting and the sarcophagus of the monastery's founder, Johann Hassenstein von Lobkowitz.

No visit to Northern Bohemia, the cradle of hop-growing, would be complete without sampling the local beer. A pleasant aroma and a spicy, resinous quality characterise the type of hop grown in the area surrounding the town of **Žatec** (Saaz). Fertile soil and favourable climatic conditions guarantee the supremacy of hops from this region, grown here since the 10th century. Today 60 percent of the total production is destined for the export market.

Chomutov (Komotau) has a number of architectural sights, including the historic town square which has an unusual arcade, and the 16th-century Collen-Luther House. A number of magnificent medieval chambers have been preserved. The little **Church of St Catherine** in the vicinity is a fine example of the early Gothic style.

The medieval town of **Most** (Brüx), lying on the trading route from Bohemia to Saxony, has become a thriving mining community. A new town has gradually replaced the original settlement. The relocation of the Gothic **Deanery church** in 1975 was an impressive technical achievement. For the first time in Europe, a total mass weighing 12,000 tons was moved in one piece. Only the altar, 17.5 metres (56 ft) high and 8 metres (26 ft) wide, was dismantled.

Of particular interest is the nearby **Jezeří Castle**. The remarkable architectural ensemble includes baroque build-

ings, a Renaissance palace and a Gothic fortress. Nonetheless, since 1973 the entire complex has been the subject of violent controversy. The coal lobby demands that the castle be demolished and the rock upon which it stands blown up, since they stand in the way of mining the brown coal. Cultural historians and ecologists object violently to these plans, and geologists have pointed out that if coal mining goes ahead the entire mountain would suffer from a landslide.

The castle in **Duchcov** (Dux) is the former residence of the von Waldstein family (*see page 39*). It contains a rare collection of historic gems. At the end of the 18th century, Giovanni Giacomo Casanova wrote his memoirs here.

The district town of **Teplice**, housing the **Krušnohorské Theatre** and an interesting museum, is the oldest spa town in Bohemia. The baths, with their radioactive springs, are used to treat circulatory disorders and malfunctions of the motor system. A visit for refreshments in one of the town's many restaurants, wine bars and cafés is recommended.

The Labe (Elbe) Valley: Litoměřice (Leitmeritz) and its hinterland are often described as the Garden of Bohemia; fruit and vines flourish here. The former Royal City also offers the visitor a wealth of historic sights and architecture. The town is characterised by its Renaissance and baroque buildings. Setting the scene are the chalice-shaped roof of the **Mráz House** and the **town hall**, of Gothic origin but rebuilt in Renaissance style. The town's skyline is dominated by **St Stephen's Cathedral**. Visitors should also make a point of visiting the **Gallery of Northern Bohemia**.

This attractive region has had its fair share of suffering at the hands of history. A particularly harsh fate befell the town of **Terezín**. It was founded in 1780 by Emperor Joseph II as a bastion against the Prussians and named in honour of Empress Maria Theresa. During the last war, the German occupying forces established the notorious concentration camp of Theresienstadt here. A memorial recalls the thousands of Jews who suffered and died (*see box page 51*).

Most (Brüx) has its fair share of environmental problems.

222

A few miles further upstream lies **Roudnice nad Labem** (Raudnitz), site of a baroque castle. An interesting gallery is housed in the former riding school. **Mount Říp** rises above the gentle hill landscape to the south. According to legend, Čech, founding father of the nation, and his entourage paused on the mountain's summit and, enchanted by the view, decided to settle in the region. The romantic **St George's Chapel** on the mountain was built in honour of a celebration marking the victory of Prince Soběslav over Emperor Lothar in the Battle of Chlumec in 1126.

Downstream from Litoměřice, the next town is **Ústí nad Labem** (Aussig). Its well-developed industry has made it the economic centre of the region. Enjoying a favourable location on the medieval Salt Road and at the confluence of the Bílina and the Labe, Ústí nad Labem became a Royal City in the 13th century. The approach to the city is marked by **Střekov Castle**, perched on a high basalt cliff overlooking the Labe (Elbe) just outside the city. A number of famous people have visited this fortress, and in 1842, Richard Wagner composed his opera *Tannhäuser* here.

The town centre has a number of other interesting sights. Since a bomb attack during World War II, the tower of the Gothic **Church of the Assumption** has had a small list. The entire building has had to be underpinned and is regarded as one of the architectural curiosities of Europe. The neighbouring baroque ensemble, comprising the **Church and Monastery of St Adalbert**, has been restored and now serves as a concert and exhibition hall. In 1972 an organ with 3,572 pipes was installed.

In the vicinity of Ústí nad Labem is **Tiské skály**, a romantic labyrinth of bizarre sandstone rock formations. A few miles further upstream, **Velké Březno Castle** is worth visiting for its interior, which retains its original features, and for the attractive 5-hectare (12-acre) park. Also worth mentioning is the village of **Stadice** in the **Bílina Valley**, the setting for *Kosmas*, the first Czech chronicler's account of Přemysl

Hops from Žatec (Saaz) give Czech beers their special flavour.

Oráč, founder of the ruling dynasty of Bohemia. According to legend, Princess Libuše married this simple farmer and inspired him to found the city of Prague. In memory of the event, the inhabitants of Stadice are said to have supplied hazelnuts for the royal table. Today the town square, with its ancient memorial stone, is a national monument.

Interesting in a very different way is the toxic waste tip in **Chabařovice**, to the west of the town. There are no precise details concerning the exact composition of the tip, which was commissioned in 1905. It is suspected that the contents of the entire Mendeleyev periodic table are represented here, offering the possibility of hitherto unknown compounds. The American government provided funds for the disposal of 40,000 tons of highly toxic hexachlorobenzol.

Děčín (Tetschen) Castle, situated on the Labe just before the German border, was occupied until recently by the Soviet army; following the 1968 invasion, they established a permanent garrison here. Although the soldiers have now

withdrawn, to date only the rose garden in the castle grounds has been made accessible to the public. Concerts are held here on summer evenings.

Nature lovers have a special affection for the area surrounding Děčín. Two Swiss artists, the painter Adrian Zingg and the engraver Anton Graff, were so enchanted by the beauty of this landscape that when they surveyed the picturesque rocky cliffs, deep ravines and narrow defiles they felt themselves transported back to their native land and lost their desire to return home. That was in 1776; since then, the area surrounding Děčín, and in particular the sandstone region near **Hřensko**, has been dubbed "Bohemia's Switzerland". One of the thrills of the area is a trip through the foaming spray of the mountain torrents in a narrow boat – with a local wild water expert at the helm, of course. Also popular is a detour to **Pravčická brána**, a remarkable natural rock formation in the sandstone plateau around Hřensko.

The sandstone mountains were formed 130 million years ago, but the region is in grave danger from today's air pollution. One crumbling sandstone block weighing about 800 tons is poised threateningly above the main road from Hřensko. It will probably have to be blown up to avoid the risk of a major catastrophe.

The district known as **Česká Lípa** (Böhmisch Leipa) is rich in unusual natural phenomena. These include the **Sloupské skály cliffs**, occupied by the sandstone castle of Sloup, and the **Panské skály cliffs**, which consist of thousands of basalt pillars. Observed from the air they resemble a honeycomb; from the side, they look more like organ pipes, which explains their nickname: *varhany*, "the organ".

Southeast of Česká Lípa, the mighty ruin of **Bezděz Castle** soars heavenwards; it is one of the most important examples of Bohemian Gothic defensive architecture. It was never rebuilt and includes an early Gothic chapel. Emperor Charles IV had the **Máchovo Lake** created near the castle. The lake is known for its carp, but it is also a popular resort area with sandy beaches and

The Labe (Elbe) near Litoměřice (Leitmeritz).

pleasantly warm water temperatures.

The Jizerské Mountains (Isergebirge):

With a population of 100,000, the town of **Liberec** (Reichenberg) is famous for its cloth production, which was begun in the Middle Ages by Flemish weavers. The weaving tradition led to tremendous prosperity in the middle of the last century, when a succession of textile factories were established. Today, a number of well preserved historic buildings still testify to the town's Golden Age. More than 40 of them are national monuments. Among the most important is the **Renaissance palace**, whose chapel is noted for its beautifully carved altar and coffered ceiling. Impressive, too, is the **Town Hall**; built in the style of the Dutch neo-Renaissance, it was designed by the Viennese architect Frans von Neuman and has definite similarities to the New Town Hall in Vienna.

A wonderful view of the town and the **Jizerské Mountains** beyond can be enjoyed from the central of the three towers. On the **Old Town Square** beneath, the 16th-century **Deanery Church of St Antony** was rebuilt in neo-Gothic style in 1879. From here the narrow Věterná ulice (Wind Alley), with its beautiful 17th-century, half-timbered **Wallenstein Houses**, leads through to the **Small Square** (Malé nám.).

The **Museum of Northern Bohemia** is situated in the north of the town. It contains an impressive collection of tapestries, furniture, pottery and glass as well as a historical and folklore section. Between 1938 and 1945, Liberec (then known as Reichenberg) was the largest town in the so-called Sudetenland. It was also the home of Konrad Henlein, the Sudeten German leader who demanded the Anschluss (union) with the German Reich and subsequently became the Gauleiter of Sudetenland and civil commissioner for Bohemia.

Some 20 km (12 miles) north of Liberec stands the forbidding fortress, **Frýdlant (Friedland) Castle**, with its impregnable round tower. It was built in 1241, on a rock above the Smědá, by a knight named Ronovec; later owners converted it into a Renaissance castle. After the Bohemian uprising of 1619,

Most of the country's energy is still derived from lignite.

the castle's Lutheran lord, Christoph von Redern, sided against the Habsburgs; his fate was sealed after defeat at the Battle of the White Mountain. In 1620 Albrecht von Wallenstein (Waldstein) bought the estate and made the castle his home.

As a token of gratitude, Ferdinand II elevated his diligent General Wallenstein to the rank of duke. But the moment of glory was to be short-lived; in 1634 Wallenstein was assassinated and the Friedland estate passed to Count Gallas, another general in the imperial army. His heirs opened the castle to the public. One of the first castle museums in Europe was created almost 200 years ago in response to the considerable interest aroused by Schiller's dramatic trilogy *Wallenstein*, written in 1799. The Lower Castle, with its meticulously renovated Renaissance facade, is linked by the Knight's Bridge to the original Gothic fortress. The latter contains luxuriously appointed salons and halls as well as a well-stocked art gallery.

Also worth visiting is **Sychrov Castle**,

Bohemian Glass

There is evidence that even during the Bronze Age the settlers of what is now the Czech Republic manufactured glass in the form of beads for necklaces and bracelets. During the Middle Ages, at about the same time as they produced the first glass drinking vessels, they learned how to make windows, panes of glass and wall mosaics.

In 1370, under Charles IV, artists created the monumental mosaic on the South Portal of St Vitus' Cathedral, depicting scenes of the Last Judgment. The magnificent windows of the Church of St Bartholomew in Kolín date from about 1380. Domestic use of glass included the manufacture of bottles and flasks, in shades of green or brown. By the turn of the 15th century there were eight glassblowers' foundries in Bohemia, five in Moravia and a further eight in territory which belonged to Bohemia at the time. The glass factory in Chřibská (Kreibitz), a town in the Lusatian hills, was first mentioned in 1427. It exerted a considerable influence on the development of the glass industry.

During the 16th century the rough-and-ready glassware produced in the Bohemian Forest no longer satisfied the refined tastes of the worldly aristocrats in the first years of Habsburg rule. Following the Venetian glass-blowing tradition, production moved towards thin glass in the harmonious forms of the Renaissance. After 1600, cylindrical tankards served as a basis for the famous enamel painting. Between 1600 and 1610 the gem cutter Caspar Lehmann from Uelzen (1563–1622) experimented with the cutting of glass at the court of Rudolf II in Prague. The manufacture of cut glass did not become widespread in Bohemia until about 1680. Nowadays, Bohemian crystal is exported all over the world.

The classic form of the Bohemian baroque wine glass with a cut pedestal foot, and the many-faceted beaker of fine, thin glass was traditionally adorned with ornate floral bouquets, garlands or grotesque decorations. After 1720 the range was enlarged by the addition of gilt glass and the black engraving in the style of Ignaz Preissler (1676–1741). Along with the local cut and polished glass, Bohemian chandeliers with cut glass prisms were also much sought after. During the 18th century crystal lustres were exported to the courts of the King of France and the Tsar.

After a period of decline at the end of the 18th century, Bohemian hyalite glass with its coloured enamel decoration established an independent reputation. Around 1800 the range of glass was further enlarged by the trend towards less ornate, finely polished and engraved Empire and Biedermeier glassware. The thick-walled coloured glass discovered by Friedrich Egermann in about 1820 revived interest in the craft further: black hyalite glassware, agate glass, Lithyalin glass and new uses for ruby glass all became popular. The status of Bohemian crystal was boosted during the 19th century by the manufacture of mirrors and tableware as well as glass coral. The latter survived until recent times in Jablonec nad Nisou (Gablonz) under the trade name Jablonex.

During the 20th century the names of Loetz, Lobmayer and Jeykal have ensured the continued worldwide reputation of Bohemian crystal through their adaptation of the fantasy, colour and metallic effects characteristic of the art nouveau style. ■ **Art nouveau glass from Bohemia.**

20 km (12 miles) south of Liberec. It was built at the end of the 17th century, but did not acquire its romantic Gothic appearance until the last century. Today's visitors to the castle tread in the footsteps of two of the greatest Czech composers, Antonín Dvořák and Josef Suk, who were frequent guests.

One of the most prominent landmarks in the region is undoubtedly the elegant tower of the television transmitter on the summit of **Mount Ještěd**. It can be reached by cable car, and the tower restaurant offers a panorama across the Krkonoše and the Jizerské mountains.

Bohemian Paradise: Adjoining the district to the south lies the nature reserve **Český raj** (Bohemian Paradise), where between Turnov (Turnau) and Jičín the massive sand deposits left by a sea covering this land during the Cretaceous Period have remained until this day. Near Jičín, there is the famous nature reserve of **Prachovské skály**, with its bizarre sandstone cliffs, vertical walls and deep, narrow grottoes.

Founded by Václav (Wenceslas) II,

Jičín is an old royal city which at various times belonged to a number of Bohemian noble dynasties. After the Battle of the White Mountain, it fell to Wallenstein who incorporated it into his Friedland estate. He wanted to make Jičín the political and cultural centre of his empire, but his plans to do so were only partially realised. But despite that, this period (the first half of the 17th century) was the most important in the town's history.

The only town gate still standing is the 50-metre (150-ft) **Valdická brána**, built in 1568. It provides a fine view of the tree-lined avenue leading to the park of **Libosad** in which Wallenstein had an attractive pleasure palace built for himself and his retinue. Further to the north are the towers of the Carthusian monastery which he founded; it was converted into a prison in 1783. Next to the gate, the **Church of St James** was also built on the orders of Wallenstein, but was only completed in the 19th century; the general's daughter is buried here. The town square is surrounded by beautiful

People have been skiing in the Krkonoše (Giant Mountains) since 1894.

Gothic, Renaissance and baroque houses. On the southern side stands **Waldstein Palace**, built by Italian architects between 1624–34. It was here, in 1813, that the Holy Alliance of the Allies against Napoleon was sealed.

The region is also characterised by its remarkable volcanic features, for example the basalt cliffs which rise above the bizarre ruins of the Gothic castle in **Trosky**. Further on the road to Turnov is the remarkable cliff town of **Hrubá Skála**, with the ruins of another medieval castle nearby.

The area retains considerable economic significance because of the presence of extensive deposits of Bohemian garnet and other precious stones. **Turnov** (Turnau) is internationally famous as a centre of gem polishing and the production of garnet jewellery. The district museum with its collection of precious stones is well worth seeing.

Following the Jizera valley to the north of Turnov, the visitor will soon arrive at the town of **Železný Brod** (Eisenbrod), which is renowned for the manufacture of ornamental glass. The town gets its name from the iron ore which has been mined here ever since the 17th century. A number of old wooden buildings are preserved, including the **belfry** next to the church of St James. Železný Brod is a good base for excursions into the Český raj.

Jablonec nad Nisou (Gablonz), the principal town in the Jizerské mountains, stands in the shadow of the highest peak in the area, the **Černá hora** (1,084 metres/3,469 ft) and is primarily important for its glass and jewellery production. During the 16th century the area was settled by German glassblowers because the wooded slopes of the Jizerské Mountains provided them with copious supplies of the charcoal needed for their craft. During the 18th century they rose to fame with their glass imitations of pearls and precious stones, and the community experienced an economic boom. Today the **Glass Museum** documents the little town's glorious heyday and the history of this traditional craft (*see page 226*).

Walkers and skiers find ample recreation possibilities in the Jizerské Mountains in summer and winter alike. Especially popular is the annual cross-country ski competition known as the Jizerská padesátka (the Iser Mountain Race), which starts in the resort of **Bedřichov**.

The Krkonose: To the east rise the peaks of the **Krkonoše** – the Giant Mountains – which as the highest mountains in Bohemia form the natural boundary between the Czech Republic and Poland. The mountain crest extends over a length of 36 km (22½ miles); the highest peak, at 1,602 metres (5,126 ft), is the **Sněžka** (Schneekoppe). Weathering and ice have produced a succession of strangely shaped seas of rock and bare pillars of stone, providing a fitting scenario for the fantastic stories of Rübezahl and other legendary characters. Almost the entire region was declared a national park in 1963; together with the adjoining area across the Polish frontier, it forms one of the largest nature conservancy areas in Europe.

The domestic buildings of the Krkonoše display a unique variety of styles, demonstrating the skill of the carpenters in this mountainous region. Also of note are the **museums** in Vrchlabí (Hohenelbe), Jilemnice, Vysoké nad Jizerou and Trutnov (Trautenau), which house extensive folklore collections and natural exhibits.

The main winter sports centres, with ski lifts, cross-country ski tracks and downhill pistes are **Špindlerův Mlyn** (Spindlermühle), **Pec pod Sněžkou** and **Harrachov**. The international ski-flying championships, the *Turné Bohemia*, are held here each year. The highlight of the winter sports season in Harrachov is the ceremonial entry of Rübezahl, the legendary ruler of the Krkonoše, at the beginning of March. The costumed parade fills the streets with an atmosphere of festivity and celebration.

East of **Trutnov**, the area surrounding **Police nad Metují** and **Teplice nad Metují** is well known to mountaineers. Erosion of the sandstone cliffs has resulted in an intricately-shaped skyline, resembling the silhouettes of town buildings. Particularly popular are the **Adršpašsko-teplické skály**, but the more

Liberec town hall: the town has been a centre of the textile industry since the late Middle Ages.

remote **Broumovské stěny** also offer spectacular views. The little town of **Broumov** is the ultimate backwater. The Benedictine monastery here – just one of the works of the Dientzenhofers in this part of the country – is a superb example of baroque architecture.

On the journey from the Krkonoše to **Hradec Králové** it is worth stopping in **Dvůr Králové**. A zoo, later expanded into a safari park, was established here in 1946. The park is stocked with a wide range of animals, including rare species such as the white rhinoceros; visitors can view the animals from the safety of a bus. A few miles to the south lies the spa town of **Kuks**, notable for the impressive baroque statues of the 18th-century artist Matthias Braun surrounding the **Church of the Holy Trinity**.

The origins of **Náchod** lie in a Gothic watchtower built to protect the long-distance trading routes. A succession of historical figures left their mark here: George of Poděbrady, Albrecht von Wallenstein, the Trčka family and the Piccolominis. During this century

Náchod was also the native town and periodic place of work of the writer Josef Škvorecký. The surrounding region provides the background for his well-known novel, *The Cowards*.

South of Náchod, you can swim in the **Rozkoš u České Skalice** – the largest reservoir in Bohemia. In **Nové Město** it is worthwhile visiting the castle and the market place, which is fringed by Renaissance-style townhouses. Another interesting destination is **Opočno**, with a magnificent arcaded Renaissance castle.

The Orlické Mountains (Adlergebirge): Two rivers, the Tichá Orlice and the Divoká Orlice, both free of industrial pollution, flow through the little towns of Letohrad, Lanskroun, Litice, Jablonné and Žamberk. Providing the backdrop are the **Orlické Mountains**, a relatively low chain covered in spruce. They reach a maximum altitude of 1,155 metres (3,696 ft). Below, in the picturesque valleys, glitter countless lakes. The most popular one lies near **Pastviny**, north of Letohrad; the best-known ski centres, with lifts, are **Deštné** and **Říčky**.

Rychnov n. Kněz Castle contains a permanent regional exhibition. The town itself, a regional centre, was traditionally the home of clothmakers and weavers; its textile manufacturing industry is still very important.

From here you can make pleasant excursions into the mountains or to the large number of castles concentrated in the immediate vicinity. Particularly recommended are **Častolovice** and **Doudleby**, as well as the imposing baroque castle in **Litice**.

Among the little towns in the foothills of the Orlické Mountains, **Žamberk** (Senftenberg) is of most historical importance. During the 17th century, Magdaléna Grambová introduced the art of **lace making** to the town from Italy. The traditional family workshops gradually expanded, until there was a flourishing industry in the town. Local lacemakers today find no shortage of customers for their delicate work. The **Municipal Museum** has a permanent exhibition dedicated to lace production; the town also has a training centre for lace workers.

Left, the source of the Labe. **Right**, downhill skiing in the Krkonoše.

Eastern Bohemia

From Prague the national road No. 333 leads to **Kutná Hora** (Kuttenberg). This attractively situated town is today a rather sleepy little regional centre, but back in medieval times it was the most important town in Bohemia after Prague. As the centre of silver mining and the royal mint, the town generated such enormous wealth that it placed the Bohemian kings among the most influential rulers in Europe, and they frequently resided here. At the insistence of Jan Hus, Wenceslas IV signed the Kuttenberg Decree, a major reform of the constitution of Prague University in favour of Czech nationals. With the victory of Jan Žižka's troops over the emperor's army of mercenaries before the city gates in 1422, Kutná Hora entered the annals of the Hussite Wars.

Approaching from Prague, your first impression on entering the town will be of the richly decorated stone fountain in the Rejskovo nám. The attractive baroque **Church of St John Nepomuk** lies in the Husova třída, leading into the Palackého nám, bordered by fine Renaissance houses which, along with the **Old Town Hall**, forms the heart of the Old Town.

The late-Gothic **Stone House** (Kamenný dům) on Námesti 1máje is of particular interest. This unusual townhouse was constructed by an unknown master builder towards the end of the 15th century; most of the statues are ascribed to Brixi, a famous stone mason from Wroclaw. The building underwent major renovation at the beginning of this century and today serves as the municipal museum.

On the way down to the River Vrchlice lies the Gothic **Church of St James**, with an 82-metre (262-ft) high tower. During the baroque period an onion dome was added; at the same time the interior acquired its share of baroque features. Next door lies the *Italian Court* (Vlasšký dvůr), originally built as the **Royal Mint** in about 1300. Florentine

Preceding pages: rape is an important cash crop. Below, brass instruments are made in Hradec Králové (Königgratz).

craftsmen minted the silver coins which served as legal tender throughout Europe: the Prague pennies. The cellars house an extensive exhibition documenting the trade. When supplies of silver ran out the mint was forced to close (mid-18th century) and later became the town hall. In about 1400, Wenceslas IV had the East Wing redesigned as a royal residence. Forming part of this complex is the **St Wenceslas Chapel**, demonstrating a surprising blend of architectural styles: under the Gothic ribbed vaulting, and framed by medieval winged altars, the art nouveau artist František Urban has executed a series of paintings narrating the well-known legend of St Wenceslas.

The Barborská ul. leads south past the fort – also formerly used as a mint – and the powerful Jesuit college to the Gothic **Cathedral of St Barbara**. The mine owners of Kutná Hora financed this magnificent place of worship and dedicated it to the patron saint of miners. Peter Parler began the building work in 1388, and Benedikt Ried designed the

nave at the end of the 15th century, but the project was not completed until 1558. Apart from the valuable frescoes in the **Smíšek Chapel**, the references to the cultural and economic history of the city are of interest. The spaces between the vaulting of the choir roof are decorated with the coats of arms of the craft guilds of the town. On the west wall of the south aisle, workers in the city's mint are depicted; a wall statue portrays a miner with tools and lamp.

Situated about 3 km (2 miles) to the northeast of Kutná Hora, **Kačina** is the finest empire-style palace in the whole of Bohemia. Built between 1802–22, it is surrounded by an attractive park, which contains a large number of rare trees. The attractions of the palace itself include the library and the theatre, as well as an agricultural museum.

In the nearby town of **Kolín**, the Old Town is laid out on a grid pattern of equal squares, a piece of town planning characteristic of the Germans who settled here at the beginning of the 13th century. The **Cathedral of St Bart-**

Kolín is the venue each June for the the world's largest meeting of brass ensembles.

PARDUBICE STEEPLECHASE

Josef Pírka, a photographer from Pardubice, vividly described the start of the hunt in the 19th century: "It was a gloomy, foggy day – typical English weather. Early in the morning we drove in a carriage decorated with twigs gathered from fir trees onto a field behind the viaduct. In the distance we could discern through the mist horsemen in formal attire, grooms, roughriders and stable lads; some of the horses bore side-saddles. At half-past eleven the sun broke through the mist, and the temperature rose. In the distance we could see the bright red riding habits of the master of hounds and his two assistants, together with the pack. The bells tolled noon, and the nobility gathered together."

The hunt soon developed into a race in which speed was what really counted. Following the English tradition, the huntsmen followed each other in hot pursuit; their goal was usually a church tower (steeple), which gave this type of race its name. This led to the founding of the Pardubice Hunt

Club in 1848, and on 5 November 1874 the signal was given for the start of the first race across a specially prepared course.

The Great Steeplechase in Pardubice is one of the most difficult and dramatic horse races in Europe. To win the Pardubice ranks with winning England's Grand National at Aintree and is every jockey's dream. Racing fans, punters and tipsters gather in their thousands on the last Sunday in March at Aintree and on the second Sunday in October in Pardubice; some try to attend both events.

The two races, however, are completely different. The Grand National is run over a closely mown grass track. Runners complete two virtually identical laps with almost 30 artificial obstacles on terrain as flat as a snooker table. The course is 7,216 metres (7,770 yards) long and the race is over within a matter of minutes.

The Pardubice course, by contrast, reflects the very different personality of the Czechs: no grass, no artificial barriers, but hedges, sand and water-filled ditches and rough ground with 31 obstacles. The course is 6,990 metres (7,456 yards) long. In the entire history of the two races, so far only one jockey – the English professional G. Williamson – has succeeded in winning at both Pardubice and Aintree. He gained the trophy in Pardubice four times, between 1890 and 1893, but at Aintree he won on just one occasion – in 1899.

The speciality of Pardubice is the Taxis Ditch, the fourth obstacle, which is rather like Beecher's Brook at Aintree. Whoever stumbles here has already lost the race. During the 1880s it was mooted that the Big Ditch, as it was then known, should be made less difficult, but the Count of Thurn und Taxis, the Postmaster-General of the Royal and Imperial Monarchy, defended the ditch, and in his honour it was renamed the Taxis Ditch. No less tricky are the Irish Bank – a natural embankment, 2 metres (6 ft) high and 2 metres wide, with small ditches on either side, the Snake's Ditch and the deceptive jump called The Gardens.

In 1990, the centenary of the race, it was a jump called the Popkovicky skok which proved to be the acid test. It is only a miniature version of the Taxis Ditch, but it was here that the two favourites fell and had to bury their hopes of victory. ■ The leap over Taxis Ditch.

holomew was begun a little later; Peter Parler subsequently added a magnificent choir. With its radiating chapels illuminated by elaborately traced windows it is one of the loveliest churches in Bohemia. The town once housed one of the largest Jewish communities in the land. Today, the only traces of Kolín's former ghetto are a semi-ruined **synagogue** and a medieval **cemetery**.

In 1757 Kolín was the site of a major battle in which the imperial forces, under Field Marshal von Daun, defeated the army of Frederick the Great, forcing the Prussians to withdraw from Bohemia.

Each June a rousing **brass band festival** is held in memory of František Kmoch, a composer who was a native son of the city; brass bands from all over the world are invited to take part.

Further down the Labe lies the spa town of **Lázně Poděbrady** (Bad Podiebrad), whose most valuable asset is the iron-rich mineral spring discovered at the beginning of this century. The spa subsequently became famous for the treatment of cardio-vascular complaints.

Renowned, too, is the Bohemian **lead crystal** from the glass foundries of Poděbrady. The town's other claim to fame is as the birthplace of its namesake, the first Hussite king of the Bohemians, George of Poděbrady, who was born in the castle in 1420.

Following the E67 in an easterly direction, you will see the Gothic castle of **Karlova Koruna** (Charles' Crown) in the little town of **Chlumec nad Cidlinou**; it is the work of the Italian architect Giovanni Santini. Chlumec went down in history as a centre of the Peasants' Revolt, which occurred here in 1775. A memorial some way outside the town bearing the popular Czech proverb "Fallen like a Peasant at Chlumec" recalls their defeat.

Continuing eastwards, the route passes the pretty little castle of **Hrádek u Nechanice**, which lies a few miles north of the E67.

Hradec Králové (Königsgrätz) grew up on the site of a prehistoric settlement at the confluence of the Labe and the Orlice. During the 14th century it be-

On the stud farm in Kladruby.

came the dowager property of the queens of Bohemia. Dating from this period is the brick Gothic **Cathedral of the Holy Ghost** (sv. Ducha), which in 1424 served as the temporary burial place of the Hussite leader Jan Žižka. As a centre of the reform movement, two years after the Battle of Lipany, in which the Hussites were defeated, the town was bold enough to defy Emperor Sigismund. The **White Tower** (Bílá vêz), which has the second-largest bell in Bohemia, the baroque **Church of St Mary**, the Jesuit College and the **Bishop's Palace** all date from the 16th century.

Northwest of Hradec lies the dreamy little town of **Chlum**, best known for the battle fought here in 1866 in which the Prussians defeated the Austrians and their Saxon allies. The 300 graves scattered between the villages of **Hořiněves**, **Číštěves** and **Sadová** are a moving legacy of the battle. On a mound near Chlum is a neo-Gothic charnel house and a memorial to the fallen.

The second most important town in Eastern Bohemia, and for many years

the rival of Hradec Králové, is **Pardubice**. The Renaissance-style town centre reflects its Golden Age under the aristocratic Pernštejn family. Among the many architectural attractions of the town are the late-Gothic **Green Gate**, the Church of St Bartholomew and the Church of the Annunciation. The **castle** was originally built for defensive purposes and later converted into a palace; it now houses the collection of the **North Bohemian Gallery**.

Today, Pardubice is a modern town with an excellent university for students of chemistry and technology. Nearby is the **Semtín chemical plant**, which produces the explosive Semtex. The main local event is the annual **steeplechase** held in Pardubice for the first time in 1874 (*see page 236*). Also in the immediate vicinity lies **Kladruby** – location of a famous **stud farm** where Spanish and Italian throroughbreds, the so-called Kladruby Greys, are bred and reared. In the mid-16th century the first horses were supplied for the Pernštejns' estate by Emperor Maximilian II.

The little wooden church at Slavanov near Nachod.

South of Pardubice, the countryside becomes more varied, with dense forests covering the hills. Every July the town of **Chrudim** attracts puppeteers from all over the world, who come for the **Marionette Festival** (Loutkarská Chrudim). The **Museum of Puppets** occupies the former Soap Boilers' House – a magnificent Renaissance building, despite its prosaic name.

The Renaissance castle in **Slatiňany**, a few miles further south, contains a remarkable gallery of paintings, engravings and sculptures on the subject of horse breeding.

The idyllic artificial lake of **Seč** in the upper reaches of the Chrudimka is surrounded by hills. The scenic beauty of the region has been protected by the designation of nature conservation areas, such as that surrounding **Polom**, which retains the essential character of the primeval forests which once covered the area. Also typical is the rural architecture, examples of which are displayed in the **Vysočina Open-Air Museum** west of **Hlinsko**.

To the east of Chrudim, passing through a varied hilly landscape, the route leads to **Vysoké Mýto** (Hohenmauth), a romantic little town still bearing traces of the original grid pattern (around the market place) as well as three 13th-century town gates.

Further along the E442 is **Litomyšl** (Leitomischl). For centuries this town has been a trading and cultural centre, and has played a dominant role in the Czech national revival during the last 200 years. Today, a **Renaissance castle** stands on the site of the former fortress. This was one of the many magnificent residences of the Pernštejns, who even installed a theatre within its walls. Also of interest in Litomyšl is the **Presbytery Church**, the **college**, the **Piarist Church** and the main square. The latter is bordered by stately baroque, Renaissance and empire-style buildings and was once one of the main centres on the trading route from Bohemia to Moravia.

Although the town has lost much of its historical, economic and social significance, it still retains some of its former glamour. Famous musicians and guests from all over the world flock here each year for the **Festival of Opera and Classical Music**, for Litomyšl was the birthplace of Bedřich Smetana. The brewery houses a museum of Czech music and a special exhibition illustrating the life and works of the renowned 19th-century composer.

The local regional centre of **Svitavy** (Zwittau) lies to the southeast of Litomyšl. Of the villages in the vicinity **Moravská Třebová** is of particular interest. It has a magnificent Renaissance-style town hall, an imposing fortress and a palace.

The Sázava Valley towards Brno: There is a motorway linking Brno (Brünn) with Prague, but travellers who prefer a more leisurely pace, or who like to travel by train, are recommended to follow the alternative route along the thickly forested **Sázava Valley**. Further downstream the river is tamed by a number of locks. In the upper reaches, however, particularly the section between **Světlá** and **Ledeč**, it finds its own way, tumbling from rapid to rapid.

The writer **Jaroslav Hašek**, author of *The Good Soldier Schweik*, lived and died in the shadow of the fortress in **Lipnice nad Sázavou**, to the west of Deutsch-Brod. He was buried in the local cemetery and his house has been turned into a fascinating memorial museum. Within the castle itself there is an informative exhibition dedicated to the author's life and work.

The little villages surrounding **Havlíčkův Brod** (Deutsch-Brod) are the home of glass-blowers and miners. It is a poor but attractive region. The town itself was rechristened in 1945 after the Czech poet and satirist Karel Havlíček Borovský; the old name, however, recalls the German miners who settled by this ford (*Brod*) from the 13th century. A fine portal of the Gothic **Church of the Assumption** still stands. The baroque church of the Holy Family (*svaté Rodiny*), some fine townhouses dating from the same period, and the rococo facade of the Krenovský dům set the tone of the Old Town. One bizarre touch is the skeleton which adorns the tower of the town hall.

BRNO

Brno (Brünn), the capital of Moravia, nestles in attractive rural surroundings at the confluence of the Svratka and the Svitava rivers. Over 30,000 years ago, settlers of the Aurignacian culture made their home in this congenial place, and a few centuries before the dawn of the Christian era, Celtic tribesmen founded a town here, which they called Brynn. The Slavs, who arrived here in the 6th century, changed the name to Brno; in about 800 they built a fortress on Mount Petrov. The earliest documented records of the castle date from the 11th century, when it is cited as the seat of a margrave of Moravia.

The stronghold guarded the crossroads of the trading routes to the Baltic and the Black Sea. A flourishing community soon grew up in its protective shadow, expanding during the 12th and 13th century due to the influx of new citizens from Germany. In 1243 it was granted a municipal charter by Wenceslas I. The town's importance grew considerably under Charles IV; from 1350, the Moravian provincial parliament met here and local assizes were held. It was not until 1462, however, that Brno was finally proclaimed the capital of Moravia in place of Olomouc (Olmütz). Charles IV issued a decree that all traders following the royal route from Austria to Poland via Moravia had to stop in the town and offer their wares for sale. This encouraged science and the arts to flourish too, a trend most strongly reflected in the foundation of new monasteries.

First textile factories: Cloth manufacturers set up factories in Brno towards the end of the 18th century. Sheep farming flourished in the surrounding grazing land, providing the raw materials. The fast-flowing rivers and local coal deposits provided the energy. Soon cloth woven in Brno penetrated the important markets of the Habsburg empire and even established itself in Western Europe in competition with fabrics produced in England. Before long, Brno was being described as "the Manchester of Moravia".

The demolition of the town fortifications during the 18th century provided space for a major rebuilding scheme including generously laid-out parks and boulevards. The architects Adolf Loos and Bohuslav Fuchs (the founder of Czech functionalism) were responsible for shaping the town's modern configuration. The best examples are found in the gracious 19th-century residential districts outside the park belt. The **Villa Tugendhat** in the Černá pole district was built in 1930 to designs by Ludwig Mies van der Rohe. In 1928 an exhibition of contemporary art and culture in the Pisárky district received attention from the international press. The exhibition halls erected for this event today form the centre of the **International Trades Fair Complex**, which hosts the International Machine Fair in autumn and the International Consumer Goods Fair in spring. Brno has emerged as a major centre of the machine building and electronics industries as well as textiles, and these fairs are very important for the country's exports.

The Old Town: The site of the original Slavic fortress is occupied by **St Peter's Cathedral** (Dóm na Petrově). Built in the high-Gothic style, the cathedral suffered severe damage when the town was besieged by the Swedish army during the Thirty Years' War. During the 18th century it was renovated in baroque style. At the beginning of the 20th century it was renovated again, this time in neo-Gothic style, and acquired twin towers. The cathedral contains a number of notable frescoes and sculptures, including the massive Gothic sculpture, the *Madonna with Child.*

One particularly interesting detail is the exterior pulpit on the north side of the church. From here, in the 15th century, the Italian Franciscan monk John of Capestrano harangued the faithful gathered in the square below. Visitors may wonder why the church bells are rung twice daily – at 11am and again at noon. It is a tradition dating from 1645, when the Swedish troops under General Linart Torstenson laid siege to Brno.

Brno

160 m / 0.1 miles

Grohova

Gorkého

Veveří

Antonínská

Mežírka

Lidická

Hotel
Continental

Obránců míru

Church of
St Thomas

Jaselská

Marešova

9. Května

Church of
St James

Gorazdova

Solniční

Česká

Veselá

Folklore
Museum

Udolní

Husova

Hotel
International

nám.
Svobody

Úvoz

Špielberk

New
Town Hall

Dominican Church
of St Michael

Panská

Dominikánská

Mečová

Old
Town Hall

Masař

Pellicova

Parnassus
Fountain

Pekařská

Kopečná

Petrská

Redo

Anenská

Moravian
Museum

St Peter's
Cathedral

Bašty

Husova

Kopečná

Vodní

Hybešova

Nové sady

Václavská

The leader of the army had sworn he would scale the town walls by noon, or else withdraw. Hearing of this, the beleaguered citizens, no longer able to resist the force of the Swedish attack, had the bells of St Peter's chime 12 o'clock when it was only 11am. The town was saved in the nick of time.

The winding Peterská ul. (St Peter's Street) leads down to the secular centre of the old town, the former **Herb Market** (Horni trh), dominated by the **Trinity Column**. The market square is always an animated spot, with stalls and stands grouped around the elaborate **Fountain of Parnassus**, a baroque fantasy of mythical figures and allegorical representations of the four seasons.

At the point where the Peterská ul. opens onto the square, the most striking complex is the **Museum of Moravia** (Moravskémuzeum), housed in a succession of medieval palazzi. The famous **Venus of Věstonice**, at 30,000 years the oldest extant Stone Age clay figure, forms the *pièce de résistance* of a comprehensive archaeological and scientific exhibition. Also worth a visit is the art gallery, containing works by Rubens and Cranach as well as Moravian painters from the 15th century to the present day. In the southeast corner lies the Reduta, opened in 1670 and thus the oldest theatre in the town.

In the north, only a few steps away along the Radnická ul., stands the oldest secular monument in Brno, the **Old Town Hall**. Dating from the 13th century, it is famous for the entrance designed by the master builder Antonín Pilgram. The Town Council held its meetings here until the end of World War II. Guarding the passage through to the courtyard is the **Dragon of Brno**, which according to local legend once gobbled up all the virgins in the city. In fact, the creature is a stuffed alligator, presented by a passing group of Turkish jugglers to Archduke Matthias, who visited Brno in 1608 to drum up support for a conspiracy against his brother, the Emperor Rudolf II. Before leaving he decided to donate the creature to the city fathers, who displayed it in a place of honour in front of the Town Hall.

Following the Mecova ul. the visitor reaches the former fish market. Here stands the baroque **Dominican Church**; the former monastery next door has served since 1945 as the New Town Hall. The Renaissance building erected above the cloister was used as long ago as 1582 as the assembly hall for the Moravian estates.

Further to the north, surrounding the Nám. Svobody (Freedom Square), lies the **Lower City**. The square served as the lower market place of the medieval town, but all that remains from this period is the former merchant's residence in the southwest corner. It dates from 1596 and has a fine entrance and inner courtyard.

The **Church of St James** (Chrám sv. Jakuba) was rebuilt following a devastating fire during the 15th century. Under the window on the south face of the high tower, Antonín Pilgram placed a little manikin who points his naked backside at the cathedral – the church of the wealthy inhabitants of the Upper Town – embracing a pretty girl as he does so.

Continuing in an easterly direction, the route passes the Jesuit church, dedicated in 1734 and regarded as the finest baroque church in town, before reaching the ring of parkland. To the left stands the contemporary **Janáček Opera House and Ballet Theatre**, to the right the Mahen Theatre, built over a century ago in the style of the French Renaissance and famous as the first stage in Europe to be lit by electric light. Behind stands the lovely **Artists' House**, built in 1911.

Špilberk Castle, dominating the town from a high plateau, is the most conspicuous landmark. It was built about 1270 on the instructions of King Otakar Přemysl II because he thought the old Slavic stronghold on Mount Petrov provided insufficient protection. By the time the Swedish army began its memorable siege during the Thirty Years' War, Italian military architects had transformed it into a virtually impregnable citadel. It withstood attack by troops from a number of countries; in 1742, Frederick the Great failed to storm the

Brno is dominated by the Cathedral of St Peter and St Paul.

fortress, but eventually Napoleon was successful in 1809.

From the 17th century the castle was one of the most feared prisons in Europe. Among the incarcerated were unrepentant heretics, peasant revolutionaries and members of the aristocracy who had fallen into disfavour at the imperial court, such as the Croatian leader, Baron Trenck. The tolerant Emperor Joseph II had it closed in 1783, but after the French Revolution the Habsburgs reopened it, to house their many political opponents. The Italian poet Silvio Pellico, for example, spent 15 years in Spilberk.

At the foot of the fortress lies the former Augustinian monastery with the Church of the Assumption, containing a charming *pietà* ascribed to Heinrich Parler the Younger and dating from about 1385. The monastery was the home of the father of genetic science, the abbot Gregor Johann Mendel (1822–84); it was in the monastery's garden that he pursued his research into inherited characteristics in plants, especially in peas. Mendel established a tradition of education and learning in the city. Today, its six ancient establishments of higher education within the city have over 20,000 students. Viktor Kaplan, the inventor of the hydraulic turbine, lectured at the **Technical University**, and the founder of the **College of Music** was the composer Leoš Janáček. His works are the focus of the annual autumn festival of classical and contemporary music.

In the vicinity of Brno: On 2 December 1805, the armies of three emperors faced each other in the Battle of Austerlitz, 20 km (12 miles) east of Brno. The French forces under Napoleon confronted the allied regiments of Austria and Russia under Emperor Francis II and Tsar Alexander I. On **Mount Žuráň**, two trees mark the position of Napoleon's command post. From here he directed 741,000 men and 250 cannon against an army which was far superior in numbers. Some 40,000 men fell in the ensuing battle. In 1911 a monument was erected in their memory on top of the

Street scenes in Brno.

Mohyla míru Heights near the village of Prace, where the slaughter was thickest.

After his victory Napoleon set up his headquarters in the baroque **Slavkov (Austerlitz) Castle** nearby. It was here, on 6 December, that he signed the peace treaty acknowledging his supremacy as the most powerful ruler in Europe. Each year, on 2 December, the **Battlefield of Austerlitz** becomes the arena for a reconstruction of the fight. Thousands of enthusiasts flood in from France and other European countries to take part in the Battle of the Three Emperors.

The Moravian Karst: North of Brno, between **Blansko** and **Sloup**, lies the **karst region** of Moravia (Moravský Kras), a landscape of romantic gorges and some 400 caves both large and small, carved out of the solid limestone by underground rivers.

There is a spectacular view down into the **Macocha Abyss**, 138 metres (440 ft) deep. A marked footpath leads down the almost vertical walls to the twin lakes at the bottom. Those with a poor head for heights are recommended to visit the **Punkevní jeskyně Caves** by boat. The breathtaking magnificence of the vaulted roofs is heightened by the forests of stalactites and stalagmites. The largest cave is the **Kateřinská** (concerts are held here to take advantage of its acoustics). The Balcarka Caves are particularly stunning. The **Sloupsko-šošůvské jeskyně** complex, on the north-eastern edge of the karst region has been the site of a number of interesting archaeological finds; the **Kůlna cavern** bears traces of human occupation some 100,000 years ago. The settlement in the **Byčí skála** cavern dates from the Palaeolithic era, and remains of a royal burial place from the 7th–6th century BC have also been found.

Evidence of early iron smelting furnaces can be found all over the Moravian karst region. The rich iron ore deposits and the ease with which charcoal could be obtained made the area a valuable source of raw material for the armament industry. Iron tools and jewellery were manufactured here, as well as swords and armour.

The International Trade Fair complex.

MORAVIAN WINE

Although the vintners of Southern Moravia like to maintain that Noah planted the very first vine after the Flood (and thereafter drank wine for 300 years, thus providing incontestable proof of wine's beneficial effect on health), it seems likely that grapevines were brought to Moravia by the ancient Romans. By the time the Kingdom of Greater Moravia was established, wine was certainly produced in the region. Excavations of settlements dating from this period have revealed evidence of grapes, so wine production in Moravia must be at least 1,100 years old.

The vine-growing regions of Southern Moravia extend over an area of more than 26,000 hectares (65,000 acres). They lie at the northern limits of the wine-producing area of Central Europe. Moravia has neither the intense sunshine of Dalmatia nor the tranquil and humid climate of the Moselle or Rhine valleys. For this reason, vines are grown only on south-facing slopes in hilly districts protected from frost and wind, and predominantly on dry, sandy soils. Despite these limitations, Southern Moravia produces light wines which are often sweeter than those from the famous wine-producing areas of France.

Among the Southern Moravian vintners, a deeply rooted tradition of professional integrity and diligence are passed on from generation to generation. During the first weeks after the grape harvest, the cellarmen supervise the process of maturation until the *burcák*, the new wine, is ready. It is allowed to "cook", as this process is known, for only a couple of hours before the vintners themselves drink a good litre of it each, on the pretext that it will cleanse their blood and provide them with the life-giving energy of the soil and the sun.

Months will pass by before the wine has settled in the barrels and it is time to taste it. Unless a vintner decides to treat a novice to his "three-man wine" – allegedly, one person actually drinks the wine while the other two have to hold him firmly to stop him from falling over – a wine tasting is a dignified procedure. "Remember it's not water!" scold the vintners when visitors drink too quickly. Before taking the first little sip one should appreciate the colour and savour the bouquet. After the first reaction to the unexpected sharpness, let the full taste slowly develop on the tongue. The entire procedure is repeated several times standing in front of a number of barrels, until the preferred wine is determined.

Two of the oldest and most famous wine cellars are Valtice and Prímetice, near Znojmo. Both were established during the baroque era and have magnificent cross vaulting. The arches were built so wide that the lord of the manor could drive through in his coach and even turn round. Another impressive cellar is in Satov, which is also near Znojmo; its walls are adorned with some amusing frescoes.

During the 16th century the Archbishop of Olomouc received his supplies of red wine from the village of Pavlov near Mikulov. And for many years the wine served in the Town Hall cellars in Vienna came from the community of Satov. Jan Amos Komensky (Comenius) was a guest in Blatnice, and even Napoleon was a fan of Archlebov wine; he celebrated his famous victory at Austerlitz with a Southern Moravian vintage. ∎

Grape-picking in Southern Moravia.

249

SOUTHERN MORAVIA

There are a number of routes from Brno into the rural heart of Southern Moravia. The tour described here runs in a clockwise direction around the region. It starts by taking the E461, which leads due south from Brno towards the Austrian border, following the Svratka to the lower reaches of the River Dyje (Thaya). The rolling landscape here is reminiscent of parts of Italy; to the south rise the **Pavlovské vrchy Mountains**, with Devon limestone cliffs and the **Pálava Nature Reserve**, famous for its rare steppe flora. In times gone by the silhouette of the Pavlovské vrchy served as a landmark for merchants; today, it is reflected in the waters of the **Nové Mlýny reservoir**.

Just to the north of the Austrian border, in a vine-growing area, is **Mikulov** (Nikolsburg). Since the 16th century this pretty little town has been connected with the name of the dukes of Dietrichstein-Mensdorff. Their castle, dating from medieval times, was rebuilt on a number of occasions and ended up as a baroque palace. One of the main attractions here is the so-called "tenner" barrel dating from 1643, which has a capacity of 1,010 litres (270 gallons). Mikulov has preserved a large number of features from the past. An old synagogue in the oriental style demonstrates the importance of the local Jewish community. The lovely **Chapel of St Sebastian**, on the Svatý Kopeček, the Holy Mountain, dominates the scene.

The castle in **Lednice**, a few miles to the east on the River Dyje, is visited by up to half a million tourists each year. It was built in the English Gothic style and is surrounded by an attractive landscaped park. Also of interest are the cast-iron framed greenhouses dating from 1834, the 60-metre (190-ft) **minaret**, replicas of historic churches and the **Janohrad**, an artificial ruin. Further south, the little town of **Veltice** has a well-known vintners' school, and the 17th-century palace of the Dukes of Liechtenstein, which is famous for its wine cellars. Also well worth visiting is the parish Church of the Assumption, whose altarpiece of the Holy Trinity is a Rubens original.

To the south of **Břeclav** (Lundenburg), an important railway junction, excavations have revealed a vast Old Slavic defensive settlement which was an important centre of the Kingdom of Great Moravia. The **archaeological museum** here merits a visit.

Southwest of Brno: The little town of **Ivančice** was the birthplace of the famous art nouveau painter Alfons Mucha. Although he spent much of his life in France, in nearby **Moravský Krumlov**, Mucha reveals to what extent he remained faithful to his Czech homeland. His famous *Slovanská epopej* – 20 vast canvasses depicting themes based on Slavic history and mythology – is exhibited in the **Knights' Hall** of the Renaissance castle.

The road rejoins the River Dyje as it irrigates the fertile Znojmo plain to the southwest of Brno. The main crops in the valley are fruit and vegetables; the slopes are reserved for the production of fine wines. The town of **Znojmo** (Znaim) was the first community in Moravia to receive its town charter, in 1226. It has successfully preserved its medieval character over the succeeding centuries. The city walls still stand, along with numerous houses and churches from the Gothic, Renaissance and baroque eras. Beneath the market place (Nám. Míru) there is a vast cellar for the storage of wine; the square itself is dominated by the fine Gothic tower – all that remained of the Town Hall at the end of World War II. The **castle** occupies the site of a former 11th-century border fortress dating from the Přemyslid kingdom. It now houses the **Museum of Southern Moravia**. The Romanesque **round church of St Catherine** contains a series of wall paintings dating form the early 12th century.

After the end of the Cold War the magnificent tract of land on the banks of the Dyje was deemed worthy of official protection as a joint Austrian–Czechoslovakian national park. Numerous footpaths and tracks lead through the Dyje valley, and the region is quite a paradise for nature lovers, anglers and walkers.

The Upper Dyje Valley: Further upstream, the Dyje has been dammed to create a vast reservoir. One mile from the barrier itself, perched on a crag above **Vranov nad Dyjí**, stands the magnificent **Castle of Frain**. Originally built as a fortress, it was later converted into a splendid baroque residence. It is worth joining a tour just to see the splendid baroque **Ancestral Hall**, not to mention the castle chapel and the lovely audience rooms. The whole building has been wonderfully restored.

A fine castle stands sentinel over the little town of **Jaroměřice** (Jarmeritz), equally famous for its lovely bridge across the River Rokytná. The castle includes its own theatre, in which the premiere of the first Czech opera, *L'origine de Jarmeritz en Moravie* (The History of the Town of Jarmeritz in Moravia) was performed in 1730. The work was composed by František Václav Miča, a valet who had been commissioned by the lord of the castle to assemble a servants' orchestra. He even arranged a number of ambitious productions of Italian operas. The tradition is perpetuated to this day in the **annual festival of classical music** held in Jaroměřice each summer, when the extensive castle grounds and the pretty little town are thronging with international visitors.

West of Brno: Třebíč (Trebitsch) is known primarily as an industrial town, but its **Basilica of St Procop**, dating from the 13th century, is well worth a visit. The triple-naved building is the most important example of the transition from Romanesque to Gothic architecture within the lands of the Bohemian crown. The basilica forms part of a monastery, in which the **Abbot's Chapel** also contains a magnificent series of 13th-century wall paintings. Part of the monastery was converted into a palace during the Renaissance period. Today it houses the **Museum of Western Moravia**, including unusual collections such as a picturesque selection of crib figures.

In the town centre, only a handful of

Market place with fountain in the romantic border town of Slavonice.

254

houses and doorways remain from the Gothic era; a hint of the Renaissance is visible in the gables of the monumental townhouses. The **Malovaný dům** was adorned with sgraffito by the Venetian merchant Francesco Calliardo; the Black House, dating from 1637, bears an allegorical depiction of Virtue, and many other buildings display fine decorative features.

Nestling amidst woodland close to **Náměšť nad Oslavou**, a charming little town west of Brno, lies a vast **Renaissance castle** which served Tomáš Garrigue Masaryk (first president of the Czechoslovak Republic in 1918) as a summer residence. Today a precious collection of Gobelin tapestries is displayed here.

In the neighbouring village of **Kralice nad Oslavou** there is a memorial museum dedicated to the *Kralická bible*, the Czech Bible, produced between 1579 and 1593. The bible is linked with the Community of the Moravian Brethren, who were known as religious reformers in Bohemia during the Middle Ages.

Telč (Teltsch) is undoubtedly one of the most beautiful towns in the whole Czech Republic. Dating from the 16th century, the central square is surrounded by historic houses linked by continuous arcades. After the Great Fire of 1530, the entire town was rebuilt in a unified Renaissance style. The region was originally covered by marshes, but during the 12th century the founding fathers of the city had these drained. By the beginning of the 14th century Telč had been awarded royal privileges; still standing within the old town centre are various late-Gothic gateways and a large number of fine old houses which date from this period. Most important among the town's religious buildings is the **Church of the Assumption**, built during the 15th century.

The sprawling **Renaissance palace** stands immediately next to the market place. It was built to replace the original fortress at the end of the 16th century, at the behest of the lords of Hradec, who were inspired by their frequent trips to sunny Italy. They added columned ar-

Southern Moravian costume.

cades, audience rooms with statues, paintings and stuccoed walls and ceilings in imitation of the Italian buildings they admired.

Visitors approaching via the Prague motorway, or planning to return to the capital by the same route, should make a point of breaking their journey in **Jihlava** (Iglau). The town was founded in 799 on a former trading route; it rose to prosperity during the 13th century when extensive silver ore deposits were discovered in the vicinity. In 1249 the town received its charter; 20 years later the citizens were awarded staple rights and permission to mint their own coins. In the **Court of Appeal of Iglau**, the ultimate authority in mining law for the entire Holy Roman Empire, cases were tried according to the Iglau Mining Laws, which were regarded as binding in many parts of the world even centuries later.

When silver mining was abandoned some 300 years later, cloth production, a complex industry introduced by Flemish weavers and dyers, became the principal driving force behind the town's economy. Jihlava is, however, particularly proud of its reputation as a centre of the arts. Its most famous native son is the composer Gustav Mahler (1860–1911), although he spent much of his life in Vienna.

Remains of the town walls, and the Náměsti Míru, whose area of 3,700 sq. metres (almost an acre) makes it the largest town square in Central Europe, bear witness to the town's historical importance. On the east side of the square, bordered by townhouses with painted arcades, stands the **Town Hall**. Dating from 1426, it provides access to the catacombs, constructed during the Middle Ages as storerooms and defensive passages. The previously mentioned miners' court met in the corner house, and the mint was housed in the building opposite. Also on this square was the headquarters of the clothmakers' guild; it now serves as a museum.

The parish **Church of St James** is the real jewel among an array of interesting churches. Begun in 1257, the building was completed at the end of the 14th century. Dating from the same period is the exquisite statue of St Catherine.

The Bohemian–Moravian Mountains: North of the motorway from Prague to Brno extend the Bohemian–Moravian Mountains. It is a landscape of wooded slopes reflected in the waters of countless lakes. Those who follow the route from Prague along the Sázava Valley (*see preceding chapter*) will pass through Deutsch-Brod before coming to **Žďár nad Sázavou**. The town serves as the starting point for a visit to the **Zdarské vrchy Nature Reserve** on the crest of the Bohemian–Moravian ridge. Here the visitor will find expanses of primeval forest, Ice Age peat moors and more than 280 lakes both large and small. In this remote region you will find the last evidence of many of the country's oldest and most interesting traditions, and in the villages the old wooden farmhouses, the so-called *dřevěnice*, can still be seen. On **Mount Žákova** 785 metres/ 2,512 ft), by the source of the Svratka, the local inhabitants welcome spring by ceremoniously opening the well. The associated celebrations are a delight.

Following a branch line of the rail link to Brno, the traveller comes to **Nové Město na Moravě**, famous for the **Horácké Museum** and its 16th-century castle. The town is a good base for walking expeditions through the mountains, which have been the setting for world championship skiing.

The enchanting **Pernštejn Castle** perches above the **Nedvědička Valley**. The massive walls have survived the march of time remarkably well. The old stonework, untouched rural surroundings and relative lack of tourists combine to produce an truly romantic atmosphere. However, you may find your visit coincides with that of film crews and production teams, for the castle provides an authentic setting for cloak-and-dagger films and popular fairy tales.

Visitors should also visit the **Porta Coeli** (Gate of Heaven) monastery in **Předklášterí** near Tišnov, a few miles before Brno. Founded in 1233, the complex includes a majestic church with a cross vaulted roof. The cloisters and the chapter house are among the finest works of Gothic architecture in Moravia.

Pernštejn, one of the largest and best-preserved castles in the Czech Republic.

NORTHERN MORAVIA

Northern Moravia has two million inhabitants, virtually all of whom are concentrated in the two conurbations around Olomouc and Ostrava; the remaining regions are rural in nature and sparsely populated. In the south lies the fertile Haná plain (Hannakei), with Olomouc at its centre. Passing through the Moravská brána, the Moravian Gate, the traveller reaches the northeastern industrial area centred upon Ostrava. To the north, the Jeseníky Mountains form a natural boundary; in the southeast the Moravian and Silesian sections of the Beskid Mountains separate the region from Slovakia.

Olomouc: The town of **Olomouc** (Olmütz) has a long and colourful history. The first written references to this settlement in the shadow of a Slavic fortress were in 1055. Eight years later, Olomouc was elevated to the rank of diocesan town. Its spiritual rulers awarded the community municipal and staple rights and encouraged the diligent Premonstratensian order to settle here along with German craftsmen and merchants, so that the town soon became the capital of Moravia. It was occupied for a number of years by Swedish troops during the Thirty Years' War, an event which was to mark the beginning of the town's slow decline. Brno, its rival in Southern Moravia, then became the provincial capital; in 1778 the university was also transferred there. Olomouc remained stuck with its reputation as a bastion of Catholicism loyal to the ruling Habsburgs, surrounded by an increasingly rebellious hinterland. For this reason the town was often referred to as the Salzburg of Moravia.

This may explain why so many historic buildings have survived in the **Old Town**. On the Náměstí Míru, the former Upper Square, the most conspicuous is the magnificent **Town Hall**. To the former town clerk's office were added a splendid banqueting hall and the late-Gothic **Chapel of St Jerome**; during the Renaissance came the elaborately decorated external staircase and the loggia. A particular attraction is the **astronomical clock** dating from 1422, whose figures move in a similar manner to the apostles on the town hall clock in Prague. Characteristic of the area is the massive 18th-century **Trinity Column**.

Half a dozen baroque fountains grace the Old Town. Two of them stand on the **Square of Peace**; others are to be found on the Lower Ring, immediately adjacent to the south side of the square, and to the north, on the square in front of the **Church of St Maurice**. Construction of the latter, a hall church housing a fine baroque organ, began in 1412; it was the place of worship of the ordinary citizens. The episcopal church was the **St Wenceslas Cathedral**, which dates from 1107, and which later acquired a 13th-century Gothic cloister that was decorated with a fine series of murals in about 1500. The **cathedral treasury** can be viewed in the crypt.

Litovel (Littau), to the northwest of Olomouc, is nicknamed the "Venice of the Hannakei". It is a pretty little town

spread across the six arms of the River Morava. Its principal historic monuments include a Gothic chapel, St Mark's Church and the **Plague Column** erected in 1724. There is an interesting local museum with displays of traditional folk costumes and prehistoric archaeological finds. Worth visiting in the hills to the west of the town is the 13th-century **Bouzov (Busau) Castle**. After suffering extensive damage during the Thirty Years' War, in 1696 the fortress and the attached estates were taken over by the Teutonic Order, which had the building converted into a magnificent palace early this century. The caves of **Javoříčko** also attract visitors to the area.

The Jeseníky Mountains, to which the town of **Šumperk** serves as gateway, are rich in scenic beauty. A little further north lies the spa town of **Velké Losiny**, scene of one of the last witchcraft trials in Europe; an exhibition of instruments of torture recalls the fateful event. The best base for a tour of the region is without doubt the spa town of **Karlova Studánka**, to the east. From here you can follow a variety of walking routes into the mountains. Particularly rewarding, if testing, is the path leading to the summit of the **Praděd**, the highest peak in the Jeseníky Mountains 1,491 metres (4,771 ft): the view stretches right across into neighbouring Poland. Another interesting path on the other side leads towards **Petrovy kameny**, and passes the scene of the Witches' Sabbath of Walpurgis Night – that is, if you believe the popular legend.

Through the Moravian Gate: Lipník nad Bečvou, to the east of Olomouc, has preserved its medieval town centre and 15th-century fortifications. Also of interest here are the Renaissance castle and the Gothic church, which was rebuilt during the Renaissance and the baroque periods.

A footpath leads from the town along the far bank of the River Becva to the 13th-century **Helfsteyn Castle**, one of the most imposing ruins in the country. Fencing displays, performed in costume, are frequently held in the castle courtyard. A few miles south of Hranice lies

Fine oriel windows in Olomouc (Olmütz).

the spa of Teplice nad Bečvou. The town is popular not so much for the rather stale-tasting warm water produced by its springs as for the **Zbrasovské aragonitové jeskyně caves**, which contain mighty stalactites and miniature lakes, emitting mysterious vapours.

Fulnek is worth visiting for its castle, built in a mixture of baroque and Renaissance styles. It is also the site of the monument to Jan Amos Komenský, better known to foreigners under his Latin name, Comenius, who lived here from 1618 to 1621.

Shortly before Opava lies the lovely palace of **Hradec nad Moravicí** (Grätz), built on the site of a 10th-century Slavic fort. Following a devastating fire, the complex was rebuilt in the empire style and subsequently rechristened The White Castle. Great composers such as Paganini and Franz Liszt stayed here at the invitation of the music-loving Prince Lichnowsky. The **Beethoven Weeks** commemorate two visits by the German master in 1806.

The name of **Opava** first cropped up in records in the 12th century. The town was the capital of the German-settled Silesian duchy of Troppau from the 13th century right up to 1918. Among the town's sights are the remains of the former town wall and the Gothic churches of St Mary, the Holy Ghost and St John. From 1618, the tower on the so-called Butterfly House (Schmetterlingshaus) was where travelling merchants stopped with their wares, which they were required to offer for sale for a period of three days. The entrepreneurial spirit of Opava has been maintained to this day; it is regarded as a model for the development of privatisation within the newly capitalist Czech Republic. Because of its German roots, many of the inhabitants still have relatives or other contacts in Germany.

Ostrava, with 350,000 inhabitants, is the third largest town in today's Czech Republic, but its history reaches back into the mists of time. Traces of a camp left by mammoth hunters have been discovered on Landek Hill. However, its turbulent modern history began at

View from the garden of Hradec nad Moravicí (Grätz Palace), in which Beethoven often stayed.

the beginning of the last century, when extensive coal deposits were discovered. This led to a massive boom in the town, which became the centre of iron and steel smelting and heavy industry. Since then, Ostrava has been the privileged bearer of the ambiguous nickname "the steel heart of the Republic".

Other industrial towns sprang up around Ostrava. Pitheads and vast factory complexes scar the landscape and noxious smoke, rarely filtered, belches forth into a leaden sky, casting a grey veil across what was once attractive foothill scenery.

The monuments worth seeing, such as the 17th-century Town Hall on **Masaryk Square**, a little wooden church in **Ostrava Hrabová** dating from the 16th century, and the Renaissance palace surrounded by a magnificent park in **Karviná**, struggle bravely to maintain their attractions in the face of this perpetual pollution

In the Beskid foothills, on both banks of the River Ostravice, lies the twin town of **Frydek-Místek**. It was founded in the 13th century as a Moravian border town. Its main attraction is a castle rebuilt in the baroque style.

The Beskids: The little town of **Hukvaldy**, with a wildlife park and shady avenues of chestnut trees, lies on the northern slopes of the Beskid Mountains in the shadow of a romantic ruined castle. The Czech composer Leoš Janáček (1854–1928) was born here.

Worth visiting nearby for its Gothic church and the well preserved Renaissance buildings surrounding the market place is **Příbor**, the town where Sigmund Freud first saw the light of day.

Only a few miles to the south lies **Štramberk**, overshadowed by the tower of a medieval castle which looks more like a mosque. The town itself is one of the loveliest in the entire country, a maze of winding narrow streets. The local culinary speciality are the delicately spiced, cone-shaped waffles known as *štramberské uši* (Stramberg Ears). The name is believed to relate to a period when the town was overrun by the Tartars. The neighbouring town of

Štramberk in the Moravian–Silesian Beskids.

Kopřivnice is famous as the home of the Tatra car production plant. Further to the West, **Nový Jičín** is a Gothic jewel with historic townhouses, a Gothic church and a castle.

The **Beskid Mountains** of Moravia and Silesia form a natural boundary to the Slovakian Republic. **Valašsko** (Wallachia) lies in the Western Beskids – without doubt one of the most fascinating regions in the Czech Republic, especially for authentic folklore (a far cry from the performances offered in restaurants and nightclubs). Old customs are still treasured and the local people are welcoming. For sports enthusiasts the Beskids offer a wide range of activities throughout the year, from mountain walks in summer to ski tours and downhill skiing in winter.

The town of **Rožnov pod Radhoštěm** provides an excellent base from which to explore. In the **Open-Air Museum of Wallachia** you can witness life as it used to be lived all over this part of the country, and hear the tinkling bells of the traditional horse-drawn carriages and the strains of dulcimer and violin playing the folk music of Wallachia. The buildings which comprise the park were removed from their sites in the immediate vicinity and rebuilt within the museum park. Later on, perfect replicas of other houses were added. In this way an entire little town of wooden buildings has been recreated, complete with a pretty church where services are held. The inn Na posledním groši serves good, satisfying meals.

The newest section of the park includes a water-driven sawmill, a water mill and a smithy which echo to the sounds of paddle wheel, saw and hammer. The weekends are devoted to traditional customs. Music and dancing are performed by people in local costumes, and traditional crafts, from wood carving to pottery, are offered for sale.

From the nearby Ráztoka Valley it is possible to take a chair lift to the summit of the **Pustevny** (1,018 metres/3,340 ft), a local mountain whose flanks are dotted with typical Wallachian wooden houses and a number of mountain ho-

Relaxing at day's end.

tels. It is worth taking the hour-long ridge walk to the **Radhošt'** (1,129 metres/3,613 ft), which is dominated by a majestic statue of the Slavic god Radegast. According to legend, those who touch the statue's stomach are bound to return here one day.

The castle in the regional centre of **Vsetín** in the Bečva Valley houses an exhibition portraying the customs and traditions of the area. Within easy reach to the southeast lies the winter sports and mountain walking paradise of **Soláň**. Equally attractive are the idyllic hamlets and wooden mountain huts. Sheep graze on the mountain slopes, and horses and oxen still draw the ploughs.

The **Lysá hora** (1,324 metres/4,237 ft) is the highest peak in the Beskids. It lies to the east and can be scaled easily from the little town of **Ostravice**. The ascent, which takes several hours, is amply rewarded by the enchanting view. On a clear day you can see the peaks of the **Malá Fatra**, the Lesser Fatra range in Slovakia. During the winter months, Lysá hora is a mecca for both downhill

and cross-country skiing enthusiasts.

Further to the east lie the remote mountain villages of **Dolni** and **Horní Lomná** – as yet an undiscovered part of Moravia. Both communities are famous for their folklore festivals. The high-altitude valley, enclosed on three sides, preserves its primeval forests in the form of a nature reserve.

Another centre of the Valašsko is the little town of **Vizovice**. The romantic castle, built on the site of a 13th-century monastery, contains an art gallery with works by Dutch, Italian and French masters; there is also a collection of fine china. Vizovice is famous for its distillery, which produces the plum schnapps *slivovice* (Slivovitz). At harvest time – and at other seasons of the year – the town holds colourful and lively festivals.

Zlín is often described as a town in the country. Originally of no particular importance, it enjoyed a boom towards the end of the 19th century, when Tomáš Bat'a had the idea of producing here the *bat'ovky*, simple and inexpensive shoes made of linen. The enterprise soon ex-

The nave of the Cistercian monastery church, Velherad.

panded to become an internationally known concern. The town itself is a typical example of inter-war development, constructed in a unified, functional style. Here, great modernist architects such as Le Corbusier and Franz Gahura realised their concepts for residential and commercial districts. In 1949 the town was rechristened Gottwaldov, after the first communist president of Czechoslovakia. In 1990, after the Bat'a heirs' claims of ownership were recognised, the old name was readopted.

The spa town of **Luhačovice**, to the east of Uherské Hradiště, basks in an atmosphere of peace and relaxation. Ten mineral springs, in particular the Vincert Spring, provide relief from disorders of the upper respiratory system. The composer Leoš Janáček is among those who have come to convalesce in this romantic little town.

On the trail of Greater Moravia: In the valley of the **River Morava** (March), in the heart of Moravian Slovakia, lies the town of **Uherské Hradiště** (Hungarian Hradisch), founded in 1257 by Přemysl

Otakar II to protect the trading routes. The name indicates that it was here, on the border of Upper Hungary (most of which now lies in the region of Slovakia), that a large group of Protestant refugees from Hungary made their home. They injected fresh life into the town. The Gothic town hall, a number of lovely churches, most of them rebuilt in the baroque style, and the **apothecary** on the market place, reconstructed in the rococo idiom, all testify to Uherské Hradiště's glorious past. The town's principal attraction, however, is the Staré Město on the West Bank. It is now a suburb, but very probably was once the site of **Velehrad**, the legendary capital of the first Slavic empire within the territory which today forms the Czech and Slovak Republics.

During the 19th century, traces of an early Slavic settlement were discovered here; it was not until a systematic excavation was undertaken in 1948 that experts were able to establish with certainty that this had been an important town, if not the actual capital, of the

A happy reaper.

Kingdom of Greater Moravia. During the 9th and 10th century its rulers established close links with Byzantium and, with the help of the Slavic apostles Cyril and Methodius, began the Christianisation of Central Europe.

Supporting such an assumption are the town's location near the Moravian Gate, at the crossroads between the Amber Road, one of the most important North–South routes in Central Europe, and the East–West trading route along the Morava valley. Thousands of urn graves dating from the 6th and 7th century have already been examined. Living quarters and a two-storey cathedral have also been unearthed, and it is well known that Velehrad, with its 5-km (3-mile) fortifications, was well protected against attack from the landward side. Nonetheless, the archaeological investigations continue, and the results to date can be inspected in a new, specially created museum, the **Památnik Velké Moravy**.

The name of the capital of Greater Moravia has been preserved a few miles to the west, in the **Cistercian Monastery of Velehrad**. It was founded in 1205 by the Margrave of Moravia, a brother of the king, Přemysl Otakar I. Its basilica, completed in 1238, is dedicated to the two Slavic Apostles, Saints Cyril and Methodius. Each year, on 5 July, the joint festival of the two saints, the monastery – now used as a sanatorium – is the focus of a colourful folkloric pilgrimage.

The **Haná Plains** (the Hannakei) extend northwards towards Olomouc. The principal town is **Kroměříž** (Kremsier), which has a beautiful historic centre that has been declared a national monument. The central square, **Riegrovo náměstí**, stands on the site of an Old Slavic settlement. In 1110 the little market town passed into the possession of the bishops of Olomouc and remained with them for centuries. Even a number of short-lived occupations by the Hussites had no effect on the the town's religious orientation.

Awarded a municipal charter in 1266, the town's advantageous location on the

Kroměříž (Kremsier): the colonnade in the Bishop's Garden.

Morava trading route attracted a large number of new residents. A castle and a cathedral were built. Both the German colonists and an active Jewish community, which since the late Middle Ages had possessed its own chamber of trade and even a town hall, had an impact on the continued development. The **Church of St Maurice**, begun in the 13th century, was finished in about 1500.

In 1643, during the Thirty Years' War, the town, the castle and the cathedral were burned to the ground by invading Swedish troops, but it wasn't long after the cessation of hostilities that reconstruction began. Under the supervision of Italian architects, work commenced on the remodelling of the fortress to create a magnificent **palace** in a combined Renaissance–baroque style.

Today the visitor can inspect not only the meticulously restored apartments, but also one of the most important art collections in the country, including works by Titian, Lucas Cranach and Pieter Brueghel, among others, and *King Charles of England and Queen Henriette*, which was painted by Antony van Dyck.

A flower garden was created just outside the estate gates; it is a stunning example of baroque garden planning. The **Květná zahrada**, a public park, is an oasis of calm in this lively city. The **music festival** in August and the film festival, **Ars-Film**, which follows it, are the liveliest times to be in the city.

Following the Morava to the south of Uherské Hradiště, after 20 km (12 miles) the road comes to the little town of **Strážnice**. It's a sleepy place for most of the year, except for the end of June when it suddenly comes to life on account of the **International Folklore Festival**. Costume groups arrive from all over Europe and beyond, to take part in the singing and dancing competitions. In the castle itself there is an interesting folklore museum.

Twenty km (12 miles) further on, **Hodonin** is an industrial town that is only worth mentioning because it is the birthplace of the country's founder president, Tomáš G. Masaryk (1850–1937).

The imperial hall in Bučovice Castle.

WESTERN SLOVAKIA

Trnava (Tyrnau), a diocesan town, lies in a fertile, vine-clad valley only 45 km (28 miles) to the northeast of Bratislava. It can be reached by means of the D61 motorway as well as by train.

In 1988 the town celebrated its 750th anniversary and, in honour of the event, it received meticulous restoration. The architectural variety of Trnava reflects its significance as one of Hungary's religious and cultural centres during the long period of Turkish rule in the southern part of the country, and helps to explain why it has been dubbed "Slovakian Rome".

In 1238 Bela IV, the reigning king of Hungary, awarded the settlement its municipal and market privileges, placing it directly under the jurisdiction of the crown. The extraordinary advantages associated with its status and its favourable location at the intersection of two long-distance trade routes encouraged Trnava's rapid growth and prosperity. In 1543 the town became the religious centre of all Hungary when the Primate of the Hungarian Church, the Archbishop of Esztergom, took refuge here because his own town and most of the rest of the country had been overrun by Turks. The foundation of a university less than a century later marked the transformation of the trading centre into a cultural metropolis. The transfer of the university to Buda in 1777 and the return of the primate to Esztergom after its liberation in 1822 would have probably resulted in Trnava's sinking into provincial oblivion once more, had Slovakian intellectuals not moved the seat of the "Company of Academics" to the town in 1792. This was the most important scientific and literary association in Slovakia, which at that time was still under Hungarian rule.

Topped by its massive twin towers, the **Cathedral of St Nicholas** dominates the panorama of the Old Town. In 1380 the present Gothic church was built on the site of a Romanesque basilica; it was subsequently extended on several occasions. The **University Church of St John the Baptist** was constructed by Italian masters commissioned by the Jesuits. In only eight years, between 1629 and 1637, they completed the largest religious building in Slovakia. Together with the **Archbishop's Palace**, it sets the architectural tone on University Square.

Soaring above the long, narrow market place is the **Town Tower**, 69 metres (220 ft) high. The elaborately stuccoed facade of the classicistic **Town Hall** dates from 1793 and bears witness to the unshakeable optimism of Trnava in a time of threatened slump, as does the **Municipal Theatre** of 1831. Also worth closer inspection are a number of beautiful private houses in the Hollého ul. and the Kapitulská ul., as well as the well-preserved town walls with the protruding bastions to the east and west of the Old Town.

Into the Váh Valley: Piešt'any (Pistyan) lies 35 km (22 miles) along the Váh Valley following the main road, No. 61, to the north. A statue in the spa quarter

bears testimony to the great expectations of this world-famous spa town; it depicts a man throwing away his crutches. As much as 3½ million litres (700,000 gallons) of hot mineral water at a temperature of 67°C (152°F) gush out of the earth here every day; patients with rheumatic complaints appreciate the sulphurous mud. There are first-class hotels and spa facilities available, and the nearby **Slňava Dam** offers good opportunities for water sports. The town is delightfully peaceful and provides a good base for excursions into the surrounding countryside. Because of the protection provided by the hills, the climate here is unusually mild.

From the 17th century increasing numbers of visitors flocked to the spa, and in 1827 the Hungarian count Erdödy, whose family owned the entire town until 1940, decided to make capital of its natural advantages. Spa halls and parks were created on the north bank; the southern **Bathing Island** with the **Napoleonic Baths** and the town's principal spring, the **Pramen Adam Trajan**,

was linked directly to the town by means of the colonnade bridge. Under the aegis of Alexander Winter, a private citizen who took on the general lease for the spa facilities, a number of art nouveau sanatoria were built. The enterprising businessman not only transformed Piešt'any into a favourite meeting place of the fashionable world, but also encouraged a social conscience. In 1893 he founded a "workers' boarding school" and persuaded public health bodies to fund spa visits for the first time. During the past decades the municipal authorities have confirmed the town's international reputation by building modern spa facilities and the **Art Museum**.

It seems that a fondness for sitting in warm mud has a long, indeed ancient, tradition. Evidence of Neanderthal settlement has been found here. Even the local love of the arts, expressed during the **International Music Festival** each summer, and the open-air exhibition of plastic arts in the spa gardens, has ancient roots. In 1939 a farmer found the **Venus of Moravany**, a small sculpture

Fresh from the Slovakian garden.

carved from the tooth of a mammoth, which is one of the oldest sculptures ever found.

Near **Čachtice**, situated 10 km (6 miles) further north, a vast castle rises threateningly out of the valley. It was formerly the residence of Countess Elisabeth Bathory. Court documents record that the "White Lady", as the countess was known, was responsible for the murder of 300 young girls. She believed that bathing in their blood was beneficial to her snow-white skin. The story has inspired a number of horror-film producers.

Trenčin, a lively little town with a long history, lies further upstream. As long ago as the 6th century, the Slavs built a fortress on the huge rock overlooking the Váh Valley. History here goes back even further, however, as the Roman inscription on the rock testifies. Dated AD 179, it records the victory of the locally stationed Roman legion over a tribe of Germanii; it is the oldest written record ever found in Slovakia.

A settlement soon developed in the protective shadow of the fortress, and was awarded market rights in 1412. From 1302 the Hungarian magnate Matuš Čák had the complex remodelled into a prestigious, well-fortified castle, from which he ruled over the whole of Western Slovakia. John of Luxembourg and his son, the future Emperor Charles IV, chose it on several occasions as the site for negotiations with the kings of Poland and Hungary. King Sigismund strengthened the bulwark against the Moravian Hussites. From the 17th century, the Counts Illésházy – who had received the town and its fortress in fief from the Habsburgs – rebuilt the complex in accordance with the latest theories of defensive architecture. Their descendants donated the entire fortress to the town in order to avoid the immense maintenance costs.

A castle chapel with a rotunda and the central **Matuš Tower** are all that remain of the medieval structure. The entire complex is extensive and includes an arsenal, casemates and an oubliette as well as the **Trenčin Gallery** with a

Vlkolínec, a village built entirely of wood.

collection of paintings by old masters.

The Gothic **parish church** was built in the shadow of the castle rock. It possesses a perfect example of a charnel house, and an elaborate alabaster altar adorns the baroque burial chapel of the Illésházys, added at a later date.

The central axis of the Old Town is formed by the Mierové námesti (Peace Square), fringed by well-kept private dwellings dating from Renaissance and baroque times. The brightly coloured frescoes in the early-baroque **Church of St Francis** are charming. The town gate with its octagonal tower provides access to an unusually large 19th-century synagogue, which reminds the visitor that the town's expansion into a cloth centre and fashion capital was a direct result of the efforts of the once flourishing Jewish community.

The **Thermal Baths of Trenčianske Teplice** lie barely 15 km (9 miles) further to the north along the Váh in the tributary valley of the Teplica, which is bordered by wooded hills. The hot springs, high in sulphur and chalk content, provide relief from rheumatism and neurosensory diseases; they were known during Roman times and the Middle Ages as Aqua Teplica but were seldom visited.

It was the enterprising Joseph Illésházy who had a pretty summer residence built here in 1729 and who subsequently attracted high society to the emerging spa town. In 1750 the fashionable **Hotel Kaštiel**, a grand hotel built in the style of a Renaissance castle, opened its doors. Under the direction of private individuals, bath houses, pump rooms and elegant restaurants were built beside the 11 springs.

The most original contribution was provided by the architect Franz Schmoranz, who designed an **oriental bath house** in Moorish style. The owner of the spa town, Iphigenie d'Harcourt, discovered the imaginative sketch at the Paris World Exhibition in 1878 and commissioned the architect to build the *hammam* as an intimate bath house with luxurious, individual, cabins. Today, visitors will find the oriental bath house is less intimate, as it is used as the men's

changing rooms for the adjoining Sina spa house.

The cradle of Slovakia: The romantic **Nitra Valley** lies to the east of the Váh Valley and can be reached either by crossing the mountains from Trenčin, or by going back along the Váh and taking the main road from Trnava. The venerable town of **Nitra**, the oldest town settlement in the Czech and Slovak Republics, lies on a broad bend in the river. It is an attractive setting and must already have been inhabited for several generations when, in 829, the Slavic feudal lord Přibina persuaded Archbishop Adalram of Salzburg to dedicate a court chapel here. From this point onwards, the history of the place is easier to follow: Mojmir I, prince of the empire of Greater Moravia, conquered the town shortly afterwards and extended it considerably.

In 880, after the message of Christianity had been spread across most of the country by the two Slavic apostles Cyril and Methodius, who are still regarded as the patron saints of the Slovaks, the pope elevated Nitra to the rank of the first diocesan town in Slovakia. Under Hungarian rule in the 11th century, the town entered its Golden Age.

The **castle** served the bishops, who were simultaneously the local feudal lords, as their administrative seat. Even today it is still the residence of Bishop Ján Chryzostom Korec, who established a reputation for himself within the Slovakian opposition. All the alleys leading uphill from the town open on to the **Square of Slovakian Cooperation**, dominated since 1750 by a column dedicated to the Virgin Mary and recalling the two cholera epidemics of the previous decades. A stone bridge lined with statues of saints leads to the first gateway and the courtyard, where a restored tower reminds us that this was a medieval stronghold.

The single-nave **Gothic cathedral** was extended on several occasions; in 1720, following a radical remodelling in the baroque style, it was adorned with original frescoes. A much older early-Romanesque church was discovered in 1930; the master builders of the inter-

Left, the magnificent oriental bath house in Trenčíanské Teplice.

vening epochs had walled in this architectural jewel. The upper classes and senior clergy lived in the Upper Town, in the shadow of the towering castle, while craftsmen and traders formed a community within the Lower Town.

Now take the Východná, which leads to a quiet square. The **Great Seminary** appears to hover between the baroque and classical styles; today it houses the **local museum** with a collection of archaeological exhibits. The **Diocesan Library** next door the famous **Nitra Codex** dating from the 11th century. Opposite stands the classical-style **Canons' House**. The builder added an Atlas to one corner, but the citizens soon recognised that the statue fulfilled no structural purpose and christened him Corgoň the Rascal. Follow the Samova ul. from here and you will arrive at the Franciscan monastery, today the **Museum of Agriculture**. The adjoining church contains wood reliefs illustrating the life of the order's founder.

The underpass beside the Studenie Gallery and the **Academy of Art** was once the only access to the castle. Beyond the square, the Saratovská ul. forms the central axis of the Old Town. Only two blocks further on and standing in the centre of the Mierové námesti (Peace Square), **St Michael's Chapel** recalls the town's two cholera epidemics. The surrounding cafés and the garden terrace of the Hotel Slovan provide a welcome chance to relax. The rest of the Lower Town can be explored easily during a gentle stroll. Turning towards the southwest, the visitor will discover a series of 11th-century frescoes in the attractively simple Romanesque **Chapel of St Stephen**. The most notable buildings in the Gudernova ul. are the baroque ensemble formed by the Grammar School and the Piarist church, which possesses a remarkable double tower. To the east, on the former main square of the medieval Lower Town, the architectural tone is set by the modern **Andrej Bagar Theatre** and the town hall.

The slopes of the **Tribeč Mountains** to the north of the town provide ideal vine-growing conditions. The vineyards are interspersed with traditional roadside inns and attractive restaurants such as the Zoborská perla. The summit of the **Zobor Peak** (588 metres/1,880 ft) provides a magnificent panorama across the town and the valley.

Half-way between Nitra and Bratislava lies the pretty little town of **Galanta**. It is the home of the legendary Esterházys, who collected castles and palaces in much the same way as other people collect postage stamps. So it's not surprising that their native town, despite its population of only 15,000, should contain no fewer than four castles. The oldest, in the centre of the built-up area, dates from the Renaissance; another, in neo-Gothic style, houses the **Museum of Local History**.

On the return journey, less than 20 km (12 miles) before Bratislava, lies the community of **Senec**, whose two lakes, crystal-clear and undeniably romantic, never fail to enchant visitors.

Downstream along the Danube: This southwest corner of Slovakia bears strong traces of Hungarian influence; in some villages, Hungarian is even the

A view of Trenčín.

main language. Travellers who want to learn more about the cultural and historical influences of the region may be tempted to make a detour across the border to Hungary, to Esztergom or even to Budapest.

Behind Bratislava, to the right of the trunk road No. 63, are lush and lovely river meadows. Unfortunately, from **Samorin** onwards they have been ruined by the construction of the reservoir and power station at **Gabčíkovo**, a scheme which has sparked off a major row between Slovakia and Hungary. The Hungarians maintain that the completion of the dam and the diversion of the river along a canal will result in enormous damage to the environment, and have demanded that the Danube be made an internationally protected area.

It is advisable to bypass the scene of the controversy by following road No. 63, along which the town of **Dunajská Streda** offers the first interesting opportunity for a break. The name of this town means Wednesday on the Danube, which alludes to the fact that since the 16th century this regional centre has been permitted to hold a market every Wednesday. The **Zity kaštiel**, the baroque Yellow Castle, is a well-stocked **museum of local history**. This, and the Gothic **Church of the Assumption**, decorated with medieval frescoes, are both well worth visiting. The recent discovery of hot springs has given new impetus to local hotellerie and gastronomy. The nature conservation area Zlatná na Ostrove, shortly before Komárno on the Danube, is still the habitat of the great bustard (*otis tarda*), the largest European scavenging bird resident in the steppes.

The history of **Komárno**, which lies at the confluence of the Váh and the Danube, mirrors almost exactly the rise and fall of the royal and imperial monarchy. The native town of Franz Lehár, whose music reflects with such lighthearted élan the many national influences at work in his homeland, has been divided since 1918. The Danube serves as the frontier – just as it did in Roman times when the *limes* ran along its course, and later during the Turkish attacks on the fortress. Worthy of particular note among the many fine churches is the **Orthodox Pravoslav Church**, which has an exceptional collection of icons and liturgical items.

The highlight of any visit to Southern Slovakia could well be a stay in **Patince** or **Štúrovo**, the idyllic spa towns lying downstream along the Danube. The region enjoys the highest average temperature in the whole of Slovakia, and it seldom rains here. Additional attractions lie in the area cradled by the arm of the Danube, in the solid comfort of the hotels and guest houses, and – a peculiarity of Southern Slovakia – in the so-called *Pussten*. These are a particular type of traditional Hungarian restaurant, where violinists play genuine gypsy music to accompany the flambéed specialities and fine wine. In Štúrovo you can even try out an unusual form of transport – the *kompa* ferry, which takes you across to the other bank of the Danube, to the ancient town of **Esztergom** with its cathedral presided over by the Hungarian bishops.

A stork with a view.

CENTRAL SLOVAKIA

Central Slovakia can be subdivided according to its clearly defined geographical areas. The mountains of the Lower Tatra gradually give way on all sides to gentle river valleys and rolling hills. There are no major conurbations in the region, but in the south in particular a number of mining communities developed as a result of the lucrative deposits of copper, silver and gold.

Old mining communities: The most interesting of these mining towns is undoubtedly **Banská Bystrica** (Neu-sohl). The Slavic inhabitants of the sleepy hamlet of Bystrica were seized by gold fever during the 13th century, when gold, silver and copper deposits were discovered outside their very doors. Encouraged by the royal privileges, German miners flocked to the new eldorado from nearby Zvolen (Altsohl). The community soon prospered and was awarded a town charter in 1255.

The Fugger dynasty from Augsburg saw the potential of the mines and stepped in, investing vast sums of capital. At the beginning of the 16th century James II, nicknamed James the Rich, acquired a large proportion of the mines, both in the town and the region, for his family business, thus establishing what was actually a monopoly on European copper production. The Fuggers and their partners made Neusohl their administrative capital, thus enabling the town to earn huge profits not only from the extraction of the ore, but also from processing, related crafts and international trade in precious metals. In those days, however, the profits were anything but fairly distributed. In 1525 the miners came out on strike.

It was from Banská Bystrica, on 29 August 1944, that the message for the Slovakians to start their revolt against the Nazis went out over the radio. Since then, the old market place has been called the **Square of the Slovakian Uprising** (SNP for short). This has always been the focal point of the busy little town. Despite some rebuilding in the Renaissance style, most of the houses surrounding the square have retained many original Gothic elements. The **Thurzo House** in the southeast corner of the long, narrow square is the most magnificent of all, for it served as the official headquarters of the mining company.

Today it houses the **Museum of Municipal History and Folklore. Benicky House** diagonally opposite is notable for its elaborately decorated facade with a loggia supported by elegant Tuscan columns.

The **Clock Tower** points the way to the **fortress**, a collection of buildings which gradually evolved into a single complex. The residence of the governor, appointed by the king to oversee the mining operations, also served as a storehouse. The building later became known as the Matthias House, for the Hungarian king Matthias Corvinus stayed here on a number of occasions. The Gothic gateway tower and the **Miners' Church** completed the castle complex; the barbican building was constructed at

Preceding pages: winter paradise in the Lower Tatra. <u>Left</u>, a blacksmith at work. <u>Right</u>, three women of Košice.

the beginning of the 16th century.

In **Zvolen**, too, you will find many buildings recalling its own Golden Age. The settlement received a town charter in 1244 and grew prosperous through the mining of its silver deposits. It is not the town itself which is of particular interest, however, but the magnificent **castle**. It was built in 1382 by King Ľudovít the Great, who planned to use it as a base for his hunting expeditions. King Matthias Corvinus also fell in love with the beautiful setting and made the hunting lodge his favourite residence. During the 16th century the Thurzos replaced the elegant lightness of the original building with massive defensive features; the Esterházys finally turned it into an imposing palace. The castle now serves as a museum exhibiting a remarkably valuable collection of medieval Slovakian art.

In the town itself, little remains of the workshops that once made this an important centre of woodcarving. However, traditional crafts are kept alive by the **International Folklore Festival** which takes place every summer, usually in July.

Banská Štiavnica (Schemnitz) traces its origins back to a mining village established in about AD 1000. During the 12th century, German miners added a number of pit shafts to the open-cast seams. The village subsequently expanded into a national mining centre. In 1244, Banská Štiavnica received its charter as a free royal city. Here, too, the Fuggers ensured that they retained the lion's share of the mining and, during the 15th and 16th century, the town became the most important supplier of silver in all Hungary. Widespread investment and high profits allowed for technical improvements in mining technology, which were soon emulated on a worldwide scale. Explosives were first used in Banská Štiavnica mines in 1627; the introduction of mechanical pumps was also an invention of local mining engineers, who from 1735 were trained in a special university college.

The most interesting buildings in the town are the former houses of the

A quaint Easter custom.

wealthy mine owners; their Renaissance-style architecture, built upon Romanesque or early-Gothic foundations, reflects the enormous prosperity that Banská Štiavnica achieved. Most of them are situated around the central Trojičné náměsti (Trinity Square), dominated by a baroque column.

The Miners' Court used to meet in house No. 47; its verdicts were based on the Schemnitz Mining Law, which was codified in 1217. Today the building houses an informative **Museum of Mines**, where the industry of the Middle Ages is documented with tools, rock samples, models and a shaft leading some 70 metres (230ft) underground. Nearby stand the Renaissance building occupied by the former Chamber of Mines, the notable **Parish Church of St Nicholas** and the Old Town Hall.

Above the Old Town rises the **Castle**. During the 13th century a Romanesque church occupied the site, but with increasing prosperity in the 16th century the citizens converted the strategically located place of worship into a fortress with thick walls and five towers. The nave became a castle courtyard.

Historically speaking, **Kremnica** (Kremnitz) is one of the most important towns in Slovakia. Mentioned in records as a Slavic settlement in the 12th century, the town owes its rapid expansion and elevation to the status of a free royal city in 1328 to the extensive gold and silver deposits in the nearby Kremnica Mountains. Precious metals are still extracted from its pits today.

From 1335, following the award of special privileges by the king of Hungary, Charles Robert, the town was permitted to mint its own gold ducats – a tradition maintained by the mint in the Horná ul. until recent times. Such was the town's prosperity that it repeatedly attracted the attention of envious conquerors; even the Hussites plundered it during their punitive expedition of 1434. Nonetheless, the town has been able to maintain its traditional appearance. The spacious Náměsti1 mája (Square of 1 May) is bordered by several dozen fine houses, mostly built during the 14th

A Slovakian wedding procession.

century and extended in contemporary style during the Renaissance. The **Municipal Museum** at No. 7 provides the visitor with an insight into the colourful history of the town. The square, built on a slight slope, is bordered by the **castle**, which from the 13th century served both as administrative headquarters and as a secure repository for precious metals. The embankments and bastions surround a Gothic church and the forbidding castle keep.

A host of castles: Apart from its picturesque towns, this region has a large number of fortresses and palaces. Totalling no fewer than 70, some of them are in good condition whilst the others survive only as ruins. **Bojnický zámok Castle**, west of the town of **Prievidza** (Priwitz), is generally considered the finest in the whole of Central Europe. Some historians claim that it was founded about AD 1000, during the reign of King Stephen of Hungary. The castle changed hands frequently over the years. The Lords of Pálffy assembled a unique collection of paintings here. Directly below the castle walls there is a popular thermal bath; the grounds contain the largest zoological gardens in Slovakia.

South of Martin, **Blatnický hrad Castle** dominates the lovely **Gaderská dolina valley**. Hidden away in a large stretch of continuous woodland, it appears all the more imposing when seen at close quarters. The castle is first mentioned in records dating from the 13th century. Access to the complex is gained by a footpath; no cars are permitted.

The course of the Váh is rich in castles. **Budatín Castle** lies at the confluence of the Kysuca and the Váh, just to the north of the town of **Žilina** (Sillein). Having grown up at the intersection of important medieval trade routes, the town remains the busiest traffic junction in all Slovakia. Of particular interest is the little church of St Stephen, one of the oldest Romanesque churches in Slovakia, whose interior is adorned with a number of striking frescoes. Žilina makes a good base for exploring the attractive region of **Orava**, in the northernmost corner of Slovakia. A well-

Oravský hrad stands sentinel above the Orava River.

developed tourist infrastructure has arisen around the Orava reservoir (Oravska nadrž). The romantic **Orava Castle**, boldly perched on a limestone crag above the river, was built to guard the trading route to Poland and was fortified on a number of occasions.It now houses a museum of local history.

The entire region is famous for its traditional folk music and extravagant **traditional costumes**. Your best chance of seeing these is if you stumble upon a wedding, which can last for three days or more. Traditional crafts such as embroidery, ceramics and pottery, as well as the painting of furniture, also retain their place in modern society. To the south of Žilina, **Čičmany** is famous far and wide for its richly embroidered costumes and its wooden houses decorated with colourful motifs.

Into the mountains: To the east of Žilina you can follow the course of the the romantic Vrátna Valley through Terchová and on to Vrátna, from where a cable car trundles up to the main ridge of the **Lesser Fatra** (Malá Fatra), beneath the highest peak of the range, Veľke Kriván 1,709 metres (5,606 ft).

The **Lower Tatra** (Nízké Tatry) is a paradise for walkers and ski enthusiasts. In the western section, the long succession of peaks makes it possible to hike along the crest, where the breathtaking views amply repay the effort involved. The descent into the valley is punctuated by mountain huts where it is possible to obtain milk and simple lamb dishes. One of the most rewarding hikes is the traverse from Šturec or Krížna in the **Greater Fatra** (Velká Fatra) to Chabenec and on to the **Chopok**, the main ridge of the Lower Tatra.

In **Liptovský Mikuláš**, the **Museum of Slovakian Karst** provides a foretaste of the wonders of nature to be experienced in the fabulous **Demänovské jaskyňe caves**, 11km (7 miles) to the south. Their chambers and galleries are ornamented with stalactites and stalagmites and are linked by a series of underground lakes, streams and waterfalls. On the southern flank of the Chopok ridge, the village of **Tále** is a good base for less experienced walkers.

The gentle ski slopes in the foothills of the **Bystrá dolina Valley** are ideal for novices. The village also has playgrounds, an open-air swimming pool, restaurants and accommodation in hotels, a motel and a campsite.

At 2,049 metres (6,722ft), **Mount Ďumbier** is the highest peak in the Lower Tatra. The ascent from **Čertovica** is equally rewarding in summer or winter: there is a magnificent view across the mountains of Slovakia from the Polish to the Hungarian frontier, from the Beskids to Branisko.

The eastern section of the Lower Tatra, between Čertovica and the **Popová Ridge**, is an unspoilt wilderness. The main crest is covered by extensive forests. The only reminder of civilisation is a hideous transmitter on the summit of the **Krakova hoľa**. There are only a few mountain huts providing accommodation for tourists, but the marked footpaths pass a succession of hunting lodges, for the entire region is rich in game. This remote corner of the continent is even inhabited by bears.

Many rare flowers in Slovakia are protected.

Eastern Slovakia

No other region of the former Czechoslovakia offers the visitor a more varied and colourful combination of natural beauty and historic sights than Eastern Slovakia. Although the inhabitants of Spiš, Šariš, Zemplín, Gemer and Košice all feel themselves to be Eastern Slovaks, there are clear differences in both dialect and folklore. The variations are most clearly reflected in the architecture of the towns and villages.

Košice (Kaschau), idyllically situated in the foothills of the Slovenské Rudohorie (Slovakian Ore Mountains), is the principal city in Eastern Slovakia. Founded by Saxon settlers, the community was awarded special privileges by the King of Hungary in 1244. In 1342 it was proclaimed a free royal city and from 1369 it was the first city in Central Europe to be allowed to bear its own coat of arms. The town became wealthy as a result of its international trade with Hungary and Poland; the university, founded in 1657, turned it into a cultural metropolis. The Golden Age lasted only until the 18th century, when internal strife, the Turkish Wars and finally the split from Hungary marked the beginning of a period of economic decline.

The historic town centre is a national monument. **St Elizabeth's Cathedral** rises above the central Námesti Slobody (Freedom Square); it is considered to be one of the most beautiful Gothic churches in the country. The north door, the *porta aurea,* dating from 1460, frames a statue of the patron saint; the magnificently carved high altar, completed a few years later, describes 12 scenes from the life of Saint Elizabeth.

The free-standing **belfry**, Urbanova věža, and the cemetery chapel, dedicated to St Michael, complete the architectural ensemble of the square. For modern citizens of Slovakia, Košice is the town of the Slovakian "magna carta", and the home of the Košice government protocol, which was proclaimed in the Committee House here on 4 April 1945,

The pedestrian precinct in Košice.

and which provided the basis of Czechoslovakia's postwar constitution.

The communist leadership decided to turn Eastern Slovakia into an industrial region. In the vicinity of Košice a vast iron and steel works was constructed, although there were lamentably inadequate supplies of water and iron ore. It proved to be the most blatant and, ecologically speaking, the most catastrophic false investment in the history of Czechoslovakia. The only positive step taken by the former regime was its expansion of the education system. The Technical University of Košice produced a large number of well qualified steel and mining engineers.

In the northeastern corner of the region lie Prešov (Preschau) and Bardéjov (Bartfeld), attractive towns which in medieval times enjoyed privileges as free royal cities, forming the Pentapolis League with Košice, Levoča and Sabinov. Fine Gothic and Renaissance houses with ornately decorated gables grace the town square of **Prešov**, now an important centre of Slovakian and Ukranian culture, possessing both a Slovakian and a Ukranian theatre. The most attractive building is the **Rákoczyho palác**, the residence of Prince Rakoczy, which until recently housed exhibits from the Museum of the Bolshevik Slovakian Soviet Republic.

In **Bardéjov** near the Polish border, the medieval city centre, dating from the town's founding year (1219), has survived to this day. Almost all the fortifications, constructed during the 15th century, can also still be seen. The houses surrounding the central square reflect the town's heyday in Gothic and Renaissance times.

The **Town Hall** dates from 1509; today it serves as municipal archives and museum. The Gothic **Church of St Aegidius** has eleven magnificent altars as well as numerous paintings and statues. The neighbouring spa town of **Bardéjovské kúpele** has operated as a spa since the 13th century. Its waters are famous for their efficacy in treating stomach disorders and illnesses of the digestive tract. It is the most important spa town in Slovakia after Piešt'any.

Vernacular churches: The remote mountain villages of Eastern Slovakia are known for their traditional **wooden churches**. Most of them were built during the 18th century and reveal an imaginative mixture of baroque and archaic elements. They frequently stand on some sort of eminence, their towers rising above the rooftops of the village. Their interiors bear witness to a Byzantine influence; many contain an iconostasis. The portraits of saints on the folding triptychs are mostly the work of anonymous local artists and craftsmen and depict religious subjects created in classical styles. The minor figures, however, are modelled on simple people, displaying the common features and ordinary clothing of the times. Also worthy of note are the decorative wall and ceiling paintings, the altars, pews and missals. There are 24 such churches in Eastern Slovakia and they are all national monuments.

In a hilly region further to the south, on the **River Ondava**, lies the **Domaša Dam** – a good tip for a longer stay. The

The famous Madonna of Košice, in St Elizabeth's Cathedral.

reservoir is popular among anglers and offers water sports facilities of all kinds.

Among the natural sights of the region are the Morské oko mountain lake in the **Vihorlat Mountains** and the lovely **Zemplínská Šírava Lake**, also known as the East Slovakian Lake. Its enchanting location on the southern slopes of the Vihorlat ensures favourable climatic conditions. The bathing season lasts for almost five months of the year, and there is an annual average of nearly 2,200 hours of sunshine. The passenger boats crossing the lake will take you on delightful outings to the pretty villages lining the shores. The restaurants have an excellent reputation; apart from fish and game, they serve regional specialities.

A caver's paradise: The scenery of the **Slovenský kras Mountains**, surrounding the mining town of **Rožňava** in the south of the region, is characterised by caves, gorges and karst landscape. The vaulted roof of the **Domica Cave** is covered with bizarre, coloured stalactites. You can take a boat trip along this underground river, through the eerie world of different colours. Equally impressive are the vast columns of ice in the **Dobšinská ľadová Cave**, north of the town of **Dobšina**. It lies adjacent to the **Slovenský raj**, the so-called Slovakian Paradise, an area of natural beauty marked by canyons, gorges and waterfalls. Particularly spectacular is the **Kyseľ Canyon**, which over a length of 5 km (3 miles) drops a distance of over 350 metres (1,000 ft). The most impressive of all, however, is the **Veľký Sokol**, also 5 km (3 miles) long and with walls rising up to 300 metres (1,000 ft) above the river, which in one place is only a metre (3 ft) across. On the edge of the Slovenský raj, the River Hornád forces its way through a 11-km (6-mile) gorge (only traversable by boat).

Further to the west, the town of Švermovo provides a convenient base for hikes into the eastern end of the Lower Tatra range, specifically the ascent of the 1,948-metre (6,391-ft) high Kráľova hoľa.

A cultural entity: Culturally speaking, northeastern Slovakia is a largely independent region. Known to the Slavs as **Spiš**, it was christened Zips by the German migrants who settled in the area from the 11th century onwards. In 1271, 24 towns within the region joined forces to form a league of free cities, choosing the royal town of Levoča (Leutschau) as their capital. Five years later they were emulated by the Seven Mountain Towns of the Zips surrounding the free royal city of Göllnitz. They prospered on their mining, trade and crafts, but the towns' history was a turbulent one. In 1412, the Emperor Sigismund pawned 13 of them to Poland for a few thousand silver pence, then refused to buy them back. The remaining towns came under pressure from the Hungarian nobility, and the Catholic Church attempted to force their inhabitants to convert to the one true faith. In 1769 the Habsburgs conquered the entire region, annexing it for their empire. It was not until 1876, however, that the Hungarians finally put an end to all autonomy.

The magnificent Gothic and Renaissance churches of the region bear wit-

Peppers thrive in the warm climate of Eastern Slovakia.

ness to this history, as do the elegant belfries, fine town halls, sprawling farms and mighty castles. Many of these monuments have been turned into museums, but a considerable number of the churches were converted or even demolished by the communist regime. Nonetheless, the centres of the cities of the Spiš have maintained their medieval appearance. Four of them have been declared national monuments: Levoča, Kežmarok, Poprad, Spišská Sobota and Spišská Kapitula.

Levoča contains a unique work of art by the local master craftsman Pavol: a **Gothic wooden altar**, no less than 18 metres (58 ft) high. It stands in the 14th-century **Parish Church of St James**, the second-largest Gothic church in Slovakia, which is situated on the Mierové námesti (Peace Square), a spacious square bordered by splendid patrician houses.

The lovely Renaissance town hall was completed in 1559 and is adorned with a massive belfry and a series of fine frescoes, depicting bourgeois morality.

Kežmarok (Käsmark) is notable for its Romanesque-Gothic parish church of the Holy Cross, its Protestant wooden church and a fortress which was later converted into a palace.

In the **Church of St Aegidius** in **Poprad**, a series of 15th-century frescoes, in particular an enchanting panorama of the High Tatra, the mountains dominating the town, has been carefully preserved. In the **Spišská Sobota** district there are historic townhouses and a Gothic parish church. Exceptionally fine examples of popular architecture are found in the remote villages of the Levoča Mountains and the valley of the River Poprad.

The northern Spiš region includes the magnificent **Pieninský narodny National Park**, where the **River Dunajec** carves its way through the Pieninský Mountains. One of the most exciting ways of exploring the river is to take a wild water trip on a raft in the company of a rafter from the Górale, a people living on both sides of the national frontier between Slovakia and Poland.

House facade in the cloth town of Bardéjov (Bartfeld).

THE HIGH TATRA

The most popular tourist region in Slovakia is a nature reserve: the Tatra National Park (Tatranský národní park). By following carefully laid out paths visitors can observe and experience a natural wilderness without damaging it. Almost all the mountain peaks in the park are accessible, and from almost any point in the park it is possible to enjoy unforgettable views of the main mountain ridge.

Extending about 64 km (40 miles) along the Slovakian–Polish frontier, the High Tatra (Vysoké Tatry) is the highest mountain range in the Central Carpathians. Although the range is much lower than the Alps and therefore lacks the permanent snowfields and glaciers, it nevertheless possesses a distinctly alpine character. The mountain slopes are covered with pine woodlands up to an elevation of 2,500 metres (6,600 ft), above which the alpine zone begins. The High Tatra supports a rich variety of fauna, including bears, chamois, marmots and eagles.

Around 300 peaks are identified by name and elevation. Until an earthquake blew off its top in the 16th century, the highest peak in the range was the Slavkovský štít, with an elevation of more than 2,700 metres (8,850 ft). Evidence of the catastrophe can be seen in the massive outcrops of rock which were hurled into the Veľká Studená dolina Valley. The highest mountain in the Tatra now is the Gerlachovský štít 2,663 metres (8,737 ft).

The highest peaks were originally over 3,000 metres (9,600 ft); during the Ice Age glaciers up to 200 metres (640 ft) thick wore away the summits and rent deep clefts in the mountain mass, thus forming the impressive hanging valleys, lakes and rock walls which characterise the Tatra today.

Glacial remains can still be found on the north faces of the mountians, in the places where the sun never penetrates. In some places you will also come across large patches of snow which do not melt, even on the warmest summer days of the year.

Wonders of nature: The 35 mountain lakes in the Slovakian Tatra have been left behind by the retreating glaciers. They are commonly referred to as "sea eyes", because the ancients believed that their deep, crystal-clear waters were directly linked with the sea. Some fill the hollows left in the rock by the ice sheets; others are contained by rock dams formed by the deposition of rocks and stones. The largest of the mountain lakes, the Veľké Hincovo, has a surface area of almost 20 hectares (50 acres) and is over 50 metres (160 ft deep).

The jewels in the crown of this mountain range are the picturesque waterfalls. The spectacular Kmeťov Falls in the Nefcerka Valley thunder 80 metres (256 ft) into the depths below. The vast Studenovodské vodopády and the Skok Falls in the Mlynická dolina Valley, as well as the Obrovský Falls in the Studenovodská dolina Valley are a magnificent natural spectacle.

Ideal climate: But the Tatra Mountains have much more to offer than just scenic beauty; the towns and villages and the bracing mountain climate are equally inviting. The massif towers above the surrounding mountains, forming a watershed and creating a microclimate unique in Central Europe.

The setting was ideal for the establishment of sanatoria for the treatment of tuberculosis, asthma, respiratory complaints and nervous diseases, all of which respond well to the oxygen-rich air. A stay in the Tatra is beneficial even during the cold, wet season, for the intensity of the healing ultraviolet rays is largely dependent upon the purity of the air. Even during the main tourist season, when there tends to be a lot of haze in the Alps, the skies in the High Tatra are generally clear. There is a partial ban on the use of private cars in operation, which means that the range is largely spared pollution from exhaust fumes, smoke and water vapour. Above the tree line, after the fog or rain has cleared, there is virtually no trace of water evaporation. The number of hours of sunshine here is as high as on the sunny plains of southern Slovakia, and amounts to between 1,800 and 2,000 hours a year.

Characteristic of the region are sudden climatic changes. While the valleys are buried under a thick layer of cloud, the upper slopes of the High Tatra often enjoy brilliant sunshine. The cold air, which is relatively heavy, sinks into the valleys and the warm air, which is less dense, moves up to the higher altitudes. Among the climatic characteristics of the Tatra region are a number of strange phenomena: a mirage effect caused by the mountains, flashes of lightning from an otherwise clear sky and *föhn* winds of up to 150 kph (94 mph). Even sand from the Sahara desert, brought by the high-altitude trade wind, is deposited on the snow-covered peaks of the High Tatra. A particular attraction is the ever-changing play of light at dawn and during the evening.

A paradise for trekkers: For those who want to hike in the High Tatra, the autumn is probably the best time of year for a visit. Although the days a shorter, the skies are at their most brilliant blue,

and the forested slopes are a riot of colour. The highlight of exploring the High Tatra is to climb through the wild, romantic valleys, past mountain lakes and across strangely formed rock terraces. The 350 km (220 miles) of clearly marked footpaths provide even inexperienced walkers with access to the mountains. But the main ridge of the High Tatra is only accessible to experienced climbers; it extends for over 26 km (16 miles) from Ľaliové sedlo to Kopské. The northern slopes in particular are steep and cold, and present a tremendous challenge to mountaineers.

Even in winter, the High Tatra and the neighbouring White Tatra (Belanske Tatry) to the east are attractive destinations, for they offer ideal conditions for cross-country and downhill skiing. The guesthouses, however, are often fully booked during the winter sports season, so prior reservations (or plenty of patience) are necessary.

The Tatra Mountains can be easily reached from other parts of the country and offer a sensitively developed tourist **An autumn hike up Mount Rysy.**

infrastructure, with accommodation ranging from top-class hotels to mountain huts offering only mattresses on shared floor space. A hundred years ago no direct roads led to this remote mountain district. Today it can be reached via the scenic route Cesta Slobody (Freedom Trail), which links the main tourist centres – Štrbské Pleso, Starý Smokovec and Tatranská Lomnica. Buses and an electrified railway line provide additional means of transport.

Starting points: Tatranská Lomnica is an ideal base for a visit to the region, since many walking tours actually begin here. Visitors who prefer not to exert themselves unduly can take one of the two cable cars to the Salnaté pleso, which lies at an altitude of 1,750 metres (5,600 ft). The **Hotel Encián** and the observatory invite one to stay longer; additional cable cars provide a link with the highest peaks of the range. The picturesque village itself houses the **Tatra National Park Museum**, where – apart from exhibits illustrating the region's folklore – visitors can admire the large collection of flora from the Spišská Magura. From Tatranská Lomnica one can continue to **Tatranská Kotlina** and visit the impressive **Belanská jaskyňa Caves**. Nearby **Ždiar** is a typical Slovakian hill community extending 7 km (4 miles) along the slopes of the Spišská Magura. On Sunday and during folk festivals the locals wear their traditional costumes.

Štrbské Pleso, the highest village in Slovakia, also makes a good base. It is the starting point for a number of interesting routes, including the popular climb to the top of Mount Rysy, whose summit provides a magnificent view of the entire Tatra range. Another much-visited destination is Mount Kriváň 2,493 metres (8182 ft), further west, the goal of many national pilgrimages.

Routes through the mountains: Every visitor to the Tatra makes for the **Cesta Slobody**, the Freedom Trail, undoubtedly the loveliest mountain road in Slovakia. For more than 70 km (44 miles) it runs parallel to the mountains from Podbanské in the west, through

Mount Kriváň is one of the most spectacular peaks in the range.

Tatranská Lomnica to Podspády and Javorina, from where it continues across the border into the Polish Zakopane. Less convenient, but every bit as attractive, is a journey by train from Poprad to Tatranská Lomnica and on to Štrbské pleso. The carriages chug slowly and laboriously through the craggy mountain landscape and seem to stop beside virtually every barn.

The main footpath through the mountains, the so-called **Magistrale**, provides the best way of getting to know the region. The route is marked in red, is well maintained along its entire length, and traverses the area between Podbanské in the west and Tatranská Kotlina at an average height of 1,300–2,000 metres (4,160–6,400 ft).

The first section passes along the shores of the Jamské pleso Lake to Štrbské Pleso, continuing to Popradské pleso and up the famous zig-zags to the summit of **Ostrava**, on over Mount Tupá, beneath Končistá and Gerlachovský štít to **Sliezsky dom**. From here the marked route runs along the slopes of **Mount Slavkovský štít** and past the Sesterské pleso lakes to the **Hrebienok**.

Skirting the mouth of the **Studentovodská dolina Valley**, the path continues past the waterfalls and uphill to Lake Skalnaté pleso, as far as the cable car leading up **Mount Lomnický štít,** which at 2,632 metres (8,635 ft) is the second highest mountain in the range. Then it is on to Velíká Svist'ovka and down into the **Zelené pleso Valley**. Near the Bielé pleso, the path starts to climb once more to the **Kopské sedlo**. Another path then traverses the ridge of the Belanske Tatry and leads the hiker down to Tatranská Kotlina.

Mountain challenges: Hiking along the Magistrale is an unforgettable experience, even for less practised walkers – especially when one combines the main walk with short detours to the nearby summits and valleys. But when attempting to climb a mountain it is imperative that the time it takes (shown on the signposts) is taken into account. The Tatra is not only a region of great beauty, it can also be a region of great danger.

Many visitors overestimate their strength, abilities and knowledge of the area and pay for their foolishness with an accident, frost bite or even death. Not only individuals, but also groups are at risk. Before undertaking an ambitious touring programme, it is absolutely essential to check with the mountain rescue association, which has a branch office in all the larger villages. The following are some of the most popular routes from west to east:

From **Podbanské**, Tri studničky or the **Furkotská chata** mountain hut hike up to **Kmet'ov** and the **Vajanského vodopád** waterfalls in the shadow of **Mount Kriváň**. Two further routes of interest in this area lead over the Kôprovské sedlo mountain crest to lakes **Hincovo pleso** and **Popradské pleso**, and the **Furkotská Valley** with the Wahlenbergové plesá lakes.

From **Štrbské pleso** in the Furkotská Valley climb up Mount Kriváň and descend into the **Mlynická dolina Valley** (ski area established in 1970), passing the **Skok Waterfall**, the **Vyšné Kozie**

Tatranská Lomnica at the foot of Lomnický štít.

and **Capie pleso** mountain lakes. From there a route continues up the **Mengusovská dolina Valley**, and past the **Popradské pleso** mountain lake, which is the starting point for the ascent to the summit of **Mount Rysy**, beneath which is the highest mountain hut in Slovakia. The trail to **Vyšné Hágy** over Mount Ostrva is also pleasant.

From Vyšné Hágy walk to the **Batizovské pleso** lake, then continue west past the Popradské pleso to Štrbské pleso, or east to Sliezsky dom and from there to **Tatranská Polianka**.

From Tatranská Polianka hike to Sliezsky dom and then continue from the **Velické pleso** mountain lake up to the **Políský hrebeň** (Polish Saddle), before descending through the **Svišt'ová** and **Bielovodská dolina** valleys to **Javorina**. From Sliezsky dom one can also hike to the top of the Hrebienok. Another attractive route leads from the Batizovské pleso mountain lake to Vyšné Hágy. Experienced walkers under the direction of a guide might also consider tackling the some of the routes up **Gerlach–ovský štít** or the **Vychodná Vysoká** from Sliezsky dom.

From **Starý Smokovec** take the cable car up the Hrebienok, and from there follow a not too arduous but long climb up the **Slavkovský štít**. An alternative is to follow the **Velíká Studená dolina** Valley to the **Zbojnická chata** hut and then continue via Prielom and Polísky hrebeň to the Sliezsky dom. Another beautiful route leads to the **Studenovodské vodopády** waterfalls and to the **Téryho chata** mountain refuge, which is run by Belo Kapolka, a well-known writer.

Set off from **Tatranská Lomnica** to the Studenovodské vodopády waterfalls and up the Hrebienok, the **Skalnaté pleso** mountain lake and on to the **Hotel Encián**. From there, climb up to the **Hrebienok Waterfalls** or down into the valley of the **Bielé pleso** (White Lake) and the **Zelené pleso** (Green Lake) and return to Tatranská Lomnica. Experienced walkers will enjoy the route from Bielé pleso to Tatranská Kotlina but novices should not attempt it.

A cosy evening after a long day's hike.